# BUILDING CYCLES

## AND THE
## THEORY OF INVESTMENT

# BUILDING
# CYCLES
## AND THE THEORY OF
## INVESTMENT

BY CLARENCE D. LONG, JR.

PRINCETON
PRINCETON UNIVERSITY PRESS
LONDON: HUMPHREY MILFORD
OXFORD UNIVERSITY PRESS

1940

SET UP AND PRINTED BY PRINCETON UNIVERSITY PRESS
AT PRINCETON, NEW JERSEY, U.S.A.

*To My Mother and Father*

# PREFACE

I<small>N</small> the course of this investigation, I have accumulated many obligations. The study was carried on with the aid of the Sanxay Felllowship at Princeton University and of numerous and generous grants by the Wesleyan University Research Committee. Dr. Otto Nathan of New York University, for two years a visiting lecturer at Princeton University, first stimulated my interest in the field of business cycle research and pointed out the need for more knowledge of cycles in the building industry. Dr. Arthur F. Burns of the National Bureau of Economic Research has given me continuous and invaluable counsel and has guided me away from many dangerous pitfalls. And during the five years devoted to this study, my wife has spent more than a thousand hours aiding me in the transcription of the basic data from the original records, in the classification and analysis of those data and in the preparation of the charts. Much of the work I have tried to do would have been nearly impossible without her aid.

I should be less than generous not to acknowledge the valuable secretarial services of Miss Ruth Brazos, and the painstaking assistance in the statistical computations and in the editing of the manuscript of Messrs. Rex Knowles, Robert Murray, Sidney Schnapp, and Joe Wannemacher, of Wesleyan University, employed under the

# PREFACE

*National Youth Administration. Professors Frank D. Graham, Archibald McIsaac, and James G. Smith of Princeton University have read parts of the manuscript and have offered valuable and constructive criticism concerning both style and substance. Officials of building departments throughout the country have been more than cooperative in compiling data to enable me to fill in the gaps resulting wherever the published documents were inadequate or unavailable. In a number of cases, the officials were kind enough to have members of their staffs work for periods of several weeks or a month gathering the data I desired. Such courtesy goes far to restore one's faith in American local government.*

*Finally, I cannot close without expressing gratitude to Professor Frank D. Graham, who of all the teachers I ever had did most to quicken my intellectual curiosity and to develop what analytical abilities I may have. In doing this, I merely echo the consensus of all his graduate students: that Professor Graham is that rare person, a truly great teacher.*

*Middletown, Conn.*
*July 1, 1940*

# CONTENTS

Preface                                                                    vii

Introduction—by Frank D. Graham                                             xv

  I. The Rôle of Investment in Economic Cycles                              3

 II. The Inducement to Invest in Buildings                                 11

III. Investment and Consumption                                            56

 IV. Explanation of the Building Data                                      95

  V. The Monthly Index of Building, 1868-1940
     Timing, Duration, Severity, and Association
     with Business and Speculative Factors, of
     Short Cycles                                                          99

 VI. Building Cycles and the Inducement to Invest                         108

VII. Long Cycles in Business, Public, and Residential
     Building
     The Data and Their Analysis                                          116

VIII. The Timing of Long Cycles                                           128

 IX. Long Building Cycles and Great Depressions                           150

  X. The Duration of Long Cycles                                          158

 XI. Severity of Long Building Cycles                                      167

XII. Severity of Long Cycles Explained                                     184

Appendix A.  The Monthly Index of Building in United
States Cities, 1868-1940                                                   213

[ ix ]

# CONTENTS

Appendix B.  Annual Indexes of Business, Public, and
Residential Building, and Alterations in United States
Cities, 1856-1935

  1. Indexes of builders' estimated cost of detached
dwellings, apartment dwellings, business building, public building, and alterations. (One to
fourteen cities)    224-5

  2. Indexes of builders' estimated cost of total residential, total nonresidential, total new building,
alterations, total building. (One to twenty-seven
cities)    226-7

  3. Indexes of number of total residential, total nonresidential and total new building. (One to
twenty-nine cities)    228-9

  4. Indexes of number of families accommodated.
(One to sixteen localities)    230

# LIST OF TABLES

1. Building Cost and Cost of Ownership      17

2. Importance of Interest Charges under Various Assumptions of Length and Distribution of Earning Life      23

3. Importance of Interest in Inducement to Invest      28

4. Elasticity of Expenditure for Housing      33

5. Continuous Expansion of Consumption, Income, and Investment      75

6. Turning Points in Building and Business      104

7. Deviations in the Turning Points of Building and Business      105

8. Length and Periodicity of Building Cycles      105

9. Relative Amplitude of Building Cycles      106

10. Turning Point Dates of Long Cycles in Detached Dwelling, Apartment House, Business, and Public Building      135

11. Turning Point Dates of Long Cycles in Residential and Nonresidential Building      136

12. Average Deviation of Turning Points in Building in the Various Cities: Detached Dwelling, Apartment House, Business, and Public Building      146

13. Average Deviations of Turning Points in Building in the Various Cities: Residential and Nonresidential Building, and Alterations      147

## LIST OF TABLES

14. Amplitudes of Long Cycles: Detached Dwelling, Apartment House, Business, and Public Building    169

15. Amplitudes of Long Cycles: Residential and Non-residential Building and Alterations    170

16. Severity of Long Cycles: Detached Dwelling, Apartment House, Business, and Public Building    171

17. Severity of Long Cycles: Residential and Non-residential Building and Alterations    172

18. Factors in the Cost of Building, New York City, 1868-1934    196-7

19. Eight Manhattan Apartment Projects: Composite Operating Data, City and Suburban Homes Company    204

[ xii ]

# CHARTS

I. The Monthly Index of Building in United States
Cities, 1868-1940                                      99

II. Indexes of Value; five basic classifications of building in fourteen cities, 1868-1935                      130

III. Indexes of Value; five comprehensive classifications
of building in twenty-seven cities, 1868-1935          131

IV. Indexes of Number; three comprehensive classifications of building in twenty-nine cities, 1856-1935   132

V. Index of Number of Families Accommodated by
all building in twelve cities and by multi-family-
dwellings in Evanston, Illinois, in all boroughs of
New York City, and in the entire state of New
Jersey, 1871-1935                                      133

VI. Factors in the Cost of Building, New York City,
1868-1934                                              195

# INTRODUCTION

THE recognition of at least three types of cycles in business activity—the short, the intermediate, and the long—lends peculiar significance to a study of fluctuations in building activity. Building is perhaps the only industry which, over a long time, is closely correlated with economic life as a whole and statistics, more or less spotty, on building in this country are available for a period now not far short of a century. There is, therefore, not only reason to expect the reflection of all types of business cycle in the building industry but we have the record in which we can carry our investigation of that reflection back over a lengthy spell of time. It is probable, indeed, that something more than a reflection will be shown, that there will be, so to speak, a reflection with causative force. There can be little doubt that building cycles are, at one and the same time, a cause and an effect of variations in general economic activity, and cases of interaction of forces afford the most difficult, and interesting, subjects of economic study. The presumptive interrelationship between activity in building and in business in general is so obvious that one would have expected it to have been thoroughly canvassed long before this. The freshness of Professor Long's study comes, therefore, as a distinct surprise. His compilations of indexes of building are the only thing of their kind. His analysis of the interaction between investment and consumption; of the repercussions of this upon activity in building and of activity on building upon it; is convincingly done. The book is, in consequence, an extremely valuable contribution to our growing knowledge of business cycles and, it is to be hoped, to our ability to limit the devastation that they cause.

FRANK D. GRAHAM

# BUILDING CYCLES

## AND THE

## THEORY OF INVESTMENT

# CHAPTER I

## THE RÔLE OF INVESTMENT IN
## ECONOMIC CYCLES

FEW economists will dispute that the industries producing durable investment goods are profitable subjects for study of causes and characteristics of business cycles. The importance of investment industries lies in their large fluctuations in production—fluctuations large both in absolute amount and in relation to the average investment flow. For example, Kuznets' estimates for 1919-1935 show that annual volume of gross capital formation averaged about fourteen billion dollars, or 19 per cent of the gross national product. If one includes consumers' durable commodities (other than residential construction already included) the volume of gross capital formation averaged twenty-one billion dollars or 31 per cent.[1] The following data give a glimpse of the extent of their fluctuation:

The various rates of decline show fluctuations much more severe in durable than in nondurable branches. The latter

[1] S. S. Kuznets, *National Income and Gross Capital Formation, 1919-35* (New York: National Bureau of Economic Research, 1937), pp. 59, 85. Included in the estimate of gross capital formation were net changes in business inventories and net changes in claims against foreign countries. These items were very small in amount, but the 2.5 billion net decrease in 1932 of business inventories made aggregate gross capital formation a smaller magnitude than construction in that year.

| | PEAK | | TROUGH | |
|---|---|---|---|---|
| | Value (Current Prices) (Billions) | | Value (Billions) | Percentage of Peak |
| Consumers' Outlay[1] | (1929) | 73.3 | (1932) 42.3 | 58 |
| Gross Capital Formation[2] | (1929) | 20.3 | (1932) 3.1 | 15 |
| Total Construction[2] | (1925) | 11.8 | (1932) 3.5 | 30 |
| Total Private Construction[2] | (1925) | 9.3 | (1933) 1.3 | 14 |
| Residential Construction[2] | (1925) | 5.2 | (1933) 0.4 | 8 |

fell during the depression only 42 per cent, whereas the total of all durable goods production fell off 85 per cent, greater relatively (though not absolutely) than the fall in ephemeral output. Although this loss of production is distressing, and embarrassing to progress, the real significance of these perturbations is (a) in the direct loss of employment, income, and purchasing power to the people dependent on capital formation for their livelihood and (b) in the indirect and cumulative effect that the loss entails for the consumption goods industries, which are *relatively* stable and would probably, were it not for these variations in income be *absolutely* stable also. It is significant, in view of this instability of durable investment, that the quantitative importance of the durable goods industries has increased secularly over the last sixty years: from 31 per cent of industrial output in 1879 to 44 per cent in 1929.[3]

[2] *ibid.*, p. 40.
[3] See Isador Lubin's testimony, using statistics of the National Bureau of Economic Research. *Hearings before the Temporary National Economic Committee,* 75th Congress, 3rd Session, Part 1, "Economic Prologue," pp. 27, 28.

As for building, its significance is to be found in some general facts about the industry. For one thing, building is, in itself, the largest single investment goods industry. During the seventeen years from 1919 to 1935 the gross value of construction in the United States averaged about eight billion dollars a year,[4] compared with the gross annual income of the nation of seventy-three billion dollars.[5] And in 1929 the number of gainfully employed workers reported to the census as being attached to the construction industry was about three million,[6] of which about two and a half million seem to have been actually employed.

Of course, building construction and employment forms only a part of total construction and employment, but it forms the largest and most violently fluctuating part and in addition exercises a strong, sympathetic influence on

[4] S. S. Kuznets, *loc. cit.*

[5] The eight billion dollars for construction represents gross income, the value added by all the materials industries that feed into the construction industry. Nevertheless, we shall see that it is the gross rather than the net investment product that is really relevant to the consideration of fluctuations in employment and purchasing power of the nation. Kuznets has left out of the construction estimate five billions annual outlays for repairs, *op. cit.*, p. 80.

[6] Fifteenth Census of the United States, 1930, *Unemployment* (Washington: Government Printing Office, 1931), Vol. I, p. 15. A report on national income by the Department of Commerce in collaboration with the National Bureau of Economic Research comments that "While the latter figure (454,824 classified under construction and maintenance of roads, sewers, and bridges) probably includes a number of gainfully occupied not engaged in construction or repair, this excess is more than offset by the number of casual workers in the construction field counted among the 1.3 million gainfully occupied for whom no industrial attachment is given." United States 73d Congress, 2d Session, Senate Doc No. 124, *National Income, 1929-32* (Washington: G.P.O.), p. 80.

the behavior of the remainder.[7] Nonbuilding construction, such as street and highway pavement, parks, fire and police equipment, sewers, gas lines, electricity generators and conduits, and telephone equipment, must take place largely at the time of building construction; such construction forms the other part of what is practically a joint demand. Consequently, when building construction rises and falls, much, perhaps most, of nonbuilding construction must rise and fall also, although not necessarily to the same extreme degree. There is little doubt that the fluctuations of the building industry may be taken as strongly representative of the fluctuations in the whole vast field of construction and, therefore, of the fluctuations in a huge amount of gross construction income and employment.

But the significance of cycles in building and nonbuilding construction does not stop with instability of income and employment occasioned for workers and employers of these industries. The effects are multiplied by the instability of the industries which are directly and indirectly dependent upon the construction industries for their markets. Of course, the eight billion dollars indicated as the gross value of the average annual volume of construction includes not only the value added by the construction industries, but also the products of the industries that supply the materials and even includes the return on the tangible and intangible capital of the builders and supply manufacturers. But it does not include the purchase price of the new machinery bought annually by building mate-

[7] Eighty-five per cent of the workers in the construction industry were attached specifically to the building industry. Fifteenth Census of the United States, 1930, *Unemployment,* Vol. I, p. 55.

rial manufacturers or the purchase price of the new equipment, such as steam rollers, work elevators, sanding machines, bought annually by builders. It does not include the purchase price of new railroad and trucking equipment needed to care for the expanding transportation needs of a booming construction industry. As for the three million men reported to have been attached to the construction industry in 1929, that figure includes only those employed directly at the site of construction. In addition, the Bureau of Labor Statistics estimates that for every hour of employment given by construction on the site, another two and a half hours of employment are given in the industries producing and handling the construction materials and equipment.[8] If this ratio is correct, the total direct and indirect employment given in 1929 must have been a little under nine millions. In the same way, it may be estimated that about one and three-quarters million men, to the extent that they could not get work elsewhere, owed their unemployment in 1929 to the construction industry. These estimates of employment influenced by construction do not include employment in the field of real estate or in the industries producing and handling furniture and other household and business equipment whose

[8] Herman B. Byer, "Employment Resulting from P.W.A. Construction, 1933 to 1937," *Monthly Labor Review*, Vol. 46 (1938), No. 1, pp. 16-26. The projects studied were non-Federal P.W.A. The additional employment created was in the "production of raw materials, fabrication, and distribution of construction materials and in administration" (p. 16). The ratio varied: On water power projects, it was found to be 2.3; and on power and light plants, it was found to be 4.4. "Estimates of indirect employment are derived in part from estimates of employment submitted by manufacturers and in part are based on studies of the labor involved in the production and transportation of certain basic construction materials" (p. 24, footnote).

demand is apt to be strongly influenced by the volume of new building.[9]

It follows that the construction industries have a significance to the problem of economic cycles that is far greater than the eight billion dollars that appears as the average annual gross value or than the three million men who were attached to the industry in 1929. It is probably impossible to compute the true multiplier that should be applied to the volume of construction in order to arrive at the aggregate influence of fluctuations in construction income and employment. However, it may not be reckless to assert that most of the rise and fall in the durable producers and consumers goods industries, estimated by Kuznets at twenty-one billion dollars annually for 1919-1935, is inextricably bound up with the rise and fall of the building industry.[10] When to this consideration is added the reflection that the perturbations of the industries engaged in gross capital formation cannot fail to disorganize the industries supplying ephemeral consumers

[9] It is impossible to separate many of these "sympathetic" industries from the industries manufacturing and handling construction materials, but the number of workers attached to the few industries which can be separated may be listed by way of suggestion:

| | |
|---|---|
| Furniture manufacturing | 39,802 |
| Furniture, carpet, rug dealers | 35,884 |
| Real estate agents and officials | 240,030 |
| Piano and organ manufacturing | 1,664 |
| Upholsterers | 51,452 |

This list does not include workers attached to industries making furnaces, refrigerators, draperies, bric-a-brac. Nor does it include people attached to the fields of fire insurance, real estate law, mortgage banking, and real estate and architectural printing, and publishing. Fifteenth Census of the United States, 1930, *Unemployment*, Vol. II (Washington: G.P.O., 1932), pp. 14-17.

[10] S. S. Kuznets, *op. cit.*

goods and services to the people who derive their income directly and indirectly from these industries, the significance of building as a part of the study of cycles should need no further urging.

Altogether, the building industry manifests two features that cause it to be the focus of the problem of great depressions. The first feature is its huge size, the fact that it is the nation's largest single industry next to agriculture, having a strategic position with regard to the production and employment of almost every other industry in the country. The second is, as we shall see, the severity of its fluctuations, the fact that swings in productive activity from valleys to peaks are the widest of any important industry.

Thus, the problem of business depressions requires a study of cycles in the building industry.[11] When have the

[11] See three articles by the present writer: "Long Cycles in the Building Industry, 1856-1935," *Quarterly Journal of Economics,* Vol. 53 (1939), pp. 371-403; "Seventy Years of Building Cycles in Manhattan," *Review of Economic Statistics,* Vol. 18 (1936), pp. 183-93; "The Building Industry—Maker and Breaker of Booms and Depression," *Dun's Review,* Dec. 1939, pp. 17-21, 50. The most thorough studies of long cycles in aggregate building are W. H. Newman, *The Building Industry and Business Cycles,* Studies in Business Administration, Vol. V, No. 4 (University of Chicago, 1935); J. R. Riggleman, "Building Cycles in the United States, 1875-1932," *Journal of the American Statistical Association,* XXVIII (1933), pp. 174-83; also *Variations in Building Activity in United States Cities* (unpublished manuscript, Johns Hopkins University Library, 1934).

Other recent studies of building activity, most of them short-period, are: H. E. Bookholtz and C. Judkins, *The Construction Industry,* Bureau of Foreign and Domestic Commerce, Market Research Series No. 10.1 (Washington: 1936); Lowell J. Chawner, *Construction Activity in the United States* (Washington: 1938); M. Bowley, "Fluctuations in Housebuilding and the Trade Cycle," *The Review of Economic Studies,* Vol. IV (1937), pp. 167-81; A. F. Burns, "Long Cycles in Residential Construction," *Economic Essays in Honor of Wesley*

building cycles occurred? How long have they lasted? What has been the extent of their fluctuations? Are they becoming more or less severe? How well have they coincided with business movements or with other significant events, and what individuality of movement, such as lead or lag, have they manifested? What have been the chief factors responsible for the timing, length, and severity of cycles in general, or the special factors responsible for unusual behavior of individual cycles? These are the questions which a study of the building industry ·in its relation to the problem of depressions must answer.

*Clair Mitchell* (New York: Columbia University Press, 1935) ; pp. 63-104; A. K. Cairncross, "The Glasgow Building Industry, 1870-1914," *Review of Economic Studies,* Vol. II (1934), pp. 1-17; L. Grebler, "Housebuilding, the Business Cycle, and State Intervention," *International Labor Review,* Vol. XXXIII (1936), pp. 337-55, 468-78; F. J. Hallauer, "Population and Building Construction," *Journal of Land and Public Utility Economics,* Vol. X (1934), pp. 35-41; H. Hoyt, *One Hundred Years of Land Values in Chicago* (Chicago: University of Chicago Press, 1933) ; *Real Estate Analysts* (St. Louis Edition, published monthly) ; C. F. Roos, "Factors Influencing Residential Building," *Dynamic Economics,* Monographs of the Cowles Commission for Research in Economics, No. 1 (Bloomington, Indiana: Principia Press, 1934), pp. 69-110; G. F. Warren and F. A. Pearson, *World Prices and the Building Industry* (New York: John Wiley & Sons, Inc., 1937) ; D. W. Wickens and R. R. Foster, *"Non-Farm Residential Construction, 1920-1936,"* National Bureau of Economic Research, Bulletin No. 65 (1937) ; C. Woodbury, "The Trend of Multi-Family Housing in Cities in the United States," *Journal of Land and Public Utility Economics,* Vol. VI (1930), pp. 225-34; Ian Bowen, "The Building Industry in War-Time," Economic Journal, Vol. 49 (1939), pp. 663-669; H. W. Robinson, *The Economics of Building* (London: P. S. King & Son, Ltd., 1939), p. 157.

# CHAPTER II

## THE INDUCEMENT TO INVEST IN BUILDINGS

### THE PROXIMATE FACTORS

COMPLEX as the ultimate forces underlying the formation of capital may be, they strike investors as a comparatively simple calculus. If capital values of projected durable agents promise to equal or exceed marginal costs of producing them, there is inducement to invest. Where capital values are with respect to production cost depends upon investors' present valuations of the series of future quasirents that durable agents are expected to yield. On what investors base their expectations and how they arrive at a present value for their expectations are, of course, not simple problems, however free from complexity they may seem to the individuals. All forces affecting the inducement to invest, including monopolistic policy, population movements, government action, wars, union wage policy, speculation, propensity to consume, inventions and discoveries, operate through three, partially distinct, channels: marginal cost of producing and owning the investment good; rate of discount or interest at which expected values of the uses of the durable agent are translated into present values; and

[ 11 ]

expectations concerning what the values of those uses will be.[1]

*Building Costs and Investment Supply*: Inducement to invest exists so long as capital values of existing structures cover marginal costs of building new ones. Inducement ceases when capital values sink below these marginal replacement costs. Since there is always at least some small flow of investment, there must always be some inducement, but whether inducement is ample to absorb all the factors not used in producing goods for ephemeral consumption is a matter of *magnitudes* of supply and demand. And the evenness of investment flow against changing magnitudes is a matter of *elasticities* of supply and demand. The more elastic the supply, the more severely investment is restricted or expanded by a fall or rise in demand; and, in the same way, the more elastic the demand, the more severely investment is restricted or expanded by a fall or rise in the supply. Importance of costs to inducement to invest is related then to intensities and elasticities of both supply and demand. The present discussion treats the connection between building costs and intensity and elasticity of supply. It also goes into the percentage part which cost of building plays in final cost of ownership, since that percentage part is significant to closeness of connection between cost and inducement.

Nothing could be less satisfying than a study of building costs and a good share of the reason is that building is

---

[1] Regarded in a slightly different way, inducement to invest exists if the expected marginal efficiency of capital equals or exceeds the long rate of interest. Marginal efficiency of capital is the ratio of the periodic value yield (after operating costs) of the agent to its original formation cost.

an integral part of the whole industrial system and its cost structure is naturally bound up in that whole system.[2]

[2] At the risk of repeating what nearly everybody knows, the following characteristics of the industry and its cost structure may be cited:

(a) The building industry is a complex of industries, producing tremendously varied complexes of utilities. Little similarity in building conditions obtains between a four-room bungalow and a chemical laboratory or a fifteen-story office building.

(b) The industry proper is made up of a huge number of small speculative and contract builders, often minutely differentiated as to function, and a small number of large contractors, engaged in erecting large unit projects primarily nonresidential in character. Competition is naturally keener in the residential than in the nonresidential branch of the industry. Back of the building industry proper lie building material and machinery producing industries, notoriously oligopolistic and dominated by every conceivable type of collusive, restrictive arrangement. Even more illuminating than a study of monopolistic elements in these industries would be a study of the extent to which price competition is able to carry on despite restrictions.

(c) The industry relies for its labor upon widely varying conditions of unionization. Most cities covered in the present study have building labor unions, but are by no means uniform as to open or closed shop or as to open or closed unions. In the small towns, villages, and open country, most building is doubtless performed under nonunion conditions. This is especially true of small residential building. See testimony of Dan Tracy and T. J. Kreps, T.N.E.C., *Hearings, op. cit.,* Part 11, "Construction Industry," pp. 5264, 5453.

(d) Capital requirements, and therefore overhead costs, are small. Direct costs are large and notoriously rigid. Although the trend in all branches of the industry is toward prefabrication, a large proportion of work is still custom-done at site with little power equipment, and this is especially true, of course, of residential building.

(e) Buildings are large in size and value and are very durable. Few industries deal in units as valuable as even a small home.

(f) Wide local differences exist in construction and cost conditions; unionization; seasonality of operations; heating, insulating, excavating; sewage; availability of water, stone, sand,

Even so, the nearly complete lack of relevant statistics of building costs is partly due to neglect. What we need are statistics for individual builders of actual unit costs of finished building structures. What we have are official statistics of materials prices and union wage rates,[3] which miss the mark as completely as data possibly could. Considering the importance which the Bureau of Labor Statistics has always attached to housing, one wonders why that excellent agency has not made at least one such unit cost study. And surely the Federal Housing Administration, with its accumulating files of appraisals, could make a study, based on relation of builder's estimated cost to appraised value of each identical dwelling, that would tell us something about cost differences among builders. Until we have data on cost differences among builders and the various percentages of direct and overhead costs we shall not know whether supply of building is elastic or inelastic. We do know that, by and large, and especially in residential building, materials and labor costs are much greater than

transportation; building regulations; legal fees; zoning codes of building materials producers.

(g) Most residential and small commercial buildings are produced ready-made for speculative sale or rent.

(h) Buildings are sold almost entirely on credit.

For further discussion of building characteristics see especially the excellent review of the structure of the construction industry, by Willard Thorp before the T.N.E.C. (pp. 5171-235) and the summarization of all the testimony on construction, by T. J. Kreps (pp. 5432-59), *op. cit.* Also see L. J. Chawner, *op. cit.,* pp. 26-7; William Newman, *op. cit.,* p. 4; H. W. Robinson, *op. cit.,* pp. 17, 53-4.

[3] Wage rates throw little or no light on labor costs. See a study by the Bureau of Labor Statistics on "Labor Cost Ratios and Hourly Wage Payments, Educational Buildings Erected with N.I.R.A. Funds, 1933-1936," T.N.E.C., *op. cit.,* p. 5587.

overhead costs.[4] But this does not give us long-run elasticity of supply.[5]

We are almost as ignorant of fluctuations of supply in the schedule sense. Naturally, it is realized that the cost schedule of buildings is influenced by whatever affects demand and price in industries that compete with building for what it uses: transportation, labor, wood, steel, copper, coal, glass, and so on. Thus recovery in national income raises the demand schedule for building, but after a certain point, and perhaps rather quickly at that, lowers the supply schedule also. Severe wars seem to affect both sides of the market adversely.[6] Technological improvements, with some exceptions, probably stimulate both supply and demand, wherever they occur. Growing or declining unionization and monopoly and variations in policies pursued by such combinations reduce or increase the supply schedule, depending upon direction of change.

---

[4] Of the five and one-half billion dollars reported as having been received for construction work in 1929, the proportion paid out for expenses that might be listed as overhead was less than 14 per cent. The great bulk was for labor and building materials. Fifteenth Census of the United States, *Construction Industry*, 1930, pp. 96, 112.

[5] A hint that variations in unit costs of individual firms may be wide is had from a Bureau of Labor Statistics study of job differences in labor productivity in the bricklaying and plastering trades. On straightaway work, costs in the same city of laying 1,000 bricks were for the highest cost job two or three times as much as for the lowest cost job. And the same wide variation characterized job differences in plastering. The study covered sixteen cities and included both union and nonunion jobs. No differences could be found between union and nonunion work in the same city. Ethelbert Stewart, "Labor Productivity and Costs in Certain Building Trades," *Monthly Labor Review*, Vol. 19 (Nov. 1924), pp. 1-15. If wide variation does characterize firm costs of building, then we have indication of low short-term elasticity of supply.

[6] *infra*, pp. 209-12.

We all realize that such developments do bring changes in cost and supply, but far from being able to attribute any given change in supply to any given development, we do not even know when and to what extent changes in supply schedule do occur. Volume of investment falls; wage rates and building material prices fall. Has supply fallen? Has it increased? No matter how adequate the data, we could not be sure;[7] but with reasonably accurate statistics of unit costs we might, at least, make intelligent guesses.

Little enough is known, then, about fluctuation and structure of building costs. Nevertheless, it seems probable that building costs, though important, and, as we shall see, more important in the aggregate than interest rates, are secondary to expectations in the inducement to invest. Not only do building costs seem less fluctuating than expectations, but, because they form only a part of cost of ownership, a given percentage change in building costs causes a less than proportional change in inducement to invest. Table 1, containing a semi-hypothetical situation of factors in ownership costs, show taxes and heating to be such important and unyielding elements that a 50 per cent reduction of building costs, including land, fees, etc., would reduce annual costs only 35 per cent. Peter Stone,

---

[7] Of course, if both cost and investment have fallen, we know that the supply schedule has either declined or is more than zero elastic, or both. If investment alone falls this must be due to a fall in both supply and demand (unless supply is perfectly elastic). If both cost and investment have fallen, this *could* be due to a fall in demand alone, supply unchanged. If cost alone has fallen, investment unchanged, this also must be due to a fall in demand and a rise in supply, unless demand or supply is zero elastic, in which case, the fall in cost could be due to a change in either one.

# INDUCEMENT TO INVEST IN BUILDINGS

## TABLE I

### *Building Cost and Cost of Ownership*

A $6,000 home in Queens cited by the Bowery Savings Bank. Amortized over 25 years.

| Assumed Original Cost of Building | Annual Taxes | Annual Insurance | Annual Heating | Annual Maintenance | Annual Interest at 5% and Amortization | Total Annual Ownership Cost |
|---|---|---|---|---|---|---|
| $6,000 | $135.96[a] | $21.00[a] | $90.00[b] | $60.00[b] | $425.70 | $732.66 |
| 5,000 | " | 17.50 | " | 50.00 | 354.75 | 648.21 |
| 4,000 | " | 14.00 | " | 40.00 | 283.80 | 563.76 |
| 3,000 | " | 10.50 | " | 30.00 | 212.85 | 479.31 |
| 2,000 | " | 7.00 | " | 20.00 | 141.90 | 394.86 |
| 1,000 | " | 3.50 | " | 10.00 | 70.95 | 310.41 |
| 0 | " | 0 | " | 0 | 0 | 225.96 |

a. F. C. Smith and R. W. Sparks, "Pioneering in Reduced-rate Lending," *Insured Mortgage Portfolio,* Federal Housing Administration, July 1939, p. 20. Taxes would not be reduced by a fall in costs in the short run and, inasmuch as costs of government would have to be met, would not be reduced even in the long run.

b. This estimate for heating and maintenance is probably conservative. Peter Stone estimates these for a $4,800 house at $144 to $180 a year "depending upon the area and type of building" (*op. cit.,* p. 9). Also generous is the assumption that maintenance will decrease proportionately to cost of building.

from a study of apartment house costs, divides the ownership dollar into half interest and depreciation, on the one hand, and half operating, maintenance, and taxes on the other, indicating that a decline of building costs of 50 per cent would increase inducement to invest hardly more than 25 per cent.[8] And the City and Suburban Homes Com-

[8] Peter A. Stone, "The Cost Elements of Housing," a paper given at the annual meeting of the American Statistical Association, Dec. 28, 1939. (From the manuscript.)

pany, a limited dividend project of eight apartment houses, showed an average total operating cost over several decades of 50 per cent. During the thirties, this percentage rose to 70 per cent.[9, 10]

*Rate of Interest*: As pointed out above, the capitalized value of a durable agent is the present value of the rents expected to accrue in the future. This present value is less than expected value on day of accrual. It is less because the market subjects expected rents to a time discount loosely referred to as the *going rate of interest*. If rate of interest helps to determine capital values of durable agents, it must form part of inducement to invest, and what it is, and how much of a part it plays are significant in the explanation of the investment process.

As the search for the going rate of interest begins, it becomes immediately apparent that there is no general market rate, even after abstracting for risks peculiar to each type of investment, but rather a complex of rates

[9] *infra*, Table 19.

[10] One should not be too quick to conclude from this that price-demand for new buildings is necessarily inelastic. After all, though a 1 per cent cost of building reduction would reduce cost of ownership perhaps only ½ per cent, nevertheless, it might still induce 1 per cent added demand for new building. Because the ½ per cent reduction will extend to all building old and new. And if ½ is the part which original cost formed of cost of ownership, then in the long run the reciprocal of that ratio should represent the ratio of total income spent each year for ownership as compared with the long-run average annual outlay needed for replacement to keep the stock of building from running down. Consequently, in the long run, a reduction of 1 per cent in cost of new building, resulting in ½ per cent reduction in cost of owning a building, would, nevertheless, induce a 1 per cent increase in demand for new buildings. Even so, it will be readily seen that building costs are secondary to expectations in the inducement to invest. In Table 1 an 11 per cent reduction in expected gross revenue could be offset only by an 18 per cent (or larger) reduction in original cost.

which includes among others a different rate for loans of every maturity. Inasmuch as these differences are wide, the student of the investment process must select from the complex of rates the rate on maturities roughly matching the expected life of the asset to be acquired. He must not, therefore, assume that because the open-market rate on loans maturing in four to six months is ½ per cent that expected rents of buildings lasting twenty to fifty years will be capitalized to form high present values and high inducement to invest. Whether he invests his own money or borrows to invest, the purchaser of a durable agent must consider the various rates which he must pay or which he could have obtained elsewhere over the whole life of that agent. And, of course, the lender must do the same. Thus the rate of interest which will prevail on a loan of twenty years will, after adjusting for greater risk of not recovering principal, be the average of the series of short term rates that are expected to prevail during the next two decades.[11] It follows that the long-term rate will, since it is a moving average of expected short-term rates, be relatively stable and that the longer the term the more stable the rate.[12] This stability of the long-term rate and the wide fluctuations of the short-term and call rates are historical facts.

This brings us to the importance of the interest rate in the investment process. It is, of course, true that the value of a given expectation is greater at a lower rate of time-

---

[11] It does not follow that these expectations are the result of very accurate or even rational forecasts. See F. R. Macaulay, *Bond Yields, Interest Rates, Stock Prices* (New York: National Bureau of Economic Research, 1938), pp. 25, 32, 33.

[12] And the higher, because of the greater risk of long maturities.

discount than at a higher one. Thus, other things equal, capitalized value of a durable agent increases with a fall in interest. This does not mean that a fall in the long rate of interest will always be accompanied by stimulated investment. If expectations fall also, the decline in interest may be more than offset.[13]

[13] The relativity of the market rate of interest to some sort of normal or standard has long been recognized: See Knut Wicksell, *Interest and Prices* (translated by R. F. Kahn, London: Macmillan and Company, Ltd., 1936), pp. 106-7; J. M. Keynes, *General Theory of Employment, Interest and Money* (New York: Harcourt Brace & Co., 1935), p. 143; A. C. Pigou, *The Theory of Unemployment* (London: Macmillan and Co., Ltd., 1933), pp. 205-6, 212-13; Joseph Schumpeter, *Business Cycles* (New York: McGraw-Hill Book Co., Inc., 1939), pp. 123-7, 603; F. A. Hayek, *Prices and Production* (London: George Routledge & Son, Ltd., 1931), p. 21.

Wicksell calls the normal the *natural rate* which "depends on the efficiency of production, on the available amount of fixed and liquid capital, on the supply of labour and land, in short on all the thousand and one things which determine the current economic position of a community; and with them it constantly fluctuates" (p. 106). Pigou refers to the *proper rate* which will maintain a "standard monetary system . . . [a system] so constructed that, for all sorts of movements in the real demand function for labour or in real rates of wages, whether they last for a long time or a short, the aggregate money income is increased or diminished by precisely the difference made to the number of work-people (or other factors of production) at work multiplied by the original rate of money wages" (pp. 205-6). Hayek changes the name of Wicksell's *natural rate* to *equilibrium rate,* or rate equalizing "the demand for real capital and the supply of savings" (p. 20). Schumpeter denies the validity of any concept of a natural rate of interest but ". . . as far as profits are the basic fact about interest and both its source and its 'cause,' they will, although no permanent returns and although not behaving exactly as that natural rate is supposed to behave, play a similar rôle in our scheme, and those relations between natural and monetary interest will in many, although not in all, respects be replaced by relations between profits and interest not *toto coelo* different from them" (pp. 127-8). Keynes replaces the concept of a natural or equilibrium rate of interest with the *prospective marginal efficiency of capital.* "For the stimulus to output depends on the marginal efficiency of a given stock of capital rising *relatively* to

Conversely, if expectations rise also, the rise in interest may be offset. On the other hand, unless variations in the long rate of interest reflect directly on expectations, that is unless changes in expectations would not occur except for changes in the rate of interest, one might say with Pigou that "In all circumstances . . . a fall in the rate of interest causes some expansion, and a rise some contraction, in the aggregate real demand function for labor."[14]

But is not the long rate of interest an expectation of the future short-term interest rates? Will not those future short-term rates depend on the relative rents of durable agents prevailing at that future time? Consequently, if expectations concerning future rents of durable agents are low, will not this represent a low expectation of the future short-term rates and therefore a low long rate representing this expectation? The answer is that there is a difference, based on the fact that money is on both sides of a loan but on only one side of a rent expectation. If future rents of buildings are expected to be low, few will wish to buy durable agents but many will wish to sell them. Their price will fall. But if future profits are expected to be low, few people will wish either to borrow or to lend. Although abundant cash balances and revenues may exist, these will not constitute a part of effective supply and there will be no borrowers market such as exists for buyers of durable

the rate of interest. . . . It is important to understand the dependence of the marginal efficiency of a given stock of capital on changes in expectation, because it is chiefly this dependence which renders the marginal efficiency of capital subject to the somewhat violent fluctuations which are the explanation of the Trade Cycle" (pp. 143-4). Keynes describes his marginal efficiency of capital as having the same sense as Irving Fisher's "rate of return over cost."

[14] *op. cit.*, p. 182.

goods. Interest rates will tend to pursue a stable course, substantially independent of the movement of expectations.[15]

We shall now examine, in an effort to secure some sort of definite appraisal of the strategic importance of interest in the inducement to invest, just how much variations in interest, if they did occur or could be made to occur, are capable of affecting the capital values of durable agents. Table 2 contains the capital values at various rates of interest of a building which is expected to yield $20,000 over its life but which may yield that $20,000 in the four different ways there described. Analysis of the various values uncovers two important generalizations: The first is, *the longer the period over which the earnings of a durable agent are distributed and the more heavily the earnings are bunched in the latter part of that period, the more important are fluctuations in the rate of interest to the capital value and therefore to the inducement to invest.* The second is, *the smaller the level about which the interest rate fluctuates, the smaller is the proportional effect of a given relative change in the interest rate on the capital value and therefore on the inducement to invest.*[16]

[15] This seems to be a better explanation of stability of the long rate than Keynes' explanation that the long rate is a "conventional" phenomenon governed by the prevailing view as to what its value is expected to be" (*op. cit.,* p. 203). For Keynes does not explain why the future long rate can be expected to be high at the same moment when future "marginal efficiency of capital" is expected to be low!

[16] The explanation for this is that as interest rates fall, capital value approaches a ceiling established by the aggregate undiscounted gross revenue. On the other hand, we shall see that a low rate of interest means a high relation and, therefore, relatively great instability of investment.

# INDUCEMENT TO INVEST IN BUILDINGS

## TABLE 2

*Importance of Interest Charges under Various Assumptions of Length and Distribution of Earning Life*

(Total Expected Net Rent Income: $20,000)

SECTION A    Earning Life: 20 years

| Interest Rate | Present Value of 20 Equal Annual Net Rent Incomes[17] | Present Value of 20 Diminishing Annual Net Rent Incomes[18] |
|---|---|---|
| 5% | $12,462.21 | $14,357.60 |
| 4 | 13,590.33 | 15,261.09 |
| 3 | 14,877.47 | 16,261.96 |
| 2 | 16,351.43 | 17,374.06 |
| 1 | 18,045.55 | 18,613.76 |
| 0 | 20,000.00 | 20,000.00 |

SECTION B    Earning Life: 50 years

| Interest Rate | Present Value of 50 Equal Annual Net Rent Incomes[17] | Present Value of 50 Diminishing Annual Net Rent Incomes[18] |
|---|---|---|
| 5% | $7,202.37 | $9,958.29 |
| 4 | 8,592.80 | 11,183.30 |
| 3 | 10,292.00 | 12,690.26 |
| 2 | 12,569.60 | 14,569.72 |
| 1 | 15,678.40 | 16,947.26 |
| 0 | 20,000.00 | 20,000.00 |

Let us examine the significance for the building industry of the first generalization. At first thought it might appear that the importance which interest variations play in the

[17] $1,000 a year for twenty years; or $400 a year for fifty years.

[18] The total expected income is $20,000 but diminishes by constant annual amounts. In case of the twenty-year earning life, the first annuity was $1,904.76 and each succeeding annuity was less than the one preceding by $95.24. In case of the fifty-year earning life, the first annuity was $780 and each succeeding annuity decreased $20.

inducement to invest in buildings would depend upon the durability of buildings, and this is true, but in a limited sense. For it is not the actual number of years that any given building proves in the end to have stood and given service, nor even, by itself, the expected number of years; but rather the combination of the latter and the extent to which the earning power of the building is expected to be sustained over the anticipated life. That is, if the building is expected to have only a short earning life and the earnings are expected to decrease rapidly after the first few years, then interest variations will be less important than if the building is expected to have a long earning life and the earnings to be well sustained up to the very end.

The question now arises, how long and how well do prospective investors expect the earning power to hold up in the case of building. This question must be answered by reference not to historical studies of the lives of actual buildings, however revealing for some purposes these may be,[19] but to actual prevailing depreciation policies. And these depreciation policies vary widely, as they might well be expected to do from the widely varying conditions surrounding the construction and use of each individual building. There is little doubt, for example, that private non-residential buildings are depreciated over a shorter life and more rapidly than are residential buildings because of

---

[19] Statistics of the *Financial Survey of Urban Housing* show that many homes sixty to one hundred years old and still standing are valued by their owners at 66 per cent to more than 100 per cent of the owner-valued homes built within a decade. Indeed the houses built before 1920 and 1910 are in the main valued by their owners at greater than original cost. (United States Department of Commerce, Bureau of Foreign and Domestic Commerce, 1937, *passim*.)

the greater risks of obsolescence and the development of conservative accounting traditions. Thus the rate of interest is a less important factor in the former than in the latter type of nonresidential building. Moreover, there are wide variations in the rate of depreciation applied within each classification. Within the field of nonresidential building, A. S. Dewing found eighteen separate estimates of proper charge of depreciation of wooden buildings, ranging from ten years to forty.[20] Fabricant lists the depreciation rates collected by the Bureau of Internal Revenue as varying from thirty years for frame dwellings to fifty years for brick and masonry. The straight line method was found to be overwhelmingly prevalent in business depreciation.[21]

The depreciation of residential buildings might seem, offhand, to offer a difficult case, because few home buyers probably have, consciously or unconsciously, any concept of depreciation. And, indeed, under conditions of home financing prevailing before last half decade, the problem was indeed puzzling. Except in the case of homes financed through the building and loan associations, unamortized mortgages were granted for, in effect, indefinite periods. Millions of owners undoubtedly regarded their homes as yielding undiminishing or even increasing quasirents in perpetuity.[22] This situation has been changed with the ad-

[20] *The Financial Policy of Corporations* (New York: The Ronald Press Co., 1934), p. 528.

[21] Solomon Fabricant, *Capital Consumption and Adjustment* (New York: National Bureau of Economic Research, 1938), pp. 140-1, p. 65.

[22] A study of apartment houses, built and operated for commercial purposes, would probably yield much the same situation. An amazing example is the City & Suburban Homes Company, a successful limited dividend corporation, studied by the Federal Housing Administra-

vent of the amortized mortgage required under the insurance provisions of the Federal Housing Administration. The fact that the great majority of mortgages granted in the future will provide for amortization in periods less than twenty-five years establishes this period as the maximum for depreciation of residential building. Obviously, it is not the expectation of the owner that counts now, but that of the agency that does the lending or insures the mortgage.[23] The owner may continue to regard his home as infinitely durable, but if he wishes to borrow money to finance it, as he usually must, he must arrange to pay for the home in twenty-five years or less and this means that the rate of interest will play a less important rôle in residential investment in the future than in the past. Moreover, to the extent that the F.H.A. has lowered the effective mortgage interest rate to the borrower, and so far this reduction has been 1 whole per cent and more,[24] then, as we saw above, we have one more reason to look for decreased importance of interest fluctuation in the future. And examination of Table 6 shows that this rôle of the rate of interest, even if it fluctuated effectively, would be secondary in the inducement to invest in residential buildings. For without any allowance for maintenance or replacements, without any consideration of the costs of heating and lighting, a fall in the mortgage rate of interest from 5

tion. No depreciation reserve for the replacement of buildings was set aside until the company had been in operation twenty years and some of the buildings were fifteen years old or more. *op. cit.*, pp. 20-4.

[23] Actually, it will always be the less optimistic of the two.

[24] According to National Association of Real Estate Boards, the dominant rate for first mortgages on new medium-priced houses has fallen from 6 to 5 per cent. In 19 per cent of the cities a 4½ per cent rate prevailed. *New York Times,* Jan. 21, 1940, R.E. 2: 7.

per cent to 0 would reduce the annual carrying charges of a $6,000 home by only 36 per cent.[25] A drop of interest of 20 per cent from 5 per cent to 4 per cent would cause a fall in carrying charges of only 7 per cent; whereas a fall in building cost of 20 per cent would reduce carrying charges by nearly 15 per cent. As pointed out above, the relative importance of interest lessens as the rate fluctuates about a lower level. A reduction of the rate of interest from 4 per cent to 2 per cent is a reduction of 50 per cent and would reduce carrying charges less than 14 per cent; whereas a reduction of 50 per cent in original cost would, even assuming no reduction in taxes and insurance, reduce carrying charges 35 per cent. Even zero interest would not in itself make building profitable if expected rent fell more than 30 per cent from equilibrium.

That under some conditions even zero interest would not stimulate investment a number of economists have pointed out. Schumpeter has said recently "There are situations in which zero interest would entirely fail to call forth any additional demand."[26] Pigou has also said, "But in times of deep depression, when industrialists see no hope anywhere, there may be *no* positive rate of money interest that will

[25] Of course, the fact that taxes and insurance costs vary from locality to locality would cause the rate of interest to be more important in some areas than in others. A study of thirty-nine apartments in New York City for 1937 by Peter A. Stone resulted in an estimate of 35 per cent of rental income for interest and return on equity. *op. cit.,* "Elements of Housing," pp. 8-9. The remainder of the owners' costs he divides between 15 per cent for depreciation, 15 per cent for taxes and assessments, and 35 per cent for operating and maintenance. (From the manuscript of the author.)

[26] *Business Cycles* (New York: McGraw-Hill Book Co., 1939), Vol. II, p. 604.

## TABLE 3

*Importance of Interest in Inducement to Invest*

A $6,000 home in Queens cited by the Bowery Savings Bank. F.H.A. insured mortgage of 90 per cent or $5,400 amortized over twenty-five years. Real estate and water taxes, fire insurance, F.H.A. insurance, $156.96 annually.[27]

| Assumed Interest Rate | Annual Charge for Interest and Amortization | Annual Cost of Taxes and Insurance | Total Annual Carrying Charge |
|---|---|---|---|
| 6% | $422.28 | $156.96 | $579.24 |
| 5(—16 2/3%) | 383.40( —9.2) | " | 540.36 |
| 4(—20%) | 345.60( —9.8) | " | 502.56 |
| 3(—25%) | 309.96(—10.4) | " | 466.92 |
| 2(—33 1/3%) | 276.48(—11.0) | " | 433.44 |
| 1(—50%) | 245.16(—11.6) | " | 402.12 |
| 0(—100%) | 216.00(—12.2) | " | 372.96 |

avail to get this money used."[28] And D. H. Robertson may have meant the same thing when he said "there may be *no* rate of money interest in excess of zero which will stimulate an unwilling (borrower)"[29]—although one might be pardoned for apprehending from both Pigou's and Robertson's statements that zero interest in itself would make investment profitable under any circumstances, which would certainly be untrue. Probably most economists who have thought about the matter would readily recognize the impotence of interest under conceivable conditions. But there is less recognition of just how closely limited the

[27] F. C. Smith and R. W. Sparks, *op. cit.,* p. 20.

[28] *Theory of Unemployment,* p. 213.

[29] *Banking Policy and the Price Level* (London: P. S. King & Son, Ltd., 1926), p. 81.

power of interest really is under realistic conditions of financial amortization.

Of course, a general interest decline might be expected to have some effect on the building costs themselves and thus have some added importance. However, the small share which interest forms of the national income would suggest that this added consideration is not greatly significant. Even before consulting the statistics of the association of interest rates and building cycles, then, we must come to the conclusion that under the most extreme circumstances interest can only exercise a minor rôle in the inducement to invest in residential buildings. What is true of the more durable residential building must be even more true of the less durable nonresidential building, except notably for public building and building in certain protected industries. And certainly if interest is a minor factor in inducing investment in the building industry, it must be minor indeed as an inducement factor in the great mass of other, less durable, classes of investment goods.[30] Of course, many argue for the importance of interest in stabilizing investment on the ground that manipulations of interest rates would be easier and neater than manipulation of cost of building with all its technical, legal, and human complications.[31] This position attaches a simplicity to the interest

[30] J. R. Hicks has recently put the matter neatly: "Interest is too weak for it to have much influence on the near future; risk is too strong to enable interest to have much influence on the far future; what place is left for interest between these two opposing perils?" He feels, however, that interest can have significance "In a state of confidence . . . (when) risk-allowances are much smaller," *Value and Capital* (Oxford: Clarendon Press, 1939), p. 226.

[31] I have no intention of deprecating the value of reducing interest as a means of helping to raise the long run standard of housing for the

rate problem that is only superficial. Not for nothing has the long rate of interest been one of the most stable prices in our economy. Some long run reduction is no doubt necessary and possible, but drastic manipulation has yet to be proven feasible. Not only might, say, a sudden halving of the long rate of interest involve just as much legal difficulty and human misery as the much smaller corresponding reduction in other costs, but the actual mechanics of reducing the rate to an effective level might involve far larger open market purchases of government and industrial bonds than even those of us who have no pathological phobia towards inflation would like to contemplate. Indeed, the volume purchased and the amounts of money that would have to be spent might well make it cheaper for the government to grant outright subsidies.

*Theory of Investment Demand*: The volume of new building demanded at any time tends to be a residual of the demand for *all* buildings. Before considering the laws of demand for *new building,* therefore, attention must first be given to laws of demand for the *total stock*. As is true of demand for any commodity, this demand is a function of two sets of variables: those which have to do with variations in price; and those which have to do with variations in income. First to be considered is demand as a func-

masses, but merely to disparage its importance as a cause for, or a stabilizer of, building fluctuations. The difference lies in the fact that expectations, which cancel out in the long run, are of overwhelming importance in cyclical periods. But even as a means of improving standards of housing, cuts in interest rates ought to be supplemented by other cost reductions: e.g. extending the amortization period, reducing materials prices, freight rates, increasing efficiency, and so on. See the testimony of T. J. Kreps before the T.N.E.C., *loc. cit.* Mr. Kreps is a strong advocate of the importance of reducing interest rates.

tion of price. And inasmuch as the cost or purchase price of a building has been seen to make up half or less of the periodic deduction from gross income, it is more accurate to speak of demand as a function of cost of ownership. What, then, is this function, and how elastic is it? Would a fall in cost of ownership, for example, bring enough of an increase in requirement for building accommodation as to increase the total outlay from an unchanged national income? Would the increased requirement be so small as to reduce the total outlay for buildings? Or would the increased requirement be likely to just match the decline in ownership costs and thus leave the total outlay, both in the aggregate and in per cent of national income, the same as before?[32] And whatever the effect of a change in the cost of ownership on the portion of the national income spent on *all buildings,* what are the probable effects of these responses on the income spent for, and the volume of, *new building?*

It is a brave man who promises precise answers to such questions. Some of the characteristics of building have already been mentioned and anybody knows that buildings vary widely in size, use, and in local conditions of cost and income. Nevertheless, it may not be far from the truth to say that the demand for *all buildings* as a function of cost of ownership is close to unit elasticity; that changes in cost of living in buildings will not be accompanied by changes in the outlay for building occupancy so long as incomes are undisturbed. The reason is that the cost of living in buildings is so large a part of

[32] Other economic forces, of course, remaining substantially the same.

national income that any appreciable change in the per cent of income so spent would involve violent disturbance to spending, living, and working habits. A doubling in the per cent of income spent for sugar which forms a small portion of income would cause hardly a ripple in the living habits of even the poor, but a change of even 1 per cent in the proportion of income spent for shelter would cut heavily into allowances for clothes, amusement, or education. Variations in expenditures for certain types of buildings might vary widely in response to cost changes, but it is unlikely that mere changes in cost would induce the aggregate expenditure for all buildings to vary much in either direction. This is reinforced by the fact that any increase in the *percentage of income* spent for one type of building almost inevitably comes, so all-pervasive are buildings in our economic life, *at the expense of some other class of building*. For example, a rise in the outlay on industrial buildings for making automobiles is likely to cut into outlays on movie theaters, railroad buildings and so on.

Statistical test of this unit elasticity of demand for the whole sweep of buildings must wait upon an investigator with greater resources than this one, but in fear and trembling the present writer does offer a coefficient of the elasticity of expenditure for housing. (See Table 4.) This coefficient was derived from statistics published by the Federal Housing Administration of the per cent of income spent on housing in relation to the varying costs of home ownership in ninety metropolitan areas. Two sets of relationships were available for both new and existing houses: (1) Relationship between the per cent of income used for gross monthly payment and the size of that pay-

# TABLE 4

*Elasticity of Expenditure for Housing*[34]

SECTION A : Per cent of Income Spent for Housing, as a Function of Cost of Ownership[35]

| | Average[36] Per cent of Income Spent on Housing $\bar{y}$ | Average[36] Monthly Cost of Ownership $\bar{x}$ | Coefficient[37] of Correlation r (P.E.) | $y = ax + b$ | Coefficient of Elasticity ($\eta$) | $m = \dfrac{.136\bar{x}}{\bar{y}}$ |
|---|---|---|---|---|---|---|
| w Houses | 17.1% | $41.04 | .485 ± .0535 | .136x + 11.52 | $.136\dfrac{(x)}{(y)}$ | .328 |
| sting Houses | 14.8% | 39.76 | .330 ± .062 | .088x + 11.30 | $.088\dfrac{(x)}{(y)}$ | .236 |

SECTION B : Ratio of Property Value to Income, as a Function of Level of Property Value[38]

| | Average[39] Ratio of Property Value to Annual Income $\bar{y}$ | Average[39] Property Value $\bar{x}$ | Coefficient[37] of Correlation (r) (P.E.) | $y = ax + b$ | Coefficient of Elasticity ($\eta$) | $m = \dfrac{.000142\bar{x}}{\bar{y}}$ |
|---|---|---|---|---|---|---|
| w Houses | 2.02 | $5,774 | .519 ± .0510 | .000142x + 1.20 | $.000142\dfrac{(x)}{(y)}$ | .406 |
| isting Houses | 1.63 | 5,213 | .464 ± .0549 | .000114x + 1.04 | $.000114\dfrac{(x)}{(y)}$ | .365 |

[4] Elasticity is presented, not in *units of housing* as a function of price, but in *per cent of ome spent for housing* as a function of price. This latter function seems much more en-itening.

[5] The Federal Housing Administration in its *Fifth Annual Report* (Dec. 31, 1938) lists, ninety-odd metropolitan areas of the United States, average percentages of income spent home-owners for gross monthly payment (including amortization, interest, insurance, es, water, special assessments), and the average levels of these gross monthly payments. e data cover only FHA insured, single-family, owner-occupied houses.

[6] Average monthly payment (x) varied from $30 to $50 in the different metropolitan areas. erage per cent of income (y) which this payment constituted varied from 13% to 20%.

[7] Ungrouped data.

[8] Source is the same as that of Section A (see footnote 35). But in this section ratio of ual income to value of property (as appraised by FHA) is taken as a function of the levels property values in the various metropolitan areas.

[9] Average ratio of value of property to income varied from 1½ to 2½. Average property ue varied from $4,000 to $8,000.

ment; and (2) Relationship between the ratio of property valuation to income and the levels of property valuation. In all cases the correlation was very close to .5 and was approximately nine times probable error. The elasticities of expenditure range between .2 and .4, which translated into coefficient of elasticity of demand, would yield an elasticity less than unity but not far from it.[40] If this is true, it means that home dwellers are torn between desire

[40] It is realized that this test suffers from a number of deficiencies: For one thing, the data are available only in groups and not by individuals so that comparison could not be made between persons of the same income levels in the different areas. Incomes differ from one area to another, and this variation might be supposed to cause variation in percentage of incomes spent quite apart from changes in cost of housing. However, the association here shows that in low income areas, which are also low housing cost areas, *low* percentages of income are spent on housing, and conversely; whereas study of the relationship between income levels and percentage income outlays in any one area shows that the poor spend much higher percentages of their incomes on housing than do the well-to-do or rich. The association between low cost of housing and low percentages of incomes spent for housing must, therefore, be due to the low housing costs and not to low income levels. It is possible, however, that these low income levels are responsible for the closeness of elasticity to unity, that, were income levels the same in all areas, percentage outlays would tend to vary even more in the same direction as cost of housing. If so, this would modify our deduction concerning the closeness to unity of the price elasticity of housing demand.

Another fault that might be found with this study is that "other things" are not equal in the different areas. Consumption habits vary and prices of other commodities vary. For example, the propensity of southern areas where housing costs are low to spend smaller percentages of income on housing may be due to higher cost of clothing and manufactured articles. Thus, this propensity might not predict their behavior if a reduction in cost were made. Again, it might be argued that housing costs are partly economic rents and that low housing costs are caused by, rather than causing, low percentage expenditures for housing. But this could be only partly true.

Still a third fault may be the selected character of the data. Home owners carefully selected as good mortgage risks may not be altogether representative of owners and renters of non-insured homes.

not to disturb habits of spending and desire not to alter habits of living, with the former tending to win out. Thus a reduction in cost of ownership of 1 per cent would tend to cause a reduction of .2 to .4 per cent in expenditure on housing, with the remaining .6 per cent to .8 per cent being taken out in additional living quarters.

As pointed out above, it is possible that the demand for one type of building, such as housing, could stray a bit from unity, but it is hardly likely that this could be true for all classes of building because of the enormous part which building and associated expenditures are of national and individual income. Therefore, if so important a part of the total stock of buildings as housing has even a mildly inelastic demand, the remainder of buildings must have demands which are even further on the elastic side.

But even if the long-run price demand for *all buildings* is known to be, or is conceded to be, close to unity,[41] our real search continues for elasticity of demand for *new buildings* and for rules that govern variations in elasticities in the short and the long run. Let us first consider elasticity of demand for new buildings in the long run. As we pointed out at the beginning of this section, demand for new buildings is really a residual of demand for all buildings. This means that the response of demand for new buildings to a change in price is related to the response of demand for all buildings to such a change. If one grants that elasticity of

[41] On the other hand, if the *real* price of buildings fell, unchanged expenditure for buildings would mean increased substitution for other real income, for more buildings and less other real income would be gotten for the same relative outlays. This would leave the *value* of the total stock of buildings undisturbed, however much it would increase its physical magnitude.

long-run demand for all buildings is unity, what, then, is elasticity of long-run demand for new buildings?

It would seem that this would depend upon the closeness with which the cost of occupying all buildings fluctuated with the cost of building new. If owners of old buildings lowered their rents to compete with the cheaper new buildings then the same division of building expenditure between old and new buildings would be maintained; and since, because of the unit elasticity of demand for all buildings, the aggregate expenditure for buildings had not changed, the same amount of money would be spent for new buildings as before. Thus, the demand for new buildings would be unity.[42] However, if owners of old buildings maintained rents of old buildings at previous high levels, then a differential would exist in favor of new buildings and expenditures for new buildings would increase. Demand for new building would be elastic. But this must be an essentially short run phenomenon. In the long run elasticity of price-demand for new buildings can hardly be otherwise than that for all buildings—unity, or close to it.

In the short run, that is for periods of two or three years or less, it would seem that the demand for new buildings

[42] Proof of this is a bit complicated. It has been seen that original cost of the building constitutes perhaps half of cost of ownership. This would induce only a ½ per cent decrease in cost of ownership from a 1 per cent decrease in cost of building new. On the surface this would seem to make the demand for new buildings inelastic. But against this is the fact that the total outlay each year for *use* of all buildings must necessarily be double the expenditure each year for replacements (since original cost is assumed to be half the ownership cost). Thus, though the users of buildings receive only half of the 1 per cent decrease in their rent bills, the result is an increase of 1 per cent in the volume of new building demanded, keeping the aggregate expenditure for new buildings the same.

could be elastic or inelastic, depending upon considerations largely psychological in nature. Well known is the principle that expectation of a further change in price in the same direction may make a demand schedule inelastic or even positively inclined. And it is generally accepted that price changes do bring expectations of further movements in the same direction: e.g. that a price reduction creates expectation of further price reductions. But it is equally true that price changes may bring expectations of subsequent price reversals. Thus the public may expect the price reduction to be temporary and to be followed by price rise. In such a case the short run demand would be elastic. On the other hand, as W. I. King points out, the public is frequently divided on the expectation formed from a price change.[43] Expectations may, therefore, be offsetting. Under circumstances when public opinion is divided about the short trend, expectations may, therefore, be neutral and short-run elasticity of price-demand for new buildings may be not different from that of long-run demand for new buildings or for all buildings.[44] This would seem to be the usual case.

Other factors besides psychological forces may cause a different elasticity for short than for long-run demand. Many of these are physical circumstances of inertia, forcing demand over on the inelastic side. Response to reduction in building cost may be hindered by lack of plans for expansion, by failure of communities to provide utilities,

---

[43] "Can Production of Automobiles be Stabilized by Making Their Prices Flexible?", *Journal of the American Statistical Association,* Vol. 34 (1939), pp. 650-1.
[44] A division of public opinion is not the same thing as public doubt.

fire protection, education. In the same way a rise of building cost will not hinder building so much if a great many plans are under way in which certain financial commitments have already been made. But many of these factors lose their power over elasticity in periods of a year or two. Consequently, for periods upwards of two years, in all except the most decisive price-trends, elasticity of demand for new buildings as a function of price probably oscillates only slightly from unity. In the moderately short run as well as in the long run, provided that income does not change, *the aggregate expenditure for new buildings, as for all buildings, would seem to be quite insensitive to price or cost of ownership.*[45]

But more important and complex than price elasticity of demand is effect on demand of changing levels of income. Income elasticity is more important, because actual income fluctuations are large quantitatively and expected income fluctuations are even larger, especially individual expectations. Incomes, both actual and anticipated, fluctuate more than mere per cent of (unchanged) income spent for buildings possibly could, spending habits being what they are. Income elasticity is more complex, because income levels are themselves functions of the volume of investment which they are supposed to influence and because income effects are intricately intangled between the actual and the expected. Without losing sight of the fact that investment

[45] It will be appreciated, of course, that the assumption of income independent of building costs may be unreal, especially if unemployment exists. A reduction of building costs, by stimulating a short-period building expansion, might induce an increase in national income and thus provide an increase in the aggregate real demand function for building without disturbing the percentage of income spent on buildings.

variations are the chief cause of income variations,[46] we shall now take up the influence on demand of actual and expected income fluctuations. Merely for convenience and without for the moment deciding which it is that really influences the demand for buildings, we shall examine first the probable effects on demand of actual income variations, as if these coincided with expected variations, and then we shall examine the significance of variations in expectations, recognizing that these often vary widely from what actually turns out to be the case.

Fluctuations in actual income payments (or incomes ex post) may vary 10 or 15 per cent a year and as much as 50 per cent in one direction over a half decade. What then is the elasticity of income-demand for building? As in the case of price demand, elasticity of demand for new buildings must be approached through elasticity of demand for all buildings.

The long-run income demand for all buildings is, it would seem, on the elastic side, i.e. an increase in income of 1 per cent would induce more than 1 per cent increase in the expenditure on all buildings, and a reduction of 1 per cent would induce more than 1 per cent reduction in expenditure on all buildings. The basis for this deduction is tied up with the propensity to consume. Larger percentages of big incomes seem to be saved and invested and it is rather difficult to conceive of any extensive amount of investment that is not incorporated in or associated with some kind of building. This elasticity would not neces-

---

[46] The reciprocal influence of investment and income is treated below (Chap. III) in the discussion of the acceleration and multiplier principles.

sarily be true of all building, however, and there is pretty certain evidence that demand for housing as a function of income is quite inelastic. The rich spend much smaller percentages of their incomes for housing than do the poor.[47] The following are the average percentages of family income spent for housing in the United States during 1935-1936:

| Annual Income | Per cent Spent for Housing |
|---|---|
| Under 1000 | 22.5 |
| 1000-1499 | 17.6 |
| 1500-2499 | 16.2 |
| 2500-4999 | 14.4 |
| 5000 and over | 10.5 |

This is understandable, and even the fact that the poor have larger families fails to rob the relationship of its validity. Nevertheless, an elastic demand for all building is perfectly compatible with an inelastic demand for residential building, for though the rich may spend less on house buildings, they spend more on other kinds of buildings: amusement, educational, charitable and so on. And, as pointed out, most of their savings must pass into buildings of some sort. All in all, then, there is a presumption that a given percentage increase in income will in the long run cause a larger than proportional rise in aggregate expenditure for buildings; and a fall in income will cause a larger than proportional fall in aggregate expenditure for buildings. But this presumption carries no quantitative estimate of what this elasticity is.

If the income demand for all buildings really is on the elastic side, what is to be expected of the income

[47] National Resources Committee, T.N.E.C., *op. cit.*, pp. 4954, 5478.

demand for *new buildings?* Here we come to the problem of the acceleration principle and care must be taken to distinguish between the operation of this principle under full, as compared with under only partial, employment of the factors of production.[48] If full employment exists, an increase in income, say, from increased productivity or repayment of debt by a foreign country, would lead to a given increase in aggregate expenditure on all buildings. But the accelerating effect on investment of new buildings would be limited to the amount of income which the nation is willing to spare from other classes of consumption. Some acceleration might be possible (that is, the volume of additional new building called for in the initial period might be greater than the added *annual* outlay for use of all buildings) if the added savings out of the increased income were devoted to building the additional new buildings which could be supported from the new income. But acceleration would be limited by the volume of these savings —not likely, in comparison, to be very great. It is clear, moreover, that taking all classes of investment into consideration, the added income could result in no acceleration if full employment were the case, but merely in a given fraction of the income being diverted from immediate consumption to the production of durable instruments. Thus, even under full employment it is possible that demand for new buildings as a function of income may be more elastic than the demand for all buildings. But considering the fact

[48] The essence of the acceleration principle has been described by Haberler as the making of heavy immediate investments, which will continue to produce for the future, in order to expand present output. Gottfried Haberler, *Prosperity and Depressions* (Geneva: League of Nations, 1937), p. 205.

that, on the one hand, savings in the long run are limited to voluntary savings and are bound to be only a fraction of the marginal income, and that, on the other, accelerating tendencies in other investment channels will compete with accelerating tendencies in building, it would seem hardly likely that long run increases in income would have very elastic effects on inducement to invest in new buildings.

Thus we must look to short-run fluctuations in income if we seek extreme elasticity of demand for new buildings. Short-run fluctuations in income are essentially fluctuations in employment of the factors of production; although fluctuations in income paid out and consumed are milder than those in income produced, the difference being made up in the accumulation and wastage of wealth. The existence of these reserves of idle factors of production makes economically possible the rapid acceleration of investment in response to comparatively mild changes in income consumed. Indeed, an extremely elastic short-run income demand for *new buildings* is quite compatible with a demand for *all buildings* that is unit elasticity or less. How this could be so? Obviously, such a relationship would have to arise out of a situation in which a given expenditure for all buildings, although less than proportional to the change in income, *might* induce a much larger expenditure on new buildings, one that would be more than proportional to the income variation. Let us examine this possibility by means of an illustration.

Assume national income to be $80,000,000,000 at full or standard employment. Annual expenditure for occupying all buildings is one-fourth of aggregate income, or $20,000,000,000, and fluctuates proportionately to income.

One-half of this annual expenditure constitutes depreciation and is normally spent to replace buildings that last, say, twenty years. No savings or net capital formation are assumed.

Now it was pointed out that any addition to national income under such conditions could not have any upwardly accelerating effects on aggregate investment. But downwardly accelerating effects might certainly result from a *decrease* in national income taking the form of unemployment. An initial 1 per cent decrease in national income would reduce annual expenditure on buildings by the same 1 per cent, or $200,000,000. Assuming, in accordance with above conditions, that only half of this constitutes net revenue to owners of buildings, nevertheless at 5 per cent discount, this would destroy (for one year only, of course) the inducement to replace about $1,250,000,000 buildings. Only $8,750,000,000 new buildings might be built in that year to replace the $10,000,000,000 of buildings that wore out. Thus an initial 1 per cent reduction in national income is capable, under circumstances that do not seem unreal, of bringing about a 12.5 per cent reduction in the volume of new building, and, of course, a further and enlarged fall in income. In this case, expenditure for use of all buildings, as a function of income, was assumed to be proportional, or unity elastic; but it is at once clear that, even if income demand for all buildings was quite inelastic, though not less than .08, variations in flow of income might still have elastic effects on demand for new buildings.

There is a lower limit to the accelerating effects, however, just as there is an upper limit established by full employment. The lower limit is reached when income and expenditure for the use of all buildings have fallen so low that practically no new buildings at all are being constructed. If income and inducement to invest fall below this point, then further reductions in income can only affect the expenditure on new buildings in subsequent years and postpone the recovery of the inducement to invest. In the same way, a rise of income is powerless to restore inducement to invest if income is at such a low level that suspension of all replacements still leaves a redundancy of buildings in comparison with the expenditure for building uses.

In addition to the rather rigid limits established by full employment and negative building there are two less rigid. but nonetheless powerful, checks on acceleration which are in potential existence at all levels of investment, although operating with greater or less force at some levels than at others. One of these is *expectation* of future net incomes or net values of uses of the durable goods; this factor is, of course, as likely to increase as to reduce the acceleration, and will be discussed at length below. The other represents all those factors which at one time may delay investment and make it more costly, and at another time may facilitate investment and make it less costly. Thus, it is certain that increases in volume of building would be held back at first by lack of plans and later on, as the level of activity increased, by transportation tie-ups; strikes, scarcity of certain classes or all classes of skilled labor, and union restrictions on productivity; restrictive city building codes; increased tax levies or assessments; increased stringency or cost of credit. All these and still other factors causing increases in costs and constituting deductions from income would postpone, or partially or wholly offset, the accelerating effects of increased income on volume of new building. For example, if a 1 per cent rise in income could induce 12.5 per cent additional outlay for buildings, a 1 per cent deduction from income could prevent that 12.5 per cent additional outlay. A 1 per cent rise of cost of building alone, other costs of ownership unchanged, would prevent perhaps half the acceleration; a 1 per cent rise in the other costs of ownership as well would prevent the other half.

All these factors making for increased cost as building volume and other business activity expanded, would also tend to make for decreased cost as declining income brought declining outlays for new buildings. But it is a familiar fact that costs do not always fall as readily or as fast as they rise. Taxes rarely fall; restrictive laws and ordinances rarely relax; labor relinquishes hard won concessions only reluctantly. Consequently, these factors are much more likely to hinder upward acceleration than they are to soften downward acceleration. Therefore, we have the familiar phenomenon that building and other forms of investment are often quick to fall but slow to recover. In two or three years, investment has been observed to lose ground that required half a decade to win.

*Expectations*: We come now to the chief modifier of the loose relation between income and demand for durable investment agents. If a given increase in annual expenditure for building uses is to induce heavy immediate investments "which will continue to bear fruit for some time into the future," those expenditures must be capitalized on the basis of expectation that they will continue to be made over the life of asset to be acquired. Hence it is obvious that the rentals or use-values capitalized by the investment market are not necessarily rents which have been or will be enjoyed, but those which are expected.[49] Whether the rents expected are high enough to constitute inducement to invest depends both on what the relevant facts of the immediate past have been and on how those facts are interpreted by the investment market. Expectations, then, depend on both "real" and psychological factors.

"Real" factors include data of the kind we have been discussing: gross rents; vacancies, indicating the effectiveness of the rent structure; foreclosures, indicating collapse of equities; and operating costs, including real estate taxes, insurance, costs of repairing and maintaining and costs of providing conventional services, such as heating, hot water, garbage collection, door and elevator service. In addition are the familiar external and semi-external forces such as wars, disasters, discoveries, changes in size and composition of population, political developments.

The psychological basis of expectations, or interpretations placed by the market on real data, constitute what is commonly known as confidence. If knowledge were perfect, expected rents would never deviate from actual rents, i.e. the correct interpretations would always be placed on the real data. Since this is not so, confidence is important. And three levels of confidence may be distinguished: *neutral* confidence; *positive* confidence; and *negative* confidence.

It is necessary to understand neutral confidence. Neutral confidence would be such a state of confidence that

[49] Keynes charges that most discussion of the marginal efficiency of capital overlooks the element of expectation. *op. cit.,* p. 138. This charge is becoming less and less true.

would not alter the outcome of the real economic forces at work. As stated, it need not consist of perfect interpretation of the real data, nor need it mean uncritical acceptance of the real data without any interpretation, for this is hardly conceivable in view of the complexity of the data and the impossibility of forming an expectation without a mental attitude. Neither need it imply mere projection of past trends, or continuance of the status quo. On the other hand, where the latter are justified, it does not obviate them. The easiest way to imagine a psychological state that would not exercise any independent effect on the outcome would be a state of divided opinion among the investing public.

Accordingly, positive confidence results in expectations and an outcome more favorable than are justified by the real forces at work, although these expectations may still be pessimistic and even contrary to the trend prevailing in the past. And negative confidence results in expectations and an outcome less favorable than are justified by the real data, although the expectations may still be optimistic and, again, even contrary to the trend prevailing in the past.

A number of characteristics of the psychology of expectations may be distinguished. For one thing, confidence is apparently susceptible to frequent and often wide alternations between positive and negative, between underestimating and overestimating the real significance of current and past events. Why confidence is rarely neutral, why it is continually fluctuating between positive and negative, altering the turning points and accentuating the movements of investment-expectations is largely, though perhaps not entirely, a problem in the psychology of social groups. If each member of an aggregation of people were isolated from the others in thought and action, it is probable that his psychology might still deviate from neutral and accentuate fluctuations in expectations induced by changes in the real data. But the deviations would not be so wide.

The fact is, however, that the investment market is not an aggregation of isolated individuals but a social group composed of members wanting somewhat the same things and communicating with and influencing each other through conversation, speeches, writings, and statistics, by means of the telephone, radio, ticker, newspapers, magazines, and letters. Moreover, having no central organization, it may be regarded as on the whole a simple, unorganized crowd. Such a crowd has the characteristics described by a social psychologist:

> "We may sum up the psychological character of the unorganised or simple crowd by saying that it is excessively emotional, impulsive, violent, fickle, inconsistent, irresolute and extreme in action, displaying only the coarser emotions and the less refined sentiments; extremely suggestible, careless in deliberation, hasty in judgment, incapable of any but the simpler and imperfect forms of reasoning; easily swayed and led, lacking in self-consciousness, devoid of self-respect and of sense of responsibility, and apt to be carried away by the consciousness of its own force, so that it tends to produce all the manifestations we have learnt to expect of any irresponsible and absolute power. Hence its behaviour is like that of an unruly child or an untutored passionate savage in a strange situation, rather than like that of its average member. . . ."[50]

[50] William McDougall, *The Group Mind* (New York: G. P. Putnam's Sons, 1920), p. 64.

The fact that the investment market is a crowd which, though it has no such thing as a collective consciousness and is not centrally organized, does consist of intercommunicating members and organizations provides the basis for self-inflammatory movements in confidence. That is, the emotions of each member are fanned by the perception of the emotions and behavior of the others. And each member, having been so stimulated, communicates his emotions to the others and thus intensifies theirs; whereupon the intensified emotions of the others are communicated back to the individual, and so the upward spiral continues until either the group is nervously exhausted or a change in the real data, developing perhaps as a result of the emotional splurge, becomes sufficiently apparent to remove the basis for the inflammation and perhaps to start a counter-inflammation.

A crowd is suggestible and reciprocally corroborative not only as to action, but quite probably also as to goal. For example, an investment boom is not only a period in which the market-crowd reciprocally convinces itself that investment will make its members rich, but it is also a period in which riches are the socially approved goals. Whereas an investment panic or depression is not only a period in which the market-crowd reciprocally convinces itself that investment is no way to get rich or achieve power and prestige, but it may also be a period in which the socially approved goals change from riches to security, from the desire for a large, however precarious, burst of income to a smaller, but more stable, flow. If this is true, and it is probable that such elemental changes do occur from the alterations of very great booms and depressions, then we have one more explanation for the autointoxication of the investment market.

A second characteristic of the psychology of expectations, which it is difficult to dissociate entirely from the first, is the sometimes intensifying interaction with real factors. The psychological reaction to a real trend may intensify the real trend and the intensified real trend may reciprocate by further intensifying the psychological reaction.[51] I say, sometimes, because the intensifying interaction with the real factors need not and does not always occur. Indeed, the fact that all general movements reverse themselves sooner or later and, on the downturn, usually before the absolute bottom is reached, would suggest that such intensifying interaction, even when it occurs, is really a temporary phase inevitably succeeded by a slowing down process in which real trend is taken as foreshadowing, not further movement in the same direction, but counter movement. Just as in the case of the intensifying interaction, the slowing-down interaction is grounded in human experience, experience teaching that no trend lasts forever without producing forces that cause its reversal. Of course, the decline would eventually slow up for real reasons, discussed in Chapter III, pp. 81-5.

[51] Pigou explains this behavior in the case of prices by pointing out that "This expectation is partly a reflection of our general tendency to expect processes that we observe in action now to continue in action at all events for some time yet. But, whatever the precise way in which the generation of these expectations comes about, there is no doubt at all that they are generated. Prices having risen, business men expect a further rise; prices having fallen, they expect a further fall. . . . The process . . . is cumulative and progressive in character . . . (and) this cumulative process is of great importance. It means that from small origins large consequences, whether of evil or of good, may be built up. *op. cit.*, pp. 241-3.

A third characteristic, not to be confused with the second, is that any given expectation may set up behavior which, depending upon the circumstances, either brings about or prevents the event expected. The circumstances upon which this depends are the type and source of the expectation. For example, if prices are expected to rise, whether they actually rise or not depends upon whether the expectation is held by the buyers or the sellers, and upon the situation in which they find themselves. If the buyers hold the expectation of rise, they may buy for speculation and thus force the price up, or they may abandon certain plans altogether and thus prevent the rise or cause a fall.[52] If sellers hold the expectation of price rise, they may withhold goods for future sale, but this is not always possible due to contracts and desire to retain good-will and the subsequent expansion of production might well prevent the rise or bring a decline. And to cite another type, an expectation of an oversupply would, if anything, cause business men to take steps to forestall such oversupply by restricting output.

A fourth characteristic of expectation psychology has been pointed out by Oskar Morgenstern:

"Only such things can be statistically analysed as can be somehow measured in the form of figures. . . . It is . . . impossible—which means in this case *inconceivable*

[52] For example, newspaper publishers fearing a price rise in newsprint paper may effect so many economies in the use of white paper as to prevent the price rise from coming about. Whether such economies would effectively block the expected rise would also depend, of course, upon the strength of cooperative restraint among publishers in refraining from bidding up the price in the attempt of each to assure himself an adequate supply. Such economies and cooperative restraints have proved to be factors in newsprint paper situation.

—to determine the feelings and expectations of individual economic subjects and entrepreneurs in this way. . . . All that we can do is to show laboriously *ex post,* by way of the repercussions it (the psychological factor) causes, that it existed at a *previous time.*"[53]

It is, of course, to this type of limited demonstration that the present statistical study shall have to confine itself.

A fifth characteristic is that the quality and extent of the mental reactions involved in expectation are largely products of the institutional background of the interpreters.[54] This means that a full understanding of the psychology of expectations must wait upon, among other things, careful study of business training, drives, and traditional modes of action or rules of thumb.[55] Perhaps the best contribution that could be made along this line would be an historical study of overt business opinion wherever it manifests itself in print, testing and analysing this opinion through various crises and stages of the business cycle. Among the many things we need to know is just how far into the future expectations normally extend and whether the length of this extension ever shows appreciable change.

[53] *The Limits of Economics* (London: Wm. Hodge & Co., Ltd., 1937), pp. 106-7.

[54] As Professor Ginzberg expresses it, since past experience is the only guide to future action, the genesis and growth of these preconceptions are crucial. Eli Ginzberg, *The Illusion of Economic Stability* (New York: Harper & Brothers, Publishers, 1939), p. 221.

[55] Although we may develop some *a priori* clues from knowledge of human nature. For example, Keynes points out that we are apt to be guided by the things we know something about and to ignore things about which we are uncertain. "For this reason the facts of the existing situation enter, in a sense disproportionately, into the formation of our long-term expectations" (*op. cit.,* p. 148). But this does not tell us much about the interpretation of these facts.

In summary then, we find that the psychology of expectations is essentially unstable due to the reciprocally corroborative quality of the unorganized investment crowd; that it often, if only temporarily, interacts cumulatively with the real factors; that, depending upon the type and source of the expectation, it may either bring about or prevent the event expected; that it is not susceptible to quantitative measurement; and that its quality and direction may be judged only by knowledge of the "preconceptions" of the interpreters.

Such characteristics would seem to rob the concept of short-run elasticity of income demand for new buildings of its precision. And to a large extent they do. Still, it may be possible to lay down a few principles concerning the behavior of expectations that would clear short-run elasticity of income demand from some of this haze. For one thing, expectations are likely to lean on the negative side during periods of doubt. This would usually operate to cause a lead on the downturn of depressions and a lag on upturn of prosperity. Reinforcement of this is had from the fact that, as Keynes has pointed out,[56] investment stagnation requires that only one party to an investment decision as between borrower and lender need be pessimistic; whereas investment activity requires that both parties be optimistic. The well-known rapidity of contraction phase and slowness of upturn phase may be partly explained by this.

Moreover, expectations are apt to deviate furthest from neutral after a long period of upward or downward movement. Doubts held by some have "proved" to be mistaken or have turned into certainty. Opinions have had a chance

[56] *op. cit.*, p. 158.

to circulate, become reinforced by the magic of numbers, and crystallize editorially or by word of mouth into rules of investment behavior accepted almost as self-evident truths. Thus in time of negative confidence, spontaneous income increases are probably never taken at face value and increases must continue for some time before being capitalized. Upward acceleration is, therefore, dampened and perhaps even nullified in periods which have been preceded by several years of continuously falling income; and downward acceleration is, of course, impossible if investment is already practically nil. Similarly in time of positive confidence, sudden or spontaneous income decreases are discounted also, though perhaps not always to the same extent. Downward acceleration may, therefore, be partly or wholly estopped in periods which have been preceded by a number of years of continuously rising income; and upward acceleration is, of course, slowed by the increasing friction of the approach to full employment. Consequently, investment acceleration will operate freely only in periods when investment is neither too high nor too low but is hanging in the balance. At either extreme, positive confidence and nearly full employment on the one hand, and negative confidence and nearly zero investment on the other, the elasticity of income demand for new building may reduce to unity or less.

The introduction of the concept of expectations helps, then, to explain a number of puzzling phenomena. In the first place, it helps explain differences in turning points of investment and income, differences which often in severe depressions take the form of a lead of investment over income on the downturn and a lag behind income on the upturn. In addition, it aids to explain the fact that fluctuations in investment have not been as great as a simple capitalization of changes in current net income would indicate. It also clears up part of the mystery of the long continued booms and depressions in investment which create in building the now familiar phenomenon of long cycles. And finally, expectations supply the link between explanations of fluctuations in investment as a function of income, and in income as a function of investment. We may avoid circular thinking by arguing that, although actual income cycles are partly determined by cycles in investment, nevertheless investment is influenced not so much by *actual* income movements, as by *expected* income movements, such expectations often pursuing strange stars.

# CHAPTER III

## INVESTMENT AND CONSUMPTION

ECONOMICS has by now pretty well satisfied itself that the theory of investment is intricately tied up with the theory of consumption. Understanding the theory involves understanding not only how consumption affects investment, but also how investment affects consumption,[1] the basic nature of the interaction being governed by technical, institutional, and psychological patterns which the mathematicians like to call determinants. These patterns do not remain the same, of course, either absolutely or relatively, and their changes, the functions of internal and external ferments, give play to wide variations in extent and quality of cyclical behavior.

With these considerations in mind, the present chapter is devoted to fixing the logical place of investment in a unified explanation of waves of employment and income. Fortunately, the many other hunters in this much explored but still little understood wilderness have blazed enough trails to give any new searching party a considerable start before it is thrown completely upon its own resources. The two main trails are the multiplier and the acceleration principles. One must beware, however, of re-

---

[1] So much attention is customarily given to the wide relative fluctuation in investment that it is worth calling attention to the fact that absolute fluctuations in consumption output are often greater than those in investment. *supra,* p. 4.

garding these as broad, straight highways, well paved, well fenced, and unmistakably indicated. Professor Hansen has told the tale of at least one brave but incautious party which started out at full speed equipped with nothing better than high-powered but too specialized and sometimes inadequately understood determinants.[2] Perhaps Professor Hansen overstated the horrors in several instances; the Harrod expedition was by no means unsuccessful, but it would certainly have done better to take along some of the shabby but serviceable equipment used by those who first advanced over this uncertain country. The present adventure will proceed tentatively, therefore, using the modern devices wherever it can, but testing them and modifying them and standing prepared to pull them out of the mire with old-fashioned empiricisms. We begin with a cautious statement of the acceleration and multiplier principles, proceed to an equally cautious synthesis, move from there to an examination of what can be rescued from the depredations of critic patrols, and end up by orienting building investment in the process which we shall have developed.

### The Acceleration Principle

There is no brief and also accurate statement of the acceleration principle. Its essence is that *under certain conditions* seemingly innocent variations in the growth of periodic consumer demand are capable of inducing wide fluctuations in the absolute level of periodic investment flow. The fundamental guilt need not be with consump-

---

[2] Hansen, A. H., "Harrod on the Trade Cycle," *Full Recovery or Stagnation?* (New York: W. W. Norton & Co., 1938), pp. 35-58.

tion, which can hardly avoid some mild deviation from the straight and narrow, but can be traced to the durability of most investment agents. This durability "necessitates" a valuable outlay in the initial period which in turn obviates for some time any further investment expenditure, except for "replacements" of worn out equipment installed at some time in the past, until there is a further periodic consumption increase of the same absolute amounts. Consequently, when consumption first rises, a large investment *may* be in order; but if periodic consumption subsequently rises by smaller absolute amounts, as would seem pretty nearly inevitable, the durable investment agents already in existence *may* require smaller and smaller additions and the periodic output of the investment goods industries such as building *may* fall even while periodic consumption is still slowly rising. If consumption stops rising, only replacements may be needed. And if consumption should fall some or all of these may be suspended until the excess capacity thus created is eliminated.

So stated, however, the acceleration principle amounts only to an exposition of what could happen under conceivable circumstances. Let us now examine the many conditions of its operation and the wide variability to which these conditions are subject. It is axiomatic that an increase in investment and an increase in consumption in the same period is possible only if there is unemployed labor and credit.[3] Otherwise, consumption must be at the expense of investment. Upward acceleration can occur

[3] Aside from increases in population and improved techniques.

therefore only during depression, during which time it is usually fed by slowly rising population.[4] (Downward acceleration can, of course, occur so long as there is any investment at all.) But not only is unemployment a condition precedent to upward acceleration; the unemployment must be distributed in occupations not too far removed from those whose demand is being stimulated. Distribution being rarely thoroughly appropriate,[5] many unemployed being of the less desirable type, and credit being at times highly immobile and inflexible, the magnification of investment is often decreased by rising labor costs and interest rates[6] and by time lags that spread the investment over several consumption periods.

Upward acceleration requires also that industrial production be in the increasing cost stage of plant utilization, in which each additional unit of output costs more than the average. This is a more accurate statement than to say that excess capacity from previous booms must have worn out, which helps give the relation between consumption and investment a spurious air of precision.[7] Excess capacity expressed in terms of unused floor space or equipment is equally useless as a definition. Defined thus it is

[4] R. F. Harrod, *The Trade Cycle* (Oxford: Clarendon Press, 1936), p. 57.
[5] Changes in skill and techniques; drifting of skilled unemployed into other occupations; death and retirement of skilled men and maturation of young, unskilled unemployed, geographical trends.
[6] To say nothing of speculative increases in land, and in other economic rents.
[7] Compare Harrod, *loc. cit.*, with S. S. Kuznets' more careful statement "Capital Goods in the Business Cycle," *Economic Essays in Honor of Wesley Clair Mitchell* (New York: Columbia University Press, 1935), pp. 238-41.

always with us and may reflect absence of demand at any price, monopolistic restriction, complete uselessness, or a healthy attitude toward obsolescence. If industrial production is in an increasing cost stage, whether due to wear and tear of time, to an increase in consumption sufficient to take it out of the decreasing cost stage, or to a wage rise (not experienced in the investment producing industries), any further increase in consumption demand may induce new investment wherever the net marginal economies promise to outweigh the costs of installing new fixed assets. Naturally this decision rests on three different sets of costs: the costs of more intensive utilization of the existing investment; the costs of operating prospective new assets; and the costs of acquiring the new assets. In addition there are considerations such as loss of orders from delays and inferior quality of product or service that might be prevented by acquiring new assets.

Far more complex than the cost problem, are expectations that form the basis of the investment decisions. The significance and perversity of this factor were discussed at length in the preceding chapter. Under no circumstances will the investment expenditures due to added consumption be larger than the discounted value of the net income anticipated from the increase in all consumption throughout the life of the investment agent. Obviously, the induced investment outlay cannot exceed the capitalized net revenue expected from the increased consumption of all future periods. The ratio of investment outlay to consumption increase cannot then exceed the ratio of the capitalized net income to that same consumption increase.[8] The size of the relation then must vary with, among other things, the long-term interest rate; the length of the period over which the consumption increase is expected to endure; the expected non-capital deductions from gross consumer outlay; and the relative cost of investing now as compared with the probable cost of investing later. Consequently, the investor will attempt to adjust the size of his investment to these expectations. For technical reasons, however, this is often impossible. Efficient agents may normally only be had in units of large value and size. For example, paper making machines for the manufacture of newsprint paper come only in million dollar units capable of producing one-fourth the requirements of a good-sized plant and characterized by great durability. In such cases—and these are the rule in large

$$[8]\ I\ <\ \frac{\Delta E}{r}\left[\frac{1-(1+r)^{-a}}{}\right];\quad \frac{I}{\Delta C}\ <\ \frac{\frac{\Delta E}{r}\left[1-(1+r)^{-a}\right]}{\Delta C}$$

I = Investment due to consumption increase.
$\Delta C$ = Expected increase in consumption.
$\Delta E$ = Expected increase in periodic net income after deduction of non-capital operating outlays.
r = Long rate of interest.
a = Expected life of the asset as reflected by depreciation or amortization schedule.

For any one stage of production net income may be only a small part of the consumption expenditure and the induced investment will be relatively small. For all stages of production, however, the induced investment may approach the full ratio of capital value to periodic net income.

The extent to which the relation is less than the ratio expressed above is dependent largely on the elasticity of investment construction supply, i.e. on the rigidity of construction costs. If costs did not vary at all with level of investment, the relation would probably be equal to this ratio.

capital industry—enterprisers bear the burden of increasing costs until their expectations fit the technical requirements of investing.

Thus the full employment of labor and credit, geographical and vocational immobility, speculative elements, the time required for investment to be consummated, the intricate and ever changing cost comparisons to be made, the many rigid technical requirements of investment, and most of all the staggering complexity of the psychological anticipations involved, enter into the formulation of the relation between advancing consumption and induced investment. To these should be added the unpredictable price and production antics of monopolies[9] in their feud with competition and the law, the operation of legal agencies in the capital and labor markets, contractual obligations and Schumpeter's well-known factor of innovation. Needless to say, decision to invest bears far from a linear or even unbroken relation to changes in expenditures on consumption.

## The Multiplier Principle

The multiplier is a convenient term for the stimulating effect which investment expenditures *may* have on consumption expenditures and thence upon the volume of income (and saving).[10] It may be stated as follows: Under

[9] Kuznets, *op. cit.*, p. 243.

[10] For a small portion of the literature see J. M. Keynes, *op. cit.*, especially pp. 89-131; J. M. Clark, "Aggregate Spending by Public Works," *Preface to Social Economics* (New York: Farrar & Rinehart, Inc., 1936), pp. 379-89; Michal Kalecki, "Investment and Income," *Essays in the Theory of Economic Fluctuations* (New York: Farrar & Rinehart, Inc., 1939), pp. 42-74; R. F. Harrod, *op. cit.*, pp. 65-74; Fritz Machlup, "Period Analysis and Multiplier Theory," *Quarterly*

*certain circumstances* an excess of actual investment outlay over planned saving[11] for the same period *may* set up a chain of consumer expenditures which, by stimulating production of goods, are capable of inducing eventual multiple additions to real income. Conversely, a deficit of actual investment outlay over planned savings may set up an opposite chain of withdrawals of consumer expenditures which, by destroying demand for goods and causing production to be suspended, are capable of inducing multiple subtractions from real income.[12] In either case the multiplying effect represents the effort of the economic system to create or destroy enough income to bring *voluntary* or planned savings into equality with actual investment. At no time, of course, are *actual* savings anything but identical with *actual* investment—that is, if you follow the right school![13]

*Journal of Economics,* Vol. 54 (Nov. 1939), pp. 1-27; Gottfried von Haberler, *op. cit.*

[11] If net investment is a negative quantity, then a deficit of actual disinvestment over planned dissaving would have the same stimulating effect.

[12] If net investment is a negative quantity, then an excess of actual disinvestment over planned dissaving would have the same depressing effect.

[13] See, however, the article by F. A. Lutz, "The Outcome of the Saving-Investment Discussion," *Quarterly Journal of Economics,* Vol. 52 (1938), pp. 588-614. Mr. Lutz shows that Robertson's definition of investment and saving are ex ante definitions. No equality of these is necessary. He feels that this terminology is more useful for process analysis than the Keynsian ex post definitions. Actually, both sets of terminology are indispensable for analysis of cumulative economic movements. Savings and investment, *ex ante,* are almost certain to be different, and savings and investment *ex post* can be defined to be identical. See also the four-sided discussions between A. P. Lerner, Oscar Lange, Myra Curtis, and F. A. Lutz in the same journal, Vol. 53 (1939), pp. 611-31.

The concept of the multiplier must be stated at least as carefully as the acceleration principle. Just as was true of the accelerating effect which comsumption may have on investment, any upward multiplying effect which investment may have on consumption can occur only in a situation of unemployment of labor. For if all labor is fully employed, investment and consumption are necessarily competitive rather than corroborative. This is not to say that unemployment is enough to permit multiplication. As is true of acceleration, the unemployment must be appropriately distributed in those industries about to be stimulated by the expenditure. Even though unemployment may exist, if it is primarily in the producers goods industries with very little unemployment in the industries making consumer goods, the operation of the principle serves chiefly to multiply prices rather than income and transfer income from the laboring to the entrepreneural classes where it may become almost entirely savings. Downward multiplication can, of course, occur so long as savings exceed investment or dissavings fall short of disinvestment.

Given then the existence of unemployment appropriately distributed, the capacity of an excess of investment over planned saving to increase real income depends upon the disposition which the recipients make of their additional money incomes. For the multiplying effect to be realized, the money has to be spent again and again with the primary factors of production so as to increase the output of these factors. Workers and entrepreneurs must be willing, therefore, to spend at least some of the money they receive for their own goods and services in turn for the goods and services of others. Their willingness to do this depends upon not only their fundamental psychological make-up which Keynes labels the psychological propensity to consume,[14] but also their expectations of the future; upon institutional factors such as distribution of income and generally accepted rules of business procedure; and upon technical or structural factors such as size of existing inventories and burden of debt. All these factors have been discussed in abundant literature on the multiplier. Whatever it is that controls the respending of the money income, the higher the per cent of additional money incomes respent, the greater is the multiplier of real consumption and real income.

But time also is the essence of the multiplier. Respendings must be considered not in the transaction sense, but in the income sense. Until a dollar spent by an income recipient has gone through all the stages involved in the creation of a dollar's worth of consumer goods, it has not completed one single respending. When a dollar spent for beer by a construction worker has been completely split up between the bartender, the saloon-keeper, the jobber, the wages and profits of the brewers, and finally the worker in the hops field, it has gone through one round of income creation and consumption and is ready to be respent and to start on another round. Each of these respendings therefore occupies a certain amount of time which, after Machlup, may be called a marginal income propagation period.[15] Such a period is, of course,

---

[14] *op. cit.*, Chap. VIII.

[15] "Period Analysis and Multiplier Theory," *Quarterly Journal of Economics,* Vol. 54 (1939), p. 10. Machlup places the length of this

only a vague kind of dispersions. Actually the spendings go through cycles of widely different durations and are staggered in such a way as to be fairly continuous. The bartender spends his share of the dollar long before the worker in the hops field receives his. The saloon-keeper may spend the day's profits in his competitor's establishment or he may place them in his Christmas club account for expenditure six months later. The length of the spending period is the sum of all the lags that enter between each successive receipt by the primary factors of production.

It is clear that the length of this income propagation is a leading determinant of the practical extent of the multiplier.[16] For example, if income propagation requires only three months, then a multiplier of 2.5 would be 92 per cent efficient within a year; whereas if income propagation requires six months, the same multiplier would be only 78 per cent efficient. Indeed, Machlup has pointed out that this time factor cuts heavily into the practical importance of large multipliers and reduces the differences between practical short-term multipliers of large and small propensities to consume.[17] The factors controlling the time element are almost as important as the factors controlling the propensity to consume.

As a matter of fact, some of them are not greatly different. The same consumption habits that influence the

period tentatively at three months, or about half the period for all income. J. M. Clark has placed the period tentatively at two months. *op. cit.*, p. 386.

[16] The full theoretical multiplier $\dfrac{1}{1-\dfrac{\Delta C}{\Delta y}}$ requires, of course, an infinite number of propagation periods.

[17] *op. cit.*, pp. 16-17.

proportion respent also influence the length of the delay in the respending. Expectations play a highly important part. So also do established business practices such as pay dates, discounts, periods of settlement and methods of communication. Distribution of income must not be overlooked: the same people who spend nearly all of their incomes are likely also to spend them quickly. Naturally many of these factors vary and the income propagation may from time to time be longer or shorter. So far as psychological factors go, one would expect that the propagation period would be longer during times of doubt and depression and shorter during periods of high expectations and rising prosperity. But the fact should not be lost sight of that the income creation period can not be shorter than that allowed by the technical problems of physical production. The multiplier involves a multiplication of *real marginal income* from marginal increases of purchasing power. This real marginal income must be produced. To be produced primary factors of production must be assembled, organized, and the goods put through the normal processing period. In the meanwhile, even though existence of stocks may prevent inconvenience to customers, incomes of primary factors are held up. If excess capacity exists, the problem of assembly and organization is much less, though even here many unforeseen problems arise to delay operations. For example the problem of training additional men of a given skill may hold up production in all the future stages.

But these lags are nothing compared to those encountered when each new series of income creations require new additions to plant capacity in all the various stages of production, i.e. when the acceleration principle comes into play. Then income propagation periods may have to be computed in terms of years rather than months.[18] For such periods it may be worth applying the term "capital propagation period." The situation at such times is further obscured by the fact that while additional plant capacity is being constructed it is always possible to produce at least some marginal real income by operating existing plants at increasing costs. The extent to which multiplication is cut down depends upon the inelasticity of the supply and steepness of the rise in prices. If the price rise is great, then there is a shift of money income from wage earners to the profit makers. This shift creates a competitive illusion which may in the end intensify to some degree the operation of the acceleration principle.[19]

[18] Added plant capacity is required only for the first respending of each fresh addition to money income. Subsequent spendings occur in subsequent periods and, becoming progressively smaller, find the provision for the first respending ample. In fact, each succeeding series of income creations finds a larger and larger capacity left over from plant provision for previous series. Eventually, plant additions begin to taper off and deceleration begins. It will be observed that the technical determinants of the income propagation period are apt to move oppositely from the psychological obstacles. During depression there are few technical obstacles and income propagation is slowed up primarily by psychological factors. During active recovery when confidence is high, technical obstacles delay the income propagation. Income propagation can move no more rapidly than the slowest of its determinants.

[19] It may do so in two ways: first, by creating an investment demand out of all proportion to the real advance in consumption; and later, by reducing the marginal propensity to consume, slowing up even that advance which is actually occurring. See Harrod, *op. cit.,* pp. 92-3. We shall see, however, that the technical effect of the production lags on the relation probably does more to reduce acceleration than the psychological effect does to increase it. (*infra,* pp. 90-1.)

## The Investment-Consumption Interaction

The idea that investment and consumption drag each other up and down the economic scale through booms and depressions is, of course, not new. But in recent years there have been brave attempts to dress the interaction with mathematical precision by fitting it into a joint pattern of acceleration and multiplication.[20] Naturally the fit is not always comfortable—the present section will point out just how wide is the variability in the operation of the interaction. But even at its worst the interaction offers plausible explanations for a number of cyclical phenomena that are not easy to explain in other ways and it will be part of our task to examine its value for this latter purpose.

## A Skeleton View of the Interaction

The outstanding feature of the business cycle process is that investment and consumption reciprocally reinforce each other and reciprocally decelerate each other on both upturn and downturn. That is, on the upturn, investment and consumption first interact to speed up the recovery of employment and income and then to slow up that recovery; on the downturn, they interact first to speed up the fall of employment and income and then to slow up that fall. The reinforcement operates in the following manner: In time of depression and unemployment, any

[20] R. F. Harrod, *op. cit.*, pp. 53-106. See especially "The Inevitability of the Cycle," pp. 102-6. Paul A. Samuelson, "A Synthesis of the Principle of Acceleration and the Multiplier," *Journal of Political Economy,* Vol. 47 (Dec. 1939), pp. 786-98.

investment expenditure that is not currently offset by planned savings represents an addition to the potential purchasing power of the community. If the recipients of this purchasing power—contractors, manufacturers, workers—do not choose to exercise it, planned savings then become equal to actual investment and the interaction stops right there. On the other hand, if they do respend part of the money for goods and services then there has been set up an additional potential demand for employment and real income. Of course, if the goods are delivered merely by allowing inventories to run down, there has been a disinvestment to offset the investment and again the interaction stops right there. But if the goods and services are currently produced or reproduced, then when the money spent has reached all the prime factors involved in the production there has been a second round of income creation and consumption.

But before this second round of income creation (the first round of consumption) can take place it may be necessary to make a new investment in capital equipment in order to produce the goods and services demanded. It would be more accurate in most cases to say that it may seem to the business man that new or additional plant capacity would make operation more economical. We have already discussed, and will have occasion to discuss further later on, the considerations that impel him to make an investment and govern his decision concerning the amount of investment outlay he should make. It is sufficient at this point that the value of the induced investment may be many times that of the induced consumption occurring in the capital propagation period.[21] This induced investment constitutes a further, magnified increase in real income and the prime factors of its production are simultaneously endowed with additional money incomes.

We now enter into a third period. Whether reinforcement occurs in this period depends upon whether the marginal consumption expenditures of this period are enough greater than those of the previous period to induce an even greater investment outlay. The responsibility for this falls on the income recipients of the previous investment expenditure and their propensities to consume, for, otherwise, respending will grow smaller and smaller in each subsequent period and the original increase in consumption flow will gradually die out. But the investment outlay in the third period must be enough greater than that of the second period to offset in the fourth period the fall in consumption due to "leakages" of money incomes of the previous periods and still provide consumption demand for even greater investment rises in the future.

Deceleration occurs if this requirement is not met. Investment, increasing by diminishing amounts, may slow consumption to a constant rate of increase; this may halt all further increases in new investment. Under theoretically conceivable circumstances, such deceleration can either lead income to level off toward an asymptote without any subsequent decline or can lead to self-dampening

21 Of course, the value of induced investment can not be larger and indeed will probably be smaller than the aggregate consumption expected to occur in all the periods over which the investment agent is to be amortized.

oscillations about an equilibrium position.[22] However, under realistic circumstances, which shall be discussed presently, such slowing down in the increase of investment and consumption must ordinarily lead to a real downturn in investment, consumption, income, and employment.

The downturn may start out with a small drop in investment due to a diminution in the periodic amounts of increase of consumption, to a drop in the relation, or to an inadequacy of credit. Whatever the reason for the fall in investment, if it is not matched by a simultaneous and equivalent reduction of savings, the multiplier now operates in reverse by inducing in the next period a further reduction in the amounts by which consumption is increasing. This, of course, reacts to reduce the absolute amount of investment even more, with further depressing effects on rising consumption. Thus investment and consumption reinforce each other downturn as well as on the upturn. When the declines in investment become greater than diminishing increases in consumption, income and employment begin to drop. And when consumption stops rising altogether, net investment may conceivably fall to zero; although if individual consumption industries are expanding some investment will probably be demanded whatever the trend of average consumption. Thus the decline accelerates itself and the acceleration may continue until net investment is wiped out and gross investment is reduced to a fraction of long-run replace-

[22] Ragnar Frisch, "The Interrelation between Capital Production and Consumer-Taking," *Journal of Political Economy*, Vol. 39 (1931), p. 649.
Samuelson, *op. cit.*, pp. 792-3.

ment need.[23] The decline in income and employment need not stop with even zero gross investment, however. So long as actual investment outlays are less than planned saving, or depreciation of aggregate investment exceeds the planned savings deficit, income consumption will continue to fall at a decelerated rate from operation of the multiplier, acting in reverse and by itself. The fall need stop only when, by action of the increasing marginal propensity to consume, planned consumption outlay exceeds expected income by an amount equal to the excess of depreciation charges over gross investment.[24] Even then recovery need not occur until time and wear and tear have reduced the quantity or quality of plant capacity to a point so far below the marginal efficiency of new capital that the net marginal economies promise to outweigh the acquisitional costs of the new capital.

Such is the mechanical, self-generative cyclical process that can be conceived to occur even under assumptions of neutral confidence, neutral money, stable efficiency rewards of labor, unchanging long-term rates of interest, constantly expanding population and labor supply, and absence of the exogenous factors of wars, great inventions and discoveries, and government intervention. Manifestly, a complete sketch of the investment process must include a careful consideration of the modifying operation of these factors. The following sections will, therefore, undertake to fill in these lights and shades as well as to com-

[23] The specialized character of most investment agents will require that a certain amount of replacement take place even in the face of enormous excess capacity.

[24] See *infra*, p. 83.

plete the outline of the mechanical process. Owing to the size and complexity of the process, it seems convenient to break the description of it into several parts.

## Turning Points of Investment and Consumption

It is *mathematically* possible for expansion of investment and consumption to continue indefinitely, either continuously accelerating, or continuously decelerating to an asymptote.[25] In Table 5 a number of cases have been drawn up to illustrate the mathematical possibilities of continuous expansion. Each case is accompanied by a list of assumptions upon which its expansion is based. It will be noted that in each case at least two fundamental assumptions are economically unreal. Every case, for example, relies upon assumption of a constant relation between increases in consumption and demand for net investment; all but one of the cases rely on marginal propensity to consume to be either unity or to be increasing; and in the same way all but one of the cases assume marginal efficiency of capital either to remain constant or to increase. Let us examine each of these assumptions in turn.

Far from remaining indefinitely constant, we have seen that the relation between consumer-taking and inducement to invest is probably the most widely variable function in our economy. And it seems certain to fall after any protracted period of expansion. If the expansion has been

---

[25] It is not necessary to lean, as does Ragnar Frisch, upon the offsetting effect of rising replacement requirements; the rôle of replacements is considered separately below. Nor is it necessary to assume, as does Paul Samuelson, a continuous flow of government expenditures.

# INVESTMENT AND CONSUMPTION

## TABLE 5

*Continuous Expansion of Consumption, Income,
and Investment*

CASE No. 1: Income and consumption increasing by amounts that increase by increasing amounts; investment increasing by increasing amounts.

| Period | Expected Income ye | $\Delta$ye | Consumption C | $\Delta$C | Savings=Investment I | Actual Income y | $\Delta$y |
|---|---|---|---|---|---|---|---|
| 1 |       |      |       |      |     | 59    | —    |
| 2 | 59    | —    | 58.05 | —    | 2.1 | 60.15 | 1.15 |
| 3 | 60.15 | 1.15 | 59.2  | 1.15 | 2.3 | 61.5  | 1.35 |
| 4 | 61.5  | 1.35 | 60.5  | 1.30 | 2.6 | 63.1  | 1.6  |
| 5 | 63.1  | 1.6  | 62.0  | 1.50 | 3.0 | 65.0  | 1.9  |
| 6 | 65.0  | 1.9  | 63.75 | 1.75 | 3.5 | 67.25 | 2.25 |
| 7 | 67.25 | 2.25 | 65.8  | 2.05 | 4.1 | 69.9  | 2.65 |
| 8 | 69.9  | 2.65 | 68.2  | 2.40 | 4.8 | 73.0  | 3.1  |

Essential assumptions basic to this case:
1. Marginal propensity to consume less than unity and diminishing.
2. Constant relation between increases in consumption and current capital formation.
3. Increasing marginal efficiency of capital.

---

proceeding more rapidly than the population growth, then the frictions of full employment begin to manifest themselves: e.g. less desirable or more independent workers; difficulty of securing labor of all skills in optimum proportions (immobility); rising efficiency wages. We may have the phenomenon of diminishing productivity of capital. This can be more than offset by a rising population and by innovations and discoveries, but these offsets need not occur in time and there is strong reason to believe that eventually the limitations of land and resources will prove too strong a depressant. Indeed, speculation in land

CASE No. 2: Income and consumption increasing by increasing amounts, investment increasing by constant amounts.

| Period | Expected Income | | Consumption | | Savings≡ Investment | Actual Income | |
|---|---|---|---|---|---|---|---|
| | ye | Δye | C | ΔC | I | y | Δy |
| 1 | | | 58.1 | | | 59 | — |
| 2 | 59 | — | 58.1 | | 2.2 | 60.3 | 1.3 |
| 3 | 60.3 | 1.3 | 59.3 | 1.2 | 2.4 | 61.7 | 1.4 |
| 4 | 61.7 | 1.4 | 60.6 | 1.3 | 2.6 | 63.2 | 1.5 |
| 5 | 63.2 | 1.5 | 62.0 | 1.4 | 2.8 | 64.8 | 1.6 |
| 6 | 64.8 | 1.6 | 63.5 | 1.5 | 3.0 | 66.5 | 1.7 |
| 7 | 66.5 | 1.7 | 65.1 | 1.6 | 3.2 | 68.3 | 1.8 |
| 8 | 68.3 | 1.8 | 66.8 | 1.7 | 3.4 | 70.2 | 1.9 |
| 9 | 70.2 | 1.9 | 68.6 | 1.8 | 3.6 | 72.2 | 2.0 |

Essential assumptions basic to this case:
1. Marginal propensity to consume less than unity but increasing.
2. Constant relation between increases in consumption and current investment.
3. Decreasing marginal efficiency of capital.

CASE No. 3: Income and consumption increasing by constant amounts; investment constant.

| Period | Expected Income | | Consumption | | Savings≡ Investment | Actual Income | |
|---|---|---|---|---|---|---|---|
| | ye | Δye | C | ΔC | I | y | Δy |
| 1 | | | 57 | | 2 | 59 | — |
| 2 | 59 | — | 58 | 1 | 2 | 60 | 1 |
| 3 | 60 | 1 | 59 | 1 | 2 | 61 | 1 |
| 4 | 61 | 1 | 60 | 1 | 2 | 62 | 1 |
| 5 | 62 | 1 | 61 | 1 | 2 | 63 | 1 |
| 6 | 63 | 1 | 62 | 1 | 2 | 64 | 1 |
| 7 | 64 | 1 | 63 | 1 | 2 | 65 | 1 |
| 8 | 65 | 1 | 64 | 1 | 2 | 66 | 1 |
| 9 | 66 | 1 | 65 | 1 | 2 | 67 | 1 |

Essential assumptions basic to this case:
1. Marginal propensity to consume unity and constant.
2. Constant relation between increases in consumption and current investment.
3. Constant marginal efficiency of capital.

CASE No. 4: Deceleration of income and consumption toward an asymptote, investment approaches zero.

| Period | Expected Income | | Consumption | | Savings≡≡ Investment | Actual Income | |
|---|---|---|---|---|---|---|---|
| | ye | Δye | C | ΔC | I | y | Δy |
| 1 | 59 | — | 59 | — | .5 | 59.5 | — |
| 2 | 59.5 | .5 | 59.5 | .5 | .25 | 59.75 | .25 |
| 3 | 59.75 | .25 | 59.75 | .25 | .125 | 59.875 | .125 |
| 4 | 59.875 | .125 | 59.875 | .125 | .0625 | 59.9375 | .0625 |
| 5 | 59.9375 | .0625 | 59.9375 | .0625 | .03125 | 59.96875 | .03125 |

Essential assumptions basic to this case:
  1. Marginal propensity to consume unity and constant.
  2. Constant relation between increase in consumption and current investment; less than 1.
  3. Constant marginal efficiency of capital.

and in durable capital agents tends to anticipate this limitation. To these should be added the stifling effect of the price policies of monopolistic and semimonopolistic groups. Harrod has furnished us with a brilliant explanation for these price policies in his diminishing elasticity of demand as income rises.[26] As consumer demand rises, it becomes less elastic, suggests Harrod, and entrepreneurs find it more profitable (individually) to raise prices than to expand their productivity in full proportion to the rise in consumer expenditures. Whether such a tendency actually exists has still to be demonstrated but it seems plausible enough.

In addition, rising profits and profit expectations in the face of institutional restrictions on the supply of credit force up the long term rate of interest. Finally,

[26] *op. cit.*, pp. 17-22 and *passim*. Increased advertising; declining price consciousness at higher incomes.

although investment psychology may be positive in the later stages of expansion and thus keep the relation artificially high for some time, such a state of affairs is precarious. Probably the greatest source of variation in the relation between consumption and inducement to invest are found in reversals of confidence and readjustment of expectations. The longer the delay in these reversals the more decisive the downturn must be when the switch occurs.

A downturn in investment and consumption after a period of expansion seems to be pretty nearly inevitable then owing to the economic impossibility of maintaining a constant relation between consumer-taking and the inducement to invest. But what about the rôle of replacements? Is it not conceivable that, as the expansion proceeds, the need for replacements may rise just as the need for new investment is falling and thus make a downturn unnecessary? This is the possibility which Ragnar Frisch takes J. M. Clark to task for not considering and which Hansen chides Harrod for ignoring.[27]

One could reply that consumer-taking depends upon *net* income. Since replacements are not a part of net income, then even though gross capital formation remains the same, net income falls when net investment declines. When net income falls, consumption falls, even though employment has not yet been affected. And of course the fall in consumption may drag down investment into a cumulative

[27] Ragnar Frisch, *op. cit.*, pp. 646-52; Clark defends himself by showing that replacements can offset only if changes in "rate of growth of consumer demand are very small." See "A Reply," pp. 814-16.
    A. H. Hansen, *Full Recovery or Stagnation?* p. 49.

downturn. This seems to be what Samuelson means when he says: "Only net investment is 'multiplied' to give the national income; as a first approximation Harrod was justified in neglecting replacement in the formal relation."[28]

However, the problem is complicated by the difficulty of drawing a line between replacements and net investment. For some purposes, replacements are that part of gross capital formation that go to offset the wear and tear and obsolescence of the existing stock of capital agents. But in spite of its simple charm, such a concept of replacements is slippery. Seldom is a capital agent constructed as mere reproduction of one that has just given up the ghost. Rarely do investors consider new agents as replacements. If the investor is not an entirely different personality embarking on a new venture in a new industry, at least the machine will be markedly different in design, quality, cost, and efficiency, tooled perhaps for a new process. Thus probably almost all gross capital formation is regarded as new investment by its projectors. Indeed, it is doubtful if actual wear and tear plays any part in short-run calculation of net investment and net income and therefore in the determination of propensity to consume. What are important are the current charges to depreciation, since these represent the actual sums deducted from current gross income to care for current depreciation of the capital stock. Reducing net income, they must also reduce consumption. The expenditure of these sums cannot, therefore, be said to increase consumption and to exercise a multiplying influence. A rise in replacements in the sense of a rise in investment paid for out of rising depreciation

[28] *op. cit.,* p. 796.

charges would not, therefore, offset a fall in investment paid for out of savings. For net income would fall, and with it consumption, and the downturn of investment would continue.

But what of a rise of replacements in the "wear and tear" sense in excess of current charges to depreciation? Even though paid for out of depreciation funds accumulated in past periods, it is clear that such replacements would constitute current net investment, since the funds spent would not be deductions from current net income, and would, therefore, offer additional purchasing power for the multiplying of consumption. It should be kept in mind, of course, that such replacements are capable of being net investment and net income only in the current or cyclical sense. If depreciation debits are below current wear and tear, net income is not really swelled by replacements in excess of depreciation. This, of course, is merely one more discrepancy between expectations and reality.[29]

Under conceivable circumstances, then, replacements may be considered as net investment and net income, but even so it is hard to build a case for continuous expansion based on replacements growing faster than current charges to depreciation. Such a situation would have to be based on failure of business to anticipate the true wear and tear of their assets. Actually, wear and tear is the easiest

---

[29] A great many investment assets are not explicitly depreciated; especially consumers' investment goods. Many of these, however, are implicitly depreciated in the form of debt amortization. Here the line between savings and depreciation and, therefore, between net and gross income is purely a psychological one. It is hard to tell the effect on consumption. Where no debt amortization or savings occurs, the owner probably considers gross and net income to be the same, and the resulting excess of consumption is equivalent to dissaving.

source of asset depreciation for business men to predict, and in any case the discrepancy could and would be quickly remedied by increased depreciation charges. Moreover, replacements of durable goods are notoriously postponable, especially in so far as obsolescence is concerned, and are most likely to fall off just when they are needed most to offset the fall in net investment. Anyway, even the physical deterioration is bound up (if it is bound up with anything, see *infra,* pp. 93-4) with the fluctuations in new installations occurring many years earlier and not with the given expansion.

But if replacements paid for out of current depreciation charges are not part of net income controlling consumption, does this mean they are not important in the cyclical process? We know that the bulk of gross capital formation merely offsets capital currently consumed.[30] Are we to ignore these billions of dollars of production and the millions of men they employ merely for this reason? Manifestly not. As Solomon Fabricant has told us, depreciation charges of business firms are outstandingly steady.[31] This being so, the wide fluctuations we know to occur in gross capital formation are bound to have serious destabilizing effects on income and employment, operating through the multiplier and acceleration principles. For example, if on the downturn of the cycle all the gross money income charged to depreciation by busi-

[30] S. S. Kuznets, *National Income and Gross Capital Formation, 1919-1935,* pp. 40, 48.
[31] *op. cit.,* pp. 196-7. Mr. Fabricant's data show that depreciation charges have been quick to follow production on the upswing of a continuous expansion but have been quite stable in the face of falling corporate production thereafter.

ness firms is not spent on replacements, it is likely to be held out in cash balances or highly liquid securities. Thus held, it is neither invested nor spent for consumption and represents a withdrawal of purchasing power exerting first a downward multiplying effect on consumption and then a downward accelerating effect on investment. As a convenient statement, it may be laid down that an increase or decrease in replacement expenditure accompanied by an equivalent increase or decrease in amount currently charged to depreciation would have no multiplying effects, but that such a change *not* accompanied by a corresponding change in charge to depreciation would have the same multiplying effects as if it were a change in net investment in the real sense. Charges to depreciation tend to move with the total stock of investment and, as we have pointed out, to remain relatively stable. *Cyclical variations in the flow of replacements are apt, therefore, to have definite multiplying effects on consumption and income.*

This leads us to consideration of the upturn of the cycle. It is true that the downturn may be brought to a halt and an upturn started by many factors. Those most frequently mentioned in business cycle literature, such as government expenditures, monopolistic price policies, inventions, wage and interest reductions, and shifts to positive confidence, are certainly extremely important in determining the time and sharpness of the upturn; no doubt they are the usual factors in inducing the upturn. Nevertheless, even without the action of these factors, an eventual upturn may be expected through the deterioration of the investment stock in the face of increasing marginal propensity to consume as incomes fall. For, as incomes fall, resistance to reduction of the living standard grows. The proportion of each remaining dollar saved becomes lower and lower until finally people may go into debt in order to keep their consumption from falling in full proportion to the decline in their incomes. Even though marginal propensity to consume may be less than unity, intended savings may become negative. Nevertheless, income may continue to fall so long as the excess of consumption over expected income is insufficient to offset the failure to respend the sums currently charged to depreciation. Purchasing power is withdrawn and the multiplier continues to work in reverse. Still, the fall in income slows up as the gap between the consumption excess and the deficit reinvestment gets smaller.

Two forces eventually close the gap entirely. One of them is the increasing marginal propensity to consume which reduces savings even to the point of making them negative. This has already been treated. The other deserves some discussion. Current charges to depreciation have been shown by Fabricant to be very stable in comparison with variations in production. The reason for this stability, though I do not believe this is the reason Fabricant gives, is largely due to the fact that such charges are naturally a function of the level of the aggregate capital stock. As the capital stock became smaller and more mature in the course of a number of years of disinvestment, such charges to depreciation would naturally decline. This decline would be aided by business reorganizations and liquidations or by the plain pressure to maintain dividends. At the same time that depreciation charges fall, the pressure to replace the depreciation of time and usage rises. Repairs, long postponed, take the form of additions and betterments. New industries and new businesses cropping up as they always do even in the depths of depression find the existing idle investment agents not exactly suited to their special needs. Either they must spend money to adapt them, or they must build new. Irritations with ancient machines and buildings accumulate with wear and tear and may suddenly become acute; when accompanied by fascinating little style changes or interesting new processes the urge to replace may become as irresistible for the business man as for the consumer.

Moreover, business men will not continue indefinitely to make charges to depreciation. Such charges have usually been drawn up on the supposition of the asset having a definite life. And conservative business practice usually dictates that depreciated life shall be shorter than potential physical life. Thus the asset matures on the books and depreciation charges stop. Once the excess of depreciation charges over current replacement is reduced to equality with the excess of planned consumption over expected income, downward multiplying effects on income are stopped. However, one may well be skeptical about the promptness of the end of decline brought by either need for physical replacement or diversion of depreciation charges to consumption expenditures. Lives of very durable agents are extremely elastic. In practice, replacements are usually regarded as new investments and their timing is a function not of wear and tear but of confidence and of innovation in product and technique. It is replacement that ordinarily precipitates discard and demolition, rather than the reverse. The more durable the good, the longer such replacement and discard may be postponed. As for depreciation charges, they seem to fall off little even in severe depressions.

But what about the upturn? It is clear that, aside from all the factors that were mentioned on pp. 82-3, an upturn will be induced when current depreciation charges fall below the aggregate made up of (a) the small flow of depression replacements, and (b) the excess of planned consumption over expected net income.[32] Aside from the increasing marginal propensity to consume, this may be brought about either by physical deterioration or by maturation on the accounting books neither giving strong promise of definite and early recovery.

But these forces merely bring about cessation of the downturn and the beginnings of an upturn by substituting an upward for a downward multiplier effect. The real recovery waits upon acceleration of investment. Whether the consumption induced by the fall in depreciation or rise in replacements will in turn induce investment in additional capital assets depends upon all the various factors in the inducement to invest, factors hidden in the "relation." The discussion in this and the preceding chapter has shown that this relation is far from an invariant function. Price policies, wage rates, interest rates, expectations, innovations, physical lags, political development—all conspire to rob the relation of any pretensions to precision and help to explain the differences in timing and rate of recoveries of different cycles.

[32] If the depression is a severe one. Otherwise the upturn would come when savings plus depreciation charges fall below aggregate gross investment.

## Severity of Cycles in Investment and Consumption

The severity of cycles has three dimensions: speed of fall; depth of fall; and slowness of recovery. Although the dimensions are capable of appearing in different combinations, there are good reasons to believe that if the fall is rapid it will also be deep, and if it is deep recovery will be slow. Leaving aside inventions, population movements and major wars, about the latter of which something will be said later, the factors most instrumental in accentuating the severity of cycles may be summarized as those which determine (a) the value and slope of the marginal propensity to consume; (b) the average size, and fluctuations in size, of the relation; and (c) the behavior of replacements.

If the marginal propensity to consume is relatively high at the peak, the multiplier will naturally be high also and the fall in consumption from any reduction in net income will be severe. Moreover, if the slope of the marginal propensity to consume is relatively mild, as it must be if the propensity is still high at the peak, this means that marginal propensity to consume rises only mildly as income falls and exercises its equilibrating effect at a low level.[33] Thus, the same high marginal propensity to consume that facilitates a close approach to full employment tends to make that position unstable. The high position is all the more unstable if it has been achieved by liberal use of consumer credit, or by high income expectations

[33] The equilibrating effect comes obviously, not from the rise in the value of the multiplier at low incomes, but from reduction of the gap between gross investment on the one hand and the sum of savings and charges to depreciation on the other.

based on positive confidence or on speculative developments. There is no reason, of course, to expect that the schedule of marginal propensity to consume will remain a constant from one cycle to another, especially in such a changing scene as the American one. Consequently, we have a contributory explanation not only for the severity of some of our cycles but also for the wide differences in their severity.

The larger the average size of the relation between an increment of current consumption and the increase in investment stock "needed" to provide for that consumption, the greater the rise and decline of investment and therefore consumption. A number of factors contribute to the determination of the size of this relation. Some of them are summarized in the expression (taken from the footnote 8 on page 61) : $\dfrac{I}{\Delta C} < r \dfrac{\dfrac{\Delta E}{\Delta C}[1-(1+r)^{-a}]^{34}}{\Delta C}$ in which

I is the increase in aggregate investment stock due to the increase in consumption, $\Delta C$; $\Delta E$ is the expected increase in periodic net yield of the investment stock and implies the level of non-capital operating costs; r is the long rate of interest; and a is the expected life of the asset, as reflected by the depreciation or amortization schedule, and expressed in time units of the same length as the capital production period. Thus, in a period known as the capital propagation period, long enough to enable the investment

---

[34] The relation is less than the ratio of capitalized increase in rents to the increase in consumption because investment is also a function of cost of construction and the supply curve of construction most certainly is less than perfectly elastic.

to be produced and to be turning out consumer goods, the relation will tend to be something less than the ratio of discounted net revenue expected from the absolute increase in consumption over the entire life of the asset—to the absolute increase in consumption in the capital propagation period. The extent to which the relation is less than this ratio depends on the elasticity of the supply curve of investment agents.

Four different factors are implied in this summarizing expression: the long-term rate of interest; consumer and business expectations; the operating costs of investment agents; and the length of the capital propagation period. A fifth factor not included but extremely important is the original investment cost. The nature of each of these has been discussed earlier, but it remains to analyze their effect on the value of the relation. A low rate of interest means that capital accumulation can be carried to a point of low marginal productivity and therefore means a high relation between consumption and investment and consequently higher peaks and lower troughs and perhaps for that reason more rapid rises and falls. We have seen that the long rate of interest has probably been falling secularly; this may be a contributing factor towards the increasing severity of cycles. Moreover, the stability of the interest rate does little to soften the acceleration effect. However, we have already observed that there are other factors in the inducement to invest more important than the interest rate.

Chief of these is the factor of consumer and producer expectations and the confidence that determines what the level of these expectations shall be. It may be difficult to conceive of a high long-run level of expectations; such a level could hardly be above the long-run marginal efficiency of capital. Still a young and buoyant economy would enjoy expectations approximating more closely to the long-run marginal efficiency of capital than would an older and more mature economy. And just as with a low rate of interest a high level of confidence and expectations would mean a high degree of durability, and generality of use of capital. Any increases of consumption expenditure will be capitalized over a longer period of time. This means a higher relation between capitalized expected rent increases and present periodic consumption increases and therefore a higher degree of instability. But perhaps even more destabilizing than a high level of expectations is a wide range of expectations. A young and buoyant nation, as a young and buoyant person, is also subject to violent changes in mood. A wide swing to positive confidence on the upsurge of the cycle would certainly increase the relation and therefore the acceleration. Then, if during the deceleration and downswing there was a marked reaction, to negative confidence, this would naturally accelerate the downward pace.

Operating costs of individual investment agents, of course, include many payments that constitute gross quasi-rents for still other investment agents. Taxes, heating costs, maintenance and repairs expenditures all such payments go partly to owners of durable goods. Consequently, the operating costs of investment agents in the aggregate are smaller than the sum of the individual amounts. Nevertheless, these operating costs, made up of pure land, labor, and managerial rewards, comprise a large part of any additional consumption expenditure and must be deducted from those expenditures before the sums capable of being labeled the net quasi-rents of capital can be computed. For only this residue of net quasi-rent can be capitalized as the demand for additions to the investment stock.

It becomes immediately obvious that the lower the percentage these non-capital payments form of the added consumption outlay, the greater the relation of new investment demand to marginal consumer expenditure. Here again it would seem that the more capitalistic the character of industry, as determined by low interest and high expectations levels, the less these non-capital payments would be, and the higher, therefore, would be the relation and the instability of investment. The rigidity of these payments is probably more important than their average level. Indeed, the rigidity of the gross operating costs such as taxes, heating, maintenance, is no less destabilizing merely because they contain capital payments also and in Chapter XII, it will be found that these operating costs may be very unyielding indeed. The relation will be all the greater on the upswing of a cycle because of the relative decline of these costs, and on the downswing all the smaller because of the relative rise.

The length of the capital propagation period has a technical effect and a psychological effect and these two effects may well work at cross purposes so far as the relation is concerned. Technically, a long capital propagation period reduces the relation by spreading the capital expenditure over a long period—perhaps several years. For it is apparent that the longer it takes to build the capital, the less the relation of this capital expenditure to the consumption expenditure—correspondingly large as the period. But the technical length of the production lag reduces the severity of cycles indirectly also. If the relation is less, not only is the addition to consumer purchasing power less, but the practical multiplier effect of what has been added is reduced also. Between each round of income creation that makes up the multiplier must occur a creation of capital equipment. Obviously, on the upswing of the cycle, once reinforcement begins to occur, the income propagation period can be no shorter than the capital propagation period. If capital construction requires a long period, it will be a long period before goods can be produced and delivered and the money income made available for respending on consumer goods. Investment is slowed up because consumption is slowed up; consumption is slowed up because production is slowed up; and production is slowed up because investment requires a long time to be consummated.

But the psychological effect of the investment lag may operate in the other direction to accentuate cycles. During the period of the capital production lag, the competitive bidding of consumers to secure the goods they want may force up prices, induce industry to work existing capacity at increasing cost. The increased ratio of marginal to average costs thus tends to cause a shift to profits and to create competitive illusions that may lead to speculative excesses in the field of investment. On the other hand, as Harrod has pointed out, a shift to profits may reduce the propensity to consume the increments of income.[35] And so the downswing is initiated, with the subsequent fall accentuated as the speculative illusionment turns to disillusionment. However, as between the modifying and the accentuating effects of the capital production lags, it is probable that the former dominates. For consumers cannot compete for consumption goods and thus push up prices unless they have received additional money incomes to enable them to do so. And the time required to produce the new capital holds up their money incomes and reduces the multiplying effect of what expenditures they do make. Thus the disparity between money income and real income is kept down and the competitive illusions are hindered from fully developing.

Fifth of the factors affecting the size of the relation and the severity of cycles is the cyclical elasticity of the investment supply. If the supply of investment agents were perfectly elastic, that is, if the cost of producing them were the same regardless of the quantity produced (i.e. stage of cycle), then the relation would be fully equal to the ratio expressed on p. 87. On the other hand, to the extent that costs rise when consumption rises, and fall when consumption falls, the increases and decreases of capital values will be offset and the relation will be less than that ratio. However, the cost changes must occur at the same time as the changes in consumption expenditure, if the relation is to be modified. Lags in the downward adjustment of cost reduce the ameliorating influence, for during the lag, the relation may have been able to exercise its full depressing effect on investment. The fall in investment may have caused, through the multiplier, a fall in consumer outlay

[35] op. cit., pp. 77-9.

and a concomitant fall in investment demand. Thus by the time the first cost reduction has made its belated appearance, still another cost reduction may be necessary to offset the acceleration effect.

So far the severity of cycles has just been discussed as if exclusively due to variations in the marginal propensity to consume and the relation of net investment to the consumption increments. Of course, this is far from the case. The major part of investment does not add to the investment stock, but merely replaces its wastage from wear and tear, fires, floods, style and efficiency obsolescence, and so on.[36] Under some circumstances, the distinction would, therefore, be important. In practice, however, we have seen that two factors destroy the significance of the distinction between net investment and replacement.

One of these is the fact that specific replacement decisions are governed only remotely by physical considerations. The pleasant little fiction, taken over as a mathematical convenience by model builders, that replacements echo the cycles in net investment of a previous life period has little foundation in actual fact, especially for the more durable agents. Not only do the conditions of production and care of different units vary so widely that the original cycles in construction can after a lapse of years no longer be distinguished in the physical fitness of the agent, but the economic life is usually much shorter than potential life any-

---

[36] See Solomon Fabricant's measures of capital consumption 1919-1935 in *Capital Consumption and Adjustment,* pp. 170-1. His estimate of wastage of business, government, and consumers capital is about fourteen billion dollars annually. See also Kuznets's estimates that capital wastage was about four-fifths of gross business capital formation during the period 1919-1937. *T.N.E.C. Hearings,* Part 9, "Savings and Investment," p. 4036.

way.[37] Consequently, the same factors: expectations, costs, interest rates, that induce the wide swing in net investment also govern the inducement to replace.

The other factor destroying the practical distinction between replacements and net investment has also been mentioned: the stability of depreciation charges. It was pointed out that variations in replacements not accompanied by direct and equivalent variations in depreciation charges would exercise the same multiplying effect on consumption and income and therefore the same accelerating effect as if the variations were in net investment.

[37] Solomon Fabricant quotes figures of Ir. H. Vos to show that the economic life of engines, boilers, motors, and transformers ranged from half to two-thirds of the technical life. *op. cit.,* p. 72. P. de Wolff shows that even for the physical life of passenger automobiles the original cycles in new production are largely obliterated in the demand for replacement. ". . . the underlying assumption of an average lifetime is too rough. The lifetime is different for different cars and there will be a distribution of lifetimes." *Econometrica,* Vol. VI (1938), pp. 115, 116. On page 127 he says: "At any rate the echo effect seems, at least for motor cars, not to be strong enough to cause important cyclical movements."

# CHAPTER IV

## EXPLANATION OF THE BUILDING DATA

THE statistics used as the basis of this long-period study of cycles in the building industry are building permits. Another type of building data, in some ways more comprehensive, are F. W. Dodge statistics of contracts awarded in thirty-seven states east of the Rocky Mountains, but reliable data in substantial detail are not available from this source before 1919.[1]

A builder who wishes to erect, alter, or repair a building is required by ordinance in most cities to apply for a permit. As a condition precedent to granting the permit, he is obliged to submit plans and specifications that conform to engineering regulations and is usually required to furnish information on: (1) purpose for which the building is to be occupied; (2) if residential, number of families that will occupy it; and (3) an estimate of probable cost of the building, usually exclusive of such things as equipment and landscaping, and always exclusive of land.

Monthly, the building department of the individual city sorts and classifies the information secured in the manner

---

[1] The F. W. Dodge data are published in the *Statistical Abstract of the United States;* for the data before 1925, see p. 847 of the 1929 volume. I am informed that the National Bureau of Economic Research has made an exhaustive study of the F. W. Dodge data and has succeeded in adjusting the data for changes in classification and nomenclature.

described, and issues monthly and annual reports of number and value of the various types of building, classified by use, that have been projected during the preceding period. If the city is large and fairly progressive, it publishes its documents, and the annual report of the building department finds its place therein. For such cities, it becomes possible to gather statistics of building long after original records have disappeared. If the city is small, it usually does not publish the annual reports of its departments and, unless the data are currently gathered, much of them becomes irrevocably lost. The Bureau of Labor Statistics since 1920 has gathered detailed data currently from hundreds of municipalities. For the period before that year, data must be gathered from annual reports of cities that have seen fit to publish their data regularly.

A few of the more important shortcomings of building permit data may be noted briefly:

*Lack of uniformity over the years*: Changes have taken place in the areas within which permits have been required;[2] in the type of building for which permits have been required;[3] and in care with which the building departments have checked the builders' estimates of value.[4]

[2] In Newark, N.J., before July 1881, very few buildings outside the fire limits were reported. An ordinance of July 1, 1881 provided that "all new building within the city limits shall be reported." No city could be discovered, however, for which this type of incomplete reporting occurred for longer than the first few years.

[3] Usually, however, all types of building except alterations have required permits from the very beginning of the building regulation. Changes have nearly always been in the direction of wider scope.

[4] The Inspector of Buildings of Boston has reported that beginning in 1929 builders' estimates of cost were more closely scrutinized. This closer scrutiny resulted, according to the report, in estimates one million dollars larger than original aggregates.

EXPLANATION OF BUILDING DATA

*Changes in the building codes*: Impending changes in building laws, threatening to tighten requirements, have occasionally, notably in New York City, caused a rush to file plans and secure permits under the old, more liberal ordinances.

*Changes in boundaries*: Most cities have hastened their growth by gathering in surrounding municipalities. The effect of these accretions has been, naturally, to disturb uniformity of permit data. However, examination of effects of more than fifty annexations in over a dozen cities produced no evidence that boundary changes seriously impair uniformity of building permits data. Most annexations involved areas at the time small in population. And in the case of the only annexation that seemed really to threaten uniformity of the data, annexation of Brooklyn to New York in 1898, the fact that separate data were available for Brooklyn obviated adjustment.

*Builders' underestimates of cost*: Real or imagined incentive exists for builders to underestimate costs of projected buildings in order to keep tax assessments low. Of thirty-five building department superintendents hazarding quantitative estimates of undervaluation, twenty-nine indicated undervaluations of 25 per cent or less and twenty-one placed the undervaluation at between 15 and 25 per cent.[5] Study of early reports uncovered no particular differ-

[5] Correspondence was established with about fifty heads of building departments, not necessarily of the cities for which building data are being used in this study. A valuable study recently made by the Bureau of Labor Statistics showed that the contract price (land, of course, excluded) of one-family houses in 1938 was 16 per cent higher than the value declared in taking out the permit. The study covered reports by both contractors and operative builders in eight cities. The range was 10 per cent to 26 per cent. Selling prices, including land costs,

ence in undervaluation from that which exists now. More-over, consensus seems to be that undervaluation is about the same during boom or depression.

*Lapses and lags in actual building*: In a statistical study made by the writer, comparison was made between build-ing permits and buildings actually completed in Richmond, Va. It was found that most building is finished in the same calendar year in which the permit is taken out.[6] A study of the Bureau of Labor Statistics showed that lag between issuance of permit and start of work is very short, less than three weeks and that the additional period required for completion is about four months. Only 2 or 3 per cent of the permits are allowed to lapse.[7]

In the aggregate the defects of building permit data just reviewed may seem to constitute a serious obstacle to the use of building permits in the analysis of building fluctua-tions. However, most of the defects prove to be more ap-parent than real. The most serious charges that may be laid against the data are that they take no account of rural building. On the whole, building permits are a workable source of information. In any case, they are the only source apparently available for a long-period study of detailed building variations.

overhead and profit, sales commissions, were 42 per cent higher. *Monthly Labor Review,* Vol. 49 (1939), No. 4, pp. 856-7.

[6] The proportion thus finished within the year is rather greater in depression than in prosperity.

[7] "Elapsed Time in Building Construction," *Monthly Labor Review,* Vol. 36 (1933), pp. 158-69. New York City plans filed show a much higher percentage of lapses because they contain projects for which approval will later be denied.

# CHAPTER V

## THE MONTHLY INDEX OF BUILDING
### 1868-1940

VASTLY more is known about the history of turbu-
lence of building than about its causes. Yet it is
inevitably easier to add to the knowledge of the
former than to that of the latter. Presentation and analysis
of the index of *monthly* building activity in the United
States for 1868-1940 (see Chart I), enabling comparison
of turning points of building and business over a period
twice as long as that permitted by previously existing data
and during the three hectic decades of the late nineteenth
century, is pretty sure to add some knowledge of history
of building waves. But it is less certain that the following
pages will add anything definite to existing knowledge of
causes of building perturbations. As is so often the com-
plaint, hunt for a solution is embarrassed not from scarcity
but from abundance of clues. Moreover, so huge and integral a part of the industrial system is the building industry that it may be useless even to try to dissociate cause
from effect or primary from secondary influences. Still, it
is hoped that analysis in terms of inducement to invest of
seventy years of monthly data—of the most important of
all channels of investment—may yield a fuller understand-

ing of investment processes and a narrowing of the wide range of clues to the fundamental initiating forces.

Naturally, the number of cities for which building could be recorded on a monthly basis over a long period is limited to those that began at an early date to report the erection of building structures. Beginning in 1868 with one city, Manhattan, the index on Chart I increases its coverage to thirty-five cities.[1] Almost all of this number are contained in the index as early as 1896. The cities are the nation's largest and, although the east naturally dominates the index, every region is represented. Alterations and repairs are included, but state and local public building are frequently excluded, federal public building is usually excluded, and rural building is always excluded. In spite of incomplete coverage the index is large. For the ten years 1921-1930, the volume of building was twenty billions, or about two billions a year. The high point, reached in 1925, was two billion, six hundred million.

## Statistical Technique

During the first half of the period, there was an increasing number of cities in the index. The problem of making

---

[1] See Appendix A for the tabulated data and annotations.

Sources of the data are the United States Bureau of Labor Statistics; reports of building inspectors, public works departments, fire departments, city engineers, departments of public safety; mayors' messages; board of trade and chamber of commerce year books; and periodicals including *Bradstreet's, American Contractor, Construction News, Chicago Economist, Real Estate Record and Builders' Guide, American Land and Title Register.*

Documents were scattered among the following libraries: New York Public Library, Congressional Library, John Crerar Library, Burton Historical Collection, University of Chicago Library, Philadelphia Public Library.

the data comparable throughout was handled by varying appropriately the number of cities included in the 1930 base. If the index started with one city, the data of the single city were divided by a base for 1930 that included data for that city only. As another city was added at a later date, the base or divisor was increased by the average monthly building for 1930 in the added city. In this way the index, though varying in content over the years, was made comparable. Even though comparable, however, an index of varying composition is obviously not free from bias.

The index has been smoothed, and random and seasonal fluctuations eliminated, by means of the Macaulay 43-term graduation, which constitutes a five month moving total of a five month moving total of an eight month moving total of a twelve month moving total, to which weights of $+ 7$, — 10,0,0,0,0,0,0, $+ 10,0,0,0,0,0,0$, — 10, $+ 7$, are applied, and which is then divided by 9600. For explanation of the advantages of this technique, see F. R. Macaulay, *The Smoothing of Time Series*.[2]

Because of distrust of all building cost data, a distrust explained in Chapter II,[3] it was felt unwise to attempt to adjust building data for fluctuations in cost of construction.

*The Timing, Length, and Severity of Building Cycles*

*Turning points*: Table 6 on p. 104 presents the turning points of cycles in building. All cycles, mild and severe, are

[2] (New York: National Bureau of Economic Research, 1931), pp. 24, 25, 73, 108.
[3] pp. 13-15.

presented in that table without regard to the secondary trend movements that make up "the long building cycle." In the same table and in Table 7 comparison is made with the corresponding turning points in the Business Annals, the Axe-Houghton-Annalist index of business activity, and the New York Federal Reserve Bank—Carl Snyder Clearings index of business activity. Association between building and business turning points proved to be close:[4]

[4] Nearly all the studies treating the connection of building and business fluctuation have recognized a definite connection between general business fluctuation and the short fluctuation in building and have noted a precedence on the part of building.

J. B. Hubbard: Building movements have corresponded with similar changes in general business conditions, have preceded corresponding general business conditions, and have agreed more closely with the movements of speculation than with those of business. "An Analysis of Building Statistics for the United States," *Review of Economic Statistics,* Vol. VI (1924), p. 32.

W. H. Newman: Building is independent of business movements in minor (random) movements and whole cycles. Building fluctuations arise to a considerable extent independently of business cycles, but are often of critical significance when direction of business is in the balance. Building shows a clear tendency to anticipate business fluctuations with a lead of three months. *op. cit.,* pp. 15-16.

W. C. Mitchell and A. F. Burns: (1) Fluctuations of building activity have conformed well to business cycles. Manhattan monthly data since 1868 (data of the present writer) show a high conformity; (2) Building in various localities conforms as closely to general business as to each other; (3) Building cycles show a lead but this may be due to the fact that permits data precede actual building by about four months. (Unpublished manuscript.)

C. D. Long, Jr.: Minor cycles in Manhattan building (annual data) tend to conform to cycles in industrial activity. The conformity seems to be best for store building, and poorest for industrial building. For residential, the conformity is moderate; this class of building displays more of a tendency to conform to the speculative movements of stock prices. *Review of Economic Statistics,* Vol. VI (1936), pp. 187-90.

J. M. Clark: (1) Industrial building shows the most regular timing and is most nearly synchronous with the general business cycle; it tends to lead on the upturn, but not on the downturn. (2) Commercial

average disparity was six months, with few turns more than a year apart; and one-to-one correspondence was high, with only two cycles in each of business and building not matched by corresponding cycles in the other. No real tendency for building to lead business on the upturn and downturn could be found, in spite of the fact that the number of turns in which building led was double the number in which building lagged. When discount is made for the fact that permits anticipate actual building by about four months[5] the two to fourth month lead of building permits becomes insufficient to establish any effective lead of actual building.

*Duration*: The seventeen cycles in building between 1870 and 1938 averaged just four years in length, or the same duration characterizing cycles in general business (Table 8). This estimate differs appreciably from the estimate of five years given by Newman.[6] Part of the difference may be traced to the shorter coverage of Newman's data, part to his use before 1903 of annual data, and part perhaps to subjective differences in defining a cycle. Variation in length from one cycle to another was wide enough, two to eight years, but not wider than that recorded in the indexes of business. Moreover, in spite of variation, cycles before 1900 averaged less than three months shorter than four years, and cycles since 1900 less than three months longer. The difference is too small to suggest any trend in length one way or another. As for relative duration of ex-

construction shows less conformity with the business cycle, but does show a lead at the upturn. (3) Residential building shows a clear tendency to lead the business cycle. *Strategic Factors in Business Cycles* (New York: National Bureau of Economic Research, 1934), pp. 27-9.
  [5] *supra*, p. 97.                                 [6] *op. cit.*, p. 11.

# TABLE 6
*Turning Points in Building and Business*[7]
Unit: One Month

| | Building | Business Annals[8] | Axe-Houghton-Annalist[9] Index of Business | New York Federal Reserve Bank-Carl Snyder[10] Clearings Index of Business |
|---|---|---|---|---|
| T | Mar. '70 | +9 | +7 | |
| P | Apr. '71 | | | |
| T | July '72 | | | |
| P | Mar. '73 | +7 | —2 | |
| T | Apr. '74 | | | |
| P | Dec. '74 | | | |
| T | May '77 | +22 | +14 | +12 |
| P | Nov. '82 | —8 | —14 | —15 |
| T | Jan. '85 | +4 | +1 | +3 |
| P | Apr. '87 | —1 | 0 | +2 |
| T | Mar. '88 | +1 | +1 | 0 |
| | | July '90 | June '90 | |
| | | May '91 | Apr. '91 | |
| P | Apr. '92 | +9 | +11 | +9 |
| T | Feb. '94 | +4 | +4 | —4 |
| P | Apr. '95 | +8 | +6 | +8 |
| T | June '98 | —12 | —19 | —15 |
| P | July '99 | —1 | +3 | —1 |
| T | May '00 | +7 | +6 | +4 |
| P | Apr. '03 | —7 | —7 | —22 |
| T | Nov. '03 | +9 | +9 | +8 |
| P | Jan. '06 | +16 | +17 | +16 |
| T | Dec. '07 | +6 | +4 | +1 |
| | | Jan. '10 | Mar. '10 | |
| | | Jan. '12 | July '11 | |
| P | Sept. '12 | +4 | +4 | —29 |
| T | Dec. '14 | 0 | 0 | 0 |
| P | Aug. '16 | +24 | —5 | +5 |
| T | Sept. '18 | +7 | —8 | +7 |
| P | Dec. '19 | +1 | +3 | +1 |
| T | Nov. '20 | +10 | +4 | +6 |
| P | Jan. '24 | —8 | —9 | —8 |
| T | Sept. '24 | —2 | —2 | 0 |
| P | Aug. '25 | +14 | +14 | +7 |
| T | May '28 | —5 | —5 | —16 |
| P | Jan. '29 | +5 | +6 | +10 |
| T | Apr. '33 | —1 | —1 | +1 |
| P | Nov. '36 | +6 | +9 | +2 |
| T | May '38 | +1 | +1 | +4 |

[7] Plus sign (+) refers to fact that building precedes, minus sign (—) to fact that building lags.

[8] W. L. Thorp and the National Bureau of Economic Research, 1926.

[9] 1868-1878, modification of the Cleveland Trust Company index; 1879-1918 three month moving average of the Axe-Houghton index; 1919-1938 *The Annalist* index. All adjusted for trend and seasonal variation. Source: *The Annalist*, Vol. 43 (1934), pp. 274, 349; Vol. 54 (1939), p. 62; *explanation*, Vol. 43 (1934), p. 96.

[10] Carl Snyder, "A New Clearings Index of Business for Fifty Years," *Journal of American Statistical Association*, Vol. 19 (1924), pp. 329-35; Federal Reserve Bank of New York.

# MONTHLY INDEX OF BUILDING

TABLE 7

*Deviations in the Turning Points of Building and Business*

Unit: One Month

| Building | Business Annals Months Turns | | Axe-Houghton Months Turns | | Snyder Index of Clearings Months Turns | |
|---|---|---|---|---|---|---|
| Leads | 174 | 21 | 124 | 19 | 106 | 18 |
| Lags | 45 | 9 | 72 | 10 | 110 | 8 |
| Average Lead or Lag | 7 | — | 6 | — | 7.4 | — |
| Average Lead | 4.1 | — | 1.7 | — | 0 | — |

pansion and contraction phases of the cycles, the former were longer than the latter during rise of the secondary trend, or long cycle, and shorter during fall of the secondary trend. As might be expected both from the upward primary trend of building throughout the seventy years

TABLE 8

*Length and Periodicity of Building Cycles*

Unit: One month

| | Building | Business Annals | Axe-Houghton | Snyder Index of Clearings |
|---|---|---|---|---|
| Duration | | | | |
| (Trough to Trough) | 48.2 | 47.7 | 47.8 | 51.7 |
| Before 1900 | 45.2 | 51.4 | 51.6 | 53.6 |
| Since 1900 | 50.9 | 45.1 | 45.1 | 50.6 |
| Periodicity | | | | |
| Range | 21-92 | 29-99 | 29-89 | 25-83 |
| Half ranges | 37-59 | 36-53 | 38-48 | 35-67 |
| Expansion | 26.5 | | | |
| Contraction | 21.5 | | | |

and from the nature of investment discussed below, expansion phases averaged five months longer than contraction phases.

*Severity*: According to Table 9, cycles in building are much more severe than those in indexes representing general business activity and are even more severe than those in speculative activity. Showing an average monthly variation of 1.7 per cent for the seventeen cycles between March 1870 and July 1938, building cycles were a third more severe than stock-price cycles; one and a half times

TABLE 9

*Relative Amplitude of Building Cycles*[11]

(Average Monthly Percentages)

| Monthly Amplitude | Building | Axe-Houghton-[12] Annalist | Clearings[12] Index | Stock[13] Prices |
|---|---|---|---|---|
| Entire Period | 1.7 | .7 | .4 | 1.2 |
| Before 1900 | 1.4 | .6 | .5 | .9 |
| Since 1900 | 1.9 | .8 | .4 | 1.5 |

[11] Peak of each cycle is taken as a percentage increase over the average of the two troughs; the cyclical amplitude is converted into monthly amplitude by dividing by the number of months in the cycle. The computation may be expressed as $200 \dfrac{[P-\frac{1}{2}(T_1+T_2)]}{N(T_1+T_2)}$ in which P = the peak value; $T_1$, the initial trough value; $T_2$, the terminal trough value; N, the number of months in the cycle.

[12] See Table 6, footnotes 9 and 10.

[13] Stock prices: Clement-Burgess average of industrials, 1868-1882; Axe-Houghton weighted average of ten industrials, 1883-1914 and twenty industrials, 1915-1929; Annalist weighted average of thirty-three industrials 1930-1939. Adjusted neither for seasonal variation nor long-time trend. Not very reliable for the period before 1883. *Annalist,* Vol. 43 (1934), pp. 274, 349; Vol. 54 (1939), p. 62; for explanation see Vol. 43 (1934), p. 96.

more severe than cycles in the Axe-Houghton-Annalist index of business; and over three times more severe than cycles in the Carl Snyder-New York Federal Reserve Bank clearings index of business. These comparisons are, of course, limited in their significance by the fact that building constitutes a single industry and that its cycles are bound to be more severe, other things equal, than those of indexes purporting to measure the activity of all industry. Nevertheless, the differences are so great as to establish a presumption that the severity of building cycles is relatively great.

It is interesting that cycles in building since 1900 were about a third more severe than those before 1900. The Axe-Houghton-Annalist index of business manifested much the same increase in severity since the turn of the century, and in the case of stock prices the increase was even greater. The clearings index of business showed somewhat less severity since 1900 than before but the period compared was shorter.

## CHAPTER VI

## BUILDING CYCLES AND THE INDUCE-
## MENT TO INVEST

### *Statistical Analysis*

I n order to appraise the factors most important in the
inducement to invest, the present analysis should be
able, under the logic of the theoretical discussion in
Chapter II, to present a single index representing the re-
sultant of all the forces acting through costs, interest rates,
and expectations of income. If this index of inducement to
invest showed a close correspondence to the volume of new
building, then, one by one, factors suspected to be of little
influence could be withdrawn until the fundamental forces
stood revealed. Unfortunately, the inadequacy of statistics
that hounds all economic investigators is no less trouble-
some here. Cost data are almost entirely worthless. All
indexes represent, not actual unit costs, but mere prices of
labor and materials. They do not, therefore reflect changes
in technology of method, quality and types of materials
used, or efficiency of labor. As price indexes, they show
the common defect of reflecting official and not "under the
counter" quotations, therefore understating the real movements. They overlook important cost factors of transportation tie-ups, strikes, and other delays; land prices; legal

costs; legal restrictions on methods of building; interest rates and bonuses on construction loans.[1] The price indexes are either local or are averages which cover up internal geographical and building-type differences in cost trends. And finally, they give not the faintest clue to marginal costs. The spread between costs of builders of various levels of efficiency are, as we have seen, important to the question of the elasticity of supply of new buildings. We may search the data in vain for an index of cost that we would be willing to use.

Interest data are much superior to cost data, but even so we have no index of effective interest rates on new mortgage loans. We must have recourse to an index of long-term bond yields. Such indexes are subject to a number of defects. Maturities keep falling, of course, and cause a downward drift until new bonds are inserted. Railroad bonds are most heavily represented because these securities and the market for them are longest established. Highest grade securities are excessively represented because of continual elimination of the unfit. Over long periods a steady secular decrease in the average yield and in the spread between yields is clearly discernable and may be due to this tendency.[2] The bond market is highly competitive and it is questionable, therefore, whether bond yields reflect rates on mortgage, which are local in character and subject to individual bargaining.

[1] For example, the cost data, because they ignore labor efficiency, transportation delays, warehousing expenses, financing charges, do not show the true high cost of building during the first World War.

[2] For discussion of the characteristics and limitations of bond yields see F. R. Macaulay, *op. cit.,* Chaps. III, IV.

After such vigorous indictment of the quality of the statistics, it seems hardly worth while to point to comparisons between volume of building and building costs and to say that comparison does not yield any significant correlation between cost at margin and the investment in new building. Building costs, as measured by the statistics, do not fluctuate widely enough, often enough, or in the expected opposite direction from building to explain the cycles in building. In so far as costs are concerned, this is the verdict of W. H. Newman: "Comparison of an index of these building costs [weighted index of materials prices and wage rates] with fluctuations in the volume of building gives no support to the hypothesis that building costs are the controlling factor in constructional activity. While costs usually moved independently of building, such connection as was found suggests that changes in building activity cause changes in building costs, rather than vice versa."[3]

But it must be kept in mind that if the statistics of wages and prices cannot claim to represent marginal unit costs of building, neither can they claim to disprove the importance of building costs in inducing investment cycles. Nor have we any intention of denying considerable importance to costs. But when we consider that all evidence, statistical and observational, points to building costs being high when building activity is high and low when activity is low, and couple this with the consideration that, even under twenty-year amortization, cost of building can only be half or less, of annual cost of ownership, the conclusion forces itself

[3] *op. cit.,* p. 24.

that we must look to other factors for the channels through which *primary* forces flow to initiate cycles in investment.

On the other hand, if primary forces do not act through building costs, there is still less evidence that they act through interest rates. In Chapter II we showed that interest rates would be a secondary factor in inducing investment cycles even if the rate rose and fell appropriately and over a wide range. The reason given is the overshadowing importance of amortization, taxes, heating, insurance, and expectations. But interest, although often moving in directions and onto levels that are entirely consistent with the volume and direction of investment activity, nevertheless shows such insignificant variation as to eliminate it as a first rank factor and relegate it to what must on the whole be a minor rôle in the explanation of any type of investment fluctuation.[4]

*Expectations*: In Chapters II and III we gave a number of theoretical reasons to believe that the real forces alternately damming and bursting the flow of long-term investment do their work principally through variations in

---

[4] W. H. Newman, although eliminating interest as a factor in major cycles and admitting the lack of any marked cyclical correspondence, suggests that bond yields "must indicate a willingness of investors to take on long-term commitments if building activity is to advance, and an unwillingness when activity contracts. . . . It appears . . . that long-term financing conditions play a vital rôle in determining minor fluctuations in building activity" (*op. cit.,* p. 31). This position would seem to reduce interest from a strategic to a mere barometric rôle and only in minor cycles at that. But even as a mere barometer of "willingness of investors to take on long-term commitments" interest should be scrutinized with a doubting eye. The great depression has taught that low interest rates often reflect only willingness of lenders to lend cheaply on high grade loans and *only unwillingness of borrowers to do much investing under any circumstances.*

expectations of income. It would be nice to say that in this section the rôle of expectations is established statistically. Honesty and caution, however, prevent us from claiming this much. Association between turning points, direction, and intensity, of fluctuation of building and of stock prices would seem to support the strategic importance of expectations. But we cannot say so positively.

Stock prices should offer a good index of changing expectations, representing as they do capitalized values of expected earnings of corporations. These earnings are supposed to represent net earnings, after depreciation, from operation of going concerns whose assets are durable producers goods, goodwill, patents and rights, and management skill. To be sure, stock prices differ from capitalized values of buildings, in that the earnings of stocks are not expected to be definitely terminable and that stock prices emerge from market conditions approximating "perfect" competition.[5] Nevertheless, stock prices and capitalized values of buildings resemble each other in the really important respects. On the one hand, both represent capitalization of incomes expected in the rather distant future, the lack of terminability of income in the case of stocks not having much potential significance. Psychology is important, therefore, to both. Second, since the substantial part of corporate assets are building and other durable goods, high stock prices imply high capitalized values of these buildings. High capital values, if interest rates are constant, imply high expected earnings and therefore strong demand for buildings. An index of stock prices, multiplied by an

[5] This "perfection" of market is often much less than it seems.

index of bond yields, ought to show something like the general movement of expectations of net income from durable agents and, in their rôle of long-term equities and principal assets of business corporations, from buildings in particular.

### Cycles in Building and Stock Prices— Statistical Association

Over the entire seventy-year period, cycles in new building and cycles in stock prices showed a high one-to-one correspondence. Only two of the seventeen building cycles were not matched by cycles in stock prices and only two of the seventeen cycles in stock prices were not matched by cycles in building. Timing of the turning points was also close: four months being the average deviation of all the thirty-four turns, six months the maximum for all but six, and one year the maximum for all but one. Association of movement was good. Aside from leads and lags of several months, there were only one or two years during which building moved in opposite direction from stock prices. Inspection of the detailed monthly movements showed that building and stock prices were either stable or moving in the same direction in 633 of the 830 months, and moving oppositely in only 197 months. The important differences in their movements consisted of (1) random movements in building already discussed as being perhaps due to the large unit size of many building projects in the large cities; and (2) one or two month leads on the part of building at the peaks and occasional lags of building at the troughs.

Even correlation of severities of the fifteen individual corresponding cycles was fair. Spearman's rank coefficient

($p$) was .425, which was three times the probable error of
.143—naturally high because of the small number of cases.
There is, of course, no reason to expect a high degree of
correlation between the severities of building cycles and
cycles in income expectations (if this is what stock prices
reveal). Effect of a change in expectations on the volume
of new building is a function of elasticity of supply of new
building, interest rate and money market conditions, and
the current situation of the total stock of all buildings in
relation to previous expectations of income. These conditions naturally vary from one cycle to the next, sometimes
modifying, sometimes accentuating, but perhaps rarely ever
preempting, the dominant rôle of expectations.

### Theoretical Significance of the Association

The association establishes, of course, no presumption of
causality. One has a choice of three explanations. (1)
Building cycles are the primary cause of stock market fluctuations; (2) stock-price cycles are the primary cause of
building cycles; or (3) both building cycles and stock-
price cycles are caused by some common force or set of
forces.

Any one of these possibilities would endow the association with significance; though the first possibility, that
building cycles independently determined and are the chief
or sole cause of variations in stock prices seems far-fetched.
Thus association between stock prices and building activity
would seem to stem from forces that are either common to
both or act through speculation in stock equities upon
speculation in building equities, with, of course, considerable interaction. What these forces are and from whence

they flow, the association cannot demonstrate. It merely suggests that the forces that whip up building cycles probably do so in part by first affecting human psychology and creating expectations that, once born, may pursue paths different in direction and sometimes more erratic than the forces that conceived them.

# CHAPTER VII

## LONG CYCLES IN BUSINESS, PUBLIC, AND RESIDENTIAL BUILDING

### *The Data and Their Analysis*

THE study of long cycles is based on detailed data of number and value of building construction, classified by type of occupancy, for all United States cities that have published their data adequately and continuously over periods of twenty-five to eighty years.

Basic materials used in the study of long cycles thus comprise about five hundred building permit series. Practically all the series are original; and, except for the series on value of total building,[1] none of the material before 1920 has, it appears, hitherto been published.[2] As indicated above, the data include series on value of building, as represented by builders' estimates of cost at the time of application for permits; on number of family accommodations;

---

[1] Several indices of the value of total building have been in existence for some time. The longest and most comprehensive is the index of John R. Riggleman, *op. cit.*

[2] Use is made of one series by Roy Wenzlick of the *Real Estate Analyst,* namely, number of family accommodations provided by new buildings erected annually in St. Louis since 1886. Since 1920, all of the series have been included in the data gathered by the United States Bureau of Labor Statistics. However, with a few exceptions all of the data, even the data since that date, were gathered from original sources. The data so gathered frequently differ somewhat from those of the Bureau of Labor Statistics, perhaps owing to differences in coverage.

and on number of permits granted or number of buildings contained in those permits.[3]

Presentation of these various types of data has involved double and even triple analysis, but the advantage of presenting and comparing *physical* measures of the volume of building with *value* measures has probably been more than worth the extra effort. Multiple analysis has not only imparted greater validity to the conclusions; it has also served in process of collation and classification as a check on accuracy of the data themselves. In addition, it has given some insight into fluctuation of building costs.

Names and classifications of data in these documents have been found to vary considerably over course of time. Fortunately, data were available in rather great detail, and substantial uniformity in occupancy-classifications used in this study was secured by copying all tables in much the same detail as that in which they were found in annual reports. This having been done, material for an individual city was surveyed in its entirety and classifications were drawn up which could be kept uniform throughout. It must be confessed, however, that homogeneity was not always achieved, and that, worse, it was not always possible even to know in a given instance whether data were uniform or not. Much uncertainty arose out of use by reporting agencies of "miscellaneous" classifications as catch-alls. With changing personnel of building departments over

[3] The terms, "building" and "permit," are usually used interchangeably, but in several large cities, particularly in New York and Philadelphia, a single permit or plan filed may represent many buildings. This is especially true of residential building. Where this is the case, the data on *buildings* rather than on *permits* or *plans filed* are the statistics used.

long periods, all classifications were bound to change somewhat; but "miscellaneous" classifications appear to have changed especially much.

Classifications set up are of nine types: detached dwelling; multifamily dwelling; total residential; public building; private nonresidential; total nonresidential; total new building; alterations; total building. Data in some degree of detail are presented for about twenty-nine cities and for all New Jersey. But data in complete detail are available for only a part of this number. New Jersey offers data only on multifamily dwellings erected in the state. Fourteen[4] cities offer data on all nine categories of building described above. Twenty-seven cities offer at least five classifications of building: total residential, total nonresidential, total new building, alterations, and total building; but all twenty-seven do not offer data on detached and multifamily dwellings, or on public building and private nonresidential. And at least fourteen cities (including all of New York City) and New Jersey give data also on number of family accommodations.

### Method of Analysis: Individual Cities

The method of analysis was marked out by the extensiveness of the data handled. In addition to analyzing composite indexes of all cities taken as a group, it was decided to analyze each series for each city individually. As a consequence, it was necessary to draw up an analytical technique adaptable to this method. In the study of timing in Chapter VIII, statistical measurements of each type of building will be presented as the consensus of the various

[4] Four of these are now boroughs of New York City.

cities analyzed individually by the method that will presently be explained, and as the measurement of the indexes
of aggregate number and value of building in the various
cities taken as a group. In the study of duration and severity, only the second type of measurement will be presented.
It has been mentioned that triple analysis of value, number,
and families data provides a valuable check on the accuracy
of the conclusions. In the same way, the *individual* analysis
of each series for each city provides another valuable check
by indicating the extent to which the cycles in national
building are typical of those in individual cities.

All data were kept in their raw form throughout the
analysis. No smoothing was applied for several reasons.
First, it was felt that the use of annual rather than monthly
data constituted in itself a smoothing out of the smaller
fluctuations within the year, and operated to dampen the
cyclical amplitudes. The National Bureau of Economic
Research analyzed the minor cycles in my annual and
monthly data on value of total new building in Manhattan
from 1868 to 1936. They discovered that the amplitudes
of cycles in annual data were less than half those in monthly
data.

Second, the method of smoothing by moving averages
would have permitted random movements to influence the
peaks and troughs. This would often have diverted the
turning points of the cycles from the actual years in which
they took place. By keeping to the raw data, it was possible,
in part at least, to disregard as turning points obviously
random movements of one year, or movements in building
following upon great fires, such as those in Baltimore
building after the great fire of 1904. Third, minor fluctu-

ations are highly irregular in their amplitudes and in their dates of recurrence. This fact makes the choice of a period for a moving average arbitrary and hazardous. Fourth, the labor involved in smoothing, even by moving averages, would have been very great. It would have been great enough to rule out the individual analysis altogether.

The effort required to fit curves of trend to so large a number of series—even to the national indexes—made that luxury also too expensive for this study. As for the conversion of the volume of building into per capita building,[5] it should be emphasized that the estimates of population for the intercensal years are too crude to justify their use on an annual basis. Moreover, some local intercensal estimates are based on the number of dwellings erected and the use of these would involve circular reasoning.[6]

The common practice of deflating the value data on building with an index of the cost of building has also been rejected. Such procedure, if the cost statistics are accurate, should reveal changes in physical volume of building. But no index of the cost of building has yet been developed which deserves such confidence in it. Labor conditions are too variable in different sections of the country; fluctuations in the efficiency of labor are too elusive for measurement; changes in technology of construction of different types of structures are too diverse, and price statistics are too deceptive—to say nothing of the problems of weighting the various factors involved. It is probably better, therefore, to present the value data in the current dollars in

[5] By per capita building is meant the ratio of volume of new building to new population.
[6] Minneapolis, Minn., *Municipal Statistics* (Feb. 28, 1917), p. 1.

which they were estimated by the builders, and to look to the number of buildings data and the number of family accommodations data for the measurements of physical volume. Thus, the double and triple analysis serves one more purpose.[7]

The first step in the individual analysis was to chart the five hundred series separately, whereupon each was inspected for major cycles, and the peaks and troughs of those cycles were marked off. The major cycles of residential building, particularly of detached residential, were usually well enough defined, but the cycles of nonresidential building and alterations often gave trouble. In the main, general sweeps in building lasting about a generation and transcending the short, nervous movements of several years were looked for. Most of the cycles were sufficiently convincing. Some, however, were extremely dubious.

The definition of a turning point was also productive of perplexity. The rule adopted was to recognize the highest or lowest point which seemed to be the focus of a cluster of high or low values. A year might thus be recognized as a turning point, the datum of which was by no means the highest or lowest in the cycle. This procedure helped to rule out random perturbations. However, the problem of flat or double peaks and troughs had to be faced. For such questions of doubt, the rule adopted was to choose the later year as the turning point. Such a rule tends to create a lopsided cycle in which the expansion phase is characterized by high average volume, and the contraction phase by low

[7] For an admirable discussion of the pitfalls of statistical deflation, see the section by W. L. Crum in Carl Snyder and W. L. Crum, "Deflated Dollar-Value Series as Measures of Business," *The Review of Economic Statistics,* Vol. VIII (1926), pp. 92-100.

average volume. But it is possible by this rule to recognize as turning points those strategic years marking the beginning and end of prosperity and depression.

Following the designation of the turning points of individual city cycles, it was necessary to average them for the various cities in order to secure the national consensus. For this purpose, each cycle was handled as a unit. For example, consider the cycle from 1918 to the recent depression. The measurements of all the cities for that cycle were averaged in order to obtain a national average. For the initial trough, the consensus was secured by placing the dates of each of the cities in an array and marking off the median year. The representativeness of this median was then measured by computing the average deviation. Exactly the same procedure was followed for the peak and the final trough. The three medians and the three average deviations constituted the timing measures of the national cycle beginning in 1918.

For the earlier cycles, the timing measures were computed by repeating this process. In taking the timing measures of the second and third cycles it was, of course, necessary to compute only the peak and initial trough, since the initial trough of each cycle constituted the terminal trough of the last.

The problem of averaging the measures of individual cycles in order to secure national consensus was complicated frequently by the lack of one-to-one correspondence. A specific type of building in one city might have more than the usual number of three long cycles from the 1870's to the present. In residential building in Manhattan, there occurred an extra cycle in the period from the depression following 1892 to 1918. The problem was partially solved in the case of timing by selecting only one peak and two troughs, those nearest the usual timing dates.

Where there were *fewer* cycles in a specific series than was usual, there was nothing to do but to take the turning points that could be recognized and to associate them with the nearest turning points usual to other cities. In number of total nonresidential building in Detroit, only two cycles occurred from 1850 to the present: one during 1880-1900, and the other during 1900-1934. The earlier fluctuation corresponded quite well with the movement of national building, but the later cycle occupied the place of two usual national cycles in total nonresidential building. The initial trough of the 1900-1934 cycle was associated with the initial trough of the cycle of national building falling between 1900 and 1918, but the peak in 1926 and the trough in 1934 were associated with the national cycle falling between 1918 and the recent depression. There could be no help from Detroit in discovering the timing of the peak and the terminal trough of the national cycle ending in 1918.

The measures of individual cities were combined in varying groups of identical cities, in order to secure comparability among national consensuses for the different types of building. Data in complete detail were available for only fourteen cities; the measures, therefore, of these fourteen cities were averaged and compared for each of the five basic types of building: detached dwelling, multifamily dwelling, public building, private nonresidential, and alterations. Data on residential and nonresidential building were available for twenty-seven cities; the measures of these twenty-seven cities were averaged and compared for each of the five comprehensive types of building: total residential, total nonresidential, total new building, alterations, and total building.

This method of computing averages for identical groups of cities was followed for both the value and number of building; except that in the case of the latter a twenty-nine instead of a twenty-seven city grouping was used. Before 1900, the number measures included more cities than the value measures; the two are not, therefore, strictly comparable.

## Method of Analysis: The Indexes

There are several advantages to supplementing the individual analysis with the analysis of composite indexes. An index provides a single picture of cyclical variation. The amplitudes of an index reflect the dampening effect of cycles occurring in the different cities at somewhat offsetting dates in a way that the consensus of the individual city amplitudes do not.

For the value data two sets of indexes were prepared. One set contained data for fourteen identical cities on five basic classifications: detached dwelling, apartment dwelling, business and public building, and alterations. The second set contained data for twenty-seven identical cities on total residential, total nonresidential, total new building, alterations, and total building.

For the number data only one set of indexes was prepared. This set included indexes for twenty-nine identical cities on total residential, total nonresidential, total new building. One index is presented also for the number of family accommodations provided annually in fourteen cities (including all New York City) and the entire state of New Jersey.

The indexes were prepared by aggregating the annual volume of building in the individual cities and converting the series of aggregates thus obtained into series of relatives. The latter was done by dividing each *annual* aggregate by the *average* annual aggregate amount of building during the eleven years 1920-1930.

Up to 1911 there was an increasing number of cities in each index. The problem of making the data comparable throughout was handled by varying appropriately the number of cities included in the 1920-1930 base. If the index started out with one city, the data of the single city were divided by a base for 1920-1930 that included data for that city only. As soon as another city was added at a later date, the base or divisor was increased by the average annual building for 1920-1930 in the added city. This process was repeated with the addition of every city. In this way the indexes, though varying in content over the years, were made fairly comparable.

This is not to deny objections to an index with a varying composition. The amplitudes of the recent cycles in building have been much greater than the earlier ones. But were it not for the dampening effect on the recent cycles of a much wider coverage in number and size of cities, it is probable that the disparity would have proved to be even greater.

Another criticism of these indexes is that New York City because of its size dominates at all times. To a certain extent, it is desirable that the indexes reflect this domination, because New York City exercises a strong influence on the building of the nation. The value of total building in that city during the decade 1921-1930 was 26 per cent of that of 257 cities (including New York) reported by the United States Bureau of Labor Statistics.[8] However, because of the smaller number of other cities represented in the early years of the indexes, the domination of New York during those early years is undoubtedly excessive.

To avoid, therefore, being influenced unduly in conclusions as to the behavior of building in the United States as a whole, it is necessary to check the indexes constantly. One check is to compare the indexes with the consensuses of the individual cities. Another is to compare the value indexes with the indexes of number and families. By constant reference to all of the various measures, a considerable extent of error can be avoided.

Appendix B contains the names of the cities and the years from which the data for each city run represented in the various indexes and consensuses. The tables reveal that chief reliance for the major cycle in *value* of building before 1900 must be placed on the two cities, New York, and Washington, since these are the only cities for which data extend back through the entire cycle. As for number data, the tables show that conclusions on the fluctuation between 1880 and 1900 are based on data for nine cities throughout, but that conclusions on the cycle between 1864 and 1880 must be derived chiefly from data on New York and Philadelphia. With respect to the cycles in the number of family accommodations, only New Haven (1871) ex-

[8] The total building in New York from 1921 to 1930 was about eight billion dollars. The total for 257 cities, including New York, during the same period, was about thirty-one billion. U.S. Bureau of Labor Statistics.

tends back over three full cycles, while six cities cover two full cycles. New York City (all boroughs) extends to 1903, and all New Jersey to 1904. All cities cover at least one major cycle.

The first measurement to be made of the indexes was, of course, that of timing. In designating the peaks and troughs of the cycles in the indexes, the same rules described above in connection with the analysis of the individual cities were followed.

The next step was to compute the *durations* of the cycles and their component phases of rise and decline. No problem was encountered here. The duration of the major cycle was computed by counting the number of years from the initial to the terminal trough.[9] The same rule was followed in computing the durations of the phases.

The amplitude or severity was the third computation in the analysis of the indexes. The method adopted of measuring the extremity of the cyclical variation was to average the initial and terminal trough of each cycle and to divide that average into the excess of the peak over this average. Thus the peak as a percentage of the preceding and subsequent troughs was obtained. As a measure of steepness of that rise and decline, the percentage was further divided by the duration of that same cycle. The result was an expression of the amplitude of each cycle as an average annual amount. With this relative measure it was possible to compare the severity of cycles of different durations.

[9] Including the year of the terminal but not of the initial trough.

# CHAPTER VIII

## THE TIMING OF LONG CYCLES

THE fact that building as a whole fluctuates in long
cycles lasting about a generation has been rather
universally observed.[1] It has never been certain,
however, that the same rhythms exist in all of the component branches of the industry. Do residential, public,
and business building and alterations show long cycles
at all? If so, do the fluctuations in each category occur
at the same time, and do the different types of building
manifest fluctuations of comparable extent and quality?
If not, what are the special reasons for the individuality
in each case. Aside from studies of residential building,
such as Roy Wenzlick's observation of pronounced long
cycles in families accommodated by new building in St.
Louis since 1886, and Arthur F. Burns' theoretical study
of "Long Cycles in Residential Construction,"[2] little attention has been given to specific categories of American

[1] J. R. Riggleman, *op. cit.; Variations in Building Activity in United
States Cities* (Baltimore: Johns Hopkins University Library, unpub-
lished manuscript, 1934); Roy Wenzlick, *Real Estate Analyst* (St.
Louis edition; published monthly); W. H. Newman, *op. cit.;* A. F.
Burns, *Production Trends in the United States since 1870* (New York:
National Bureau of Economic Research, 1934); A. K. Cairncross, *op.
cit.;* G. F. Warren and F. A. Pearson, *op. cit.;* Emmy Reich, *Der
Wohnungsmarkt in Berlin von 1840-1910* (Berlin, 1912), Staats-und
Sozialwissenschaftliche Forschungen, Heft 164 (1912).

[2] *Economic Essays in Honor of Wesley Clair Mitchell.*

building. In this and the succeeding two chapters the rhythmical patterns of the building types are examined, and the cycles of the various types of building are compared with each other and with cycles of business in general.

Tables 10-13 contain for various groups of cities the timing measures of cycles in the various building classifications. These timing measures are of three types: (1) the turning points of the indices, not given in the tables, but shown graphically in Charts II-V; (2) the medians of the individual city turning points shown in Tables 10 and 11, representing the consensus of data of the individual cities; and (3) the average deviations, given in Tables 12 and 13, of the individual city peaks and troughs from the medians just referred to. As announced in the last chapter, independent analysis is also made in those tables of the value and number data.

### General Characteristics of the Long Cycles

Inspection of Charts II-V, reinforced by examination of the separate classifications of building in each of the individual cities, shows rather conclusively that long cycles in building appear in all types of building in all localities at all times. These cycles appear as great sweeps of enormous height and depth that last from trough to trough on the average almost twenty years. Although the industry is torn by random perturbations and constantly disturbed by short cycles averaging four years in length, these are the cycles from which it suffers chiefly.

On the whole, the cycles are well pronounced and the cases in which the long building cycles are so obscured by

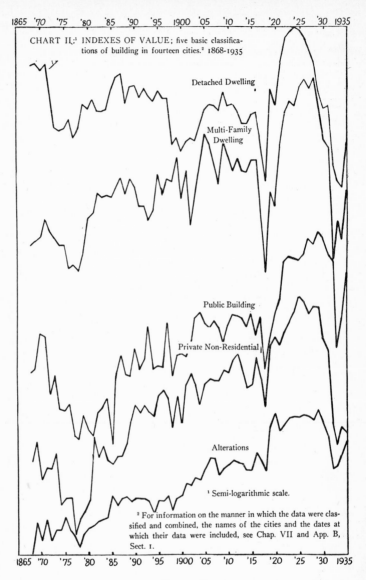

CHART II.[1] INDEXES OF VALUE; five basic classifications of building in fourteen cities.[2] 1868-1935

Detached Dwelling

Multi-Family Dwelling

Public Building

Private Non-Residential

Alterations

[1] Semi-logarithmic scale.

[2] For information on the manner in which the data were classified and combined, the names of the cities and the dates at which their data were included, see Chap. VII and App. B, Sect. 1.

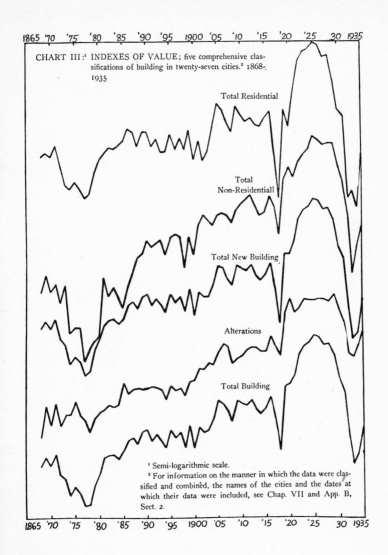

CHART III:[1] INDEXES OF VALUE; five comprehensive classifications of building in twenty-seven cities.[2] 1868-.
1935

Total Residential

Total Non-Residential

Total New Building

Alterations

Total Building

[1] Semi-logarithmic scale.
[2] For information on the manner in which the data were classified and combined, the names of the cities and the dates at which their data were included, see Chap. VII and App. B, Sect. 2.

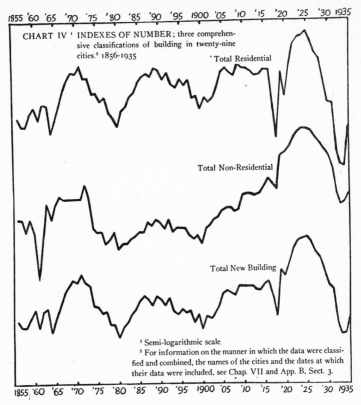

CHART IV [1] INDEXES OF NUMBER; three comprehensive classifications of building in twenty-nine cities.[2] 1856-1935

Total Residential

Total Non-Residential

Total New Building

[1] Semi-logarithmic scale.
[2] For information on the manner in which the data were classified and combined, the names of the cities and the dates at which their data were included, see Chap. VII and App. B, Sect. 3.

other movements as to be unrecognizable are unusual and are confined to alterations[3] and nonresidential building, especially public building, in scattered cities: Examples are

[3] Indeed, no type of new building possessed cycles which were less conventional, which differed so markedly from city to city, and which assumed so many sizes and shapes. In some cities, such as Boston, the cycles were very mild; but in others, such as Detroit, they were nearly as extreme as the fluctuations of new building. In other cities again, the cycles were even and regular; elsewhere, they were quite the opposite. Indeed, irregularity was much more often met with than not.

1865 '70  '75  '80  '85  '90  '95  1900  '05  '10  '15  '20  '25  '30  1935

CHART V:¹ INDEX OF NUMBER OF FAMILIES ACCOMMODATED; by all
building in twelve cities and by multi-family-dwellings in Evanston, Ill.,
in all boroughs of New York City, and in the entire state of New Jer-
sey.² 1871-1935

¹ Semi-logarithmic scale.
² For information on the manner in which the
data were classified and combined, the names of
the cities and the dates at which their data were
included, see Chap. VII and App. B, Sect. 4.

1865 '70  '75  '80  '85  90  '95  1900  '05  '10  '15  '20  '25  '30  1935

the value of private nonresidential building in Philadelphia; nonresidential building and alterations in Richmond
Borough of New York City; and nonresidential building
and alterations in Providence. The best-defined cycles are
found in detached dwelling construction. Separate data on
detached dwellings were gathered for twenty-one cities.
All the series agreed rather well with the graph on Chart
II in manifesting even, regular undulations with wide valleys and relatively smooth, well-rounded peaks.[4]

[4] These characteristics of detached dwelling cycles gather importance
from the fact that this class of building by reason of its volume dominates total residential building. Although total residential does reveal

The chief explanation for infrequency of random distortion in detached residential is undoubtedly the large volume of construction occurring regularly in this class and the small and uniform size of the one- and two-family units. There is much less chance for specific building projects to distort the total. In the case of public and business buildings, as well as in apartment house construction, the fact that aggregate volume is often very small and that cost of a single unit may well be a hundred

the influence of the more turbulent apartment house construction, this influence is due almost entirely to New York City multiple dwelling construction. The close resemblance of the total residential cycle pattern to that of detached dwellings was clearest, therefore, when comparisons were made for each individual city and abstraction thus made from New York. The outside cities for which a comparison was possible indicated almost no trace of apartment house influence on total residential. But even with New York included the predominate pattern of detached dwellings stands out in bold relief.

Not only does detached dwelling construction dominate in total residential, but it also dominates in total new building. A majority of the cities indicated predominance for residential building in the cycles of the total. Some cities manifested no predominance for either type, the cycles revealing the modifying influences equally of both categories. A few cities indicated that a more important rôle was played by non-residential building. The instances of the latter were Louisville, Atlanta, New Haven, Manhattan, the Bronx, Providence and Washington. The dominance of nonresidential building in New Haven may be attributed, for the later years at least, to the huge building program of Yale University. Manhattan Borough is notoriously a commercial and industrial city with a disproportionate day population. And Washington, D.C., manifests a dominance of nonresidential building only for the recent cycle, which apparently includes the building program of the Federal Government.

In spite of the fact that residential building seemed to be more influential in shaping the pattern of total new building, the latter was obviously modified in all cities by the inclusion of nonresidential construction. The troughs, while usually more pronounced than those of nonresidential, were rarely as deep as those of residential building. And the peaks or periods of prosperity were wider than those of the latter. These observations held for both number and value data.

## TABLE 10

*Turning Point Dates of Long Cycles in Detached Dwellings, Apartment House, Business, and Public Building*
(Median Dates of the Various Cities) [5]

| Building Type | | Post-Civil-War Cycle | | Last 19th-Century Cycle | | Pre-First-World-War Cycle | | | Post-First-World-War Cycle | |
|---|---|---|---|---|---|---|---|---|---|---|
| | | Trough | Peak | Trough | Peak | Trough | Peak | Trough | Peak | Trough |
| Detached Dwelling | Value | — | — | 76 | 90 | 00 | 09 | 18 | 24 | 34 |
| | Number | — | — | 78 | 91 | 00 | 09 | 18 | 24 | 34 |
| Multifamily Dwelling | Value | — | — | — | — | 02 | 09 | 18 | 26 | 35 |
| | Number | — | — | 78 | 88 | 02 | 05 | 18 | 26 | 35 |
| Public Building | Value | — | — | 79 | 93 | 98 | 06 | 18 | 29 | 33 |
| | Number | 63 | 72 | 78 | 92 | 98 | 07 | 18 | 28 | 33 |
| Private Non-residential | Value | — | — | 77 | 90 | 00 | 12 | 18 | 26 | 33 |
| | Number | 63 | 71 | 77 | 92 | 99 | 06 | 18 | 24 | 34 |

[5] For names of the cities from which these medians were taken, see Appendix B.

## TABLE II

Turning Point Dates of Long Cycles in Residential and Nonresidential Building
(Median Dates of the Various Cities)[6]

| Building Type | | Post-Civil-War Cycle | | Last 19th-Century Cycle | | Pre-First-World-War Cycle | | | Post-First-World-War Cycle | |
|---|---|---|---|---|---|---|---|---|---|---|
| | | Trough | Peak | Trough | Peak | Trough | Peak | Trough | Peak | Trough |
| Residential | Value Data | — | — | '77 | '89 | '00 | '12 | '18 | '25 | '34 |
| | Number Data | '64 | '71 | '78 | '92 | '00 | '12 | '18 | '25 | '34 |
| Nonresidential | Value Data | — | — | '77 | '91 | '98 | '12 | '18 | '27 | '33 |
| | Number Data | '63 | '71 | '77 | '92 | '00 | '13 | '18 | '24 | '34 |
| Alterations | Value Data | — | — | '78 | '90 | '97 | '11 | '17 | '26 | '33 |
| | Number Data | — | — | '79 | '94 | '98 | '13 | '18 | '24 | '33 |

[6] For names of the cities from which these medians were taken, see Appendix B.

thousand or a million dollars makes a smooth flow of building almost impossible. Even alterations occasionally involve expenditures of tens and hundreds of thousands of dollars.

In view of what has just been said about the effect of the huge costs of individual projects, it is interesting that the number data, in which cost does not enter, show fewer blind movements and therefore show cycles that are more even and regular.

## Agreement of the Turning Points in the Medians and Indexes

The turning points of long building cycles have been established by two independent criteria: the indexes and the medians of the turning points in the individual cities. A comparison of turning points as indicated by the indexes and medians shows that agreement is on the whole good but occasionally leaves something to be desired. Corresponding turning dates usually coincided, and although they sometimes deviated one or two years, they only infrequently deviated as much as three, and indeed the three-or-more-than-three-year deviations occurred very largely in the peak before the World War. There is reason to believe that the influence of New York City, through its huge volume of building and large unit size of buildings, has been unduly great upon the index. Thus, the cycle before the War shows the greatest variation between indexes and medians, and the prewar period is the period in which New York City building show the greatest individuality. The trough of the 1890's was much shallower in New York and the prewar peak came much earlier than was usual elsewhere. It is significant that in the number data the agreement between index and median peaks and troughs is considerably greater. In general about the same conclusions concerning timing and duration of long building cycles will be obtained from either type of measure, but for precise results in fixing any particular peak or trough, the dates found in the medians or in the number indexes are to be preferred to those in the indexes of value, dominated as the latter are by the large cities.

### Agreement of the Turning Points in the Number and Value Data

Owing to occasional upheavals in the price level and in the costs of construction, the value data, which reflect the builders' estimates of probable cost of erection, are open to the charge that they do not always reflect fluctuations in the actual physical volume of buildings projected. A sharp, upward movement in building costs such as occurred during and immediately after the War may conceivably obscure the true turning point in building activity and exaggerate the violence of the cycle in actual construction. The usual statistical device to adjust for such cost fluctuations is that of deflation, in which the index of value of building operations is divided by an index of building costs. However, for reasons given above (pp. 13-14, 108-9, 120), such a device has been rejected in this study and a triple analysis which in addition to the value data makes use also of the number of buildings and the number of families accommodated was adopted instead. There is good reason to believe that these two latter types of data reflect rather faithfully the actual physical volume of construction.[7]

At any rate, the timing of the turning points in these three types of data has been fairly close. Corresponding peaks and troughs usually coincided or varied one and two years. Variations of more than three years are infrequent and are largely confined to the prewar peak (see the comparison of the medians and indexes in the preceding section). The chief discrepancy between the findings of the number and value data is perhaps the absence of the second cycle in the nonresidential number data of twenty-nine cities. Aside from this discrepancy, the same general timing is revealed by all of three types of data. Timing of the troughs is in particularly close agreement.

*The Turning Points of the Various Classes of Building*

A number of important conclusions may be derived from study of the turning points of building. The first conclusion is that in the matter of timing of turning points of different classes of building, the troughs show high correspondence, usually coinciding or varying perhaps one or two years, with variations of more than two years extremely rare; whereas the peaks vary considerably, showing few cases of coincidence and a good many deviations of three and four years, especially in the indexes.

A second conclusion is that leads and lags exist between turns in the various types of building. Except for the prewar peak in value, the tendency seems persistent for public building to lag on the downturn of the cycle. In

---

[7] Any changes in size and quality of buildings are probably changes of trend rather than of cyclical variation.

the earlier cycles alterations exhibited definite tendencies to lead total new building on both the upturn and downturn. The value of alterations in thirty-four cities led the value of total new building by one to five years in every turn from the 1878 trough through the prewar peak. During the trough of the World War and the recent depression, the turns of alterations and total new building coincided, however, and in the boom of the 1920's, for the only time in the study, it lagged by three or four years. Finally, the value of residential tends to lead the value of nonresidential on the downturn, but the evidence is by no means conclusive. No such tendency is found in the number data; and no lead or lag is found in the upturn in either the number or value of residential.

The explanation for the advance of alterations cycles at the upturn is not far to seek. Repairs are notoriously less postponable than new building. Once erected, a building constitutes a fixed cost: that is, it is usually cheaper to use it than not to use it. But in order to secure the most economical use—or ultimately even to secure any kind of use—the owner must keep the building in repair. The same considerations may necessitate alterations and additions as well. Thus, it may occur that even after a building has been altered or enlarged, it does not yield sufficient revenue, after operating expenses, to cover taxes and interest on the over-all investment; yet the owner of the building may find such an operation profitable nevertheless. It suffices only that the improvement yield an *additional* revenue greater than the *additional* expense— that the outlay for the improvement result in a smaller net deficit than if the outlay had not been made. It follows

that owners of existing structures are more easily con-
vinced of the profitability of altering or repairing than
are prospective builders of the profitability of erecting
new structures, and will not always wait the full return of
favorable building conditions before resuming operations.

The lead of alterations at the downturn is less easy
to rationalize. It may be due to the inelasticity in short
periods of the stock of buildings upon which repairs or
improvements may be made. With the demand thus relatively fixed, the peak in alterations is more quickly reached.
Another possible explanation is the fact that, in the midst
of boom psychology, the building of new structures may
seem more attractive to business men and even to government agencies and eleemosynary institutions than the repair or improvement of old ones. Such a shift would lend
a fillip to new construction at the expense, of alterations,
prolonging the prosperity of the former, and cutting short
the prosperity of the latter.[8]

The explanation for the lag of public building may be
the complete lack of speculative activity in public
and quasi-public building. Ready-made construction of

[8] Offsetting the tendency of substitution of new building to cause
alterations to turn down before new construction is the tendency of the
percentage of old buildings needing repairs often to continue increasing
even after new construction has been discontinued. The importance of
this latter fact will vary. If the upward trend of new building has not
been long sustained, the buildings added will not have had time to age
sufficiently to need much repair. Under these conditions, there may be
no tendency to prolong the boom in alterations. On the other hand, if
there have been several decades of rapid upward movement in the new
building industry, the volume of added old buildings needing repair will
have had time to accumulate. Alterations may then continue to rise for
some time after new building turns down. This latter condition may be
the explanation for the lag of alterations in the recent cycle.

churches, colleges, hospitals, or schools is all but inconceivable. So rigid are the requirements as to utility and location that it is clearly impracticable to estimate them in advance. Such structures will be built only upon demand and according to precise specifications. In residential building, however, and to a lesser extent in business building, speculation is an established phenomenon. Speculative overbuilding may take place in these types relatively early in the boom, so that during the later stages of business prosperity, business and residential building decline while the oversupply is being absorbed. Public building, in which speculation is impossible and in which premature overbuilding is therefore much less likely, may continue so long as business prosperity holds up. In fact, public building may be well sustained for some time after the decline in business. Municipal revenues tend to lag behind business movements on both the upswing and downswing. In fact, if the recession is mild, no effect on revenues may be observed at all.[9] The same is probably true of endowments for quasi-public organizations.

The tendency of residential building to lead nonresidential on the downturn may be due to the much greater element of speculation in the former. Speculation is impracticable for much nonresidential construction, because the latter is by nature highly specialized. Once designed for a specific business or industry, a building can be adapted to another use only at great expense, if at all. Location is also an important factor; for an unfortunate

[9] The per capita net revenue receipts of 146 cities increased through 1930 and fell off only slightly in 1931. The mild recession of 1927 had no retarding effect on the revenues (*Statistical Abstract* (1935), p. 217).

site may destroy the value of a building otherwise quite satisfactory to a specific industry. As a consequence, much, perhaps most, nonresidential building must be "tailor made."

The utility offered by residential buildings, on the other hand, is very adaptable: almost any such structure can be converted to serve some kind of housing purpose; and almost any location within a given area is as good as another so long as it possesses adequate transportation facilities and is reasonably free from the various residential "blights." This adaptability of residential structures has made it possible for a certain class of builder to anticipate the future demand for dwellings and to build residences "ready made" for an estimated market. Builders of this class are called speculators; and speculative building is exposed to error arising not only from the bad judgment of the ultimate purchasers of buildings, error to which nonresidential "tailor made" building is also subject, but to bad guesses on the part of the speculative builder as well.[10] The degree of speculation in residential building is, of course, large only relatively. Even in nonresidential building, there is much that lends itself to speculative activity. Small stores, hotels, office buildings, storage garages, and loft buildings are types of structures which may be constructed and sold (or rented) ready made. The difference between residential and nonresidential building in the matter of speculative overbuilding is necessarily one of degree.

[10] A conscious attempt may even be made by the latter to schedule the building program during periods of building inactivity in order to secure lower costs.

The effects of this difference between residential and nonresidential construction are that nonresidential building is more apt to fluctuate with the *actual requirements* of the various industries; that nonresidential buildings will be constructed more in accordance with the degree of profitability of business at any given time; and that since the tendency for overbuilding at any one time is less, nonresidential structures will be erected so long as business is profitable and future expectations are reasonably sanguine.

Residential construction, on the other hand, need not fluctuate so closely with income and the real demand for additional dwellings. There is much greater possibility that the speculators will overbuild in the earlier part of the boom so that during the last stages of the boom the building industry finds the expanding residential requirements have already been anticipated. Residential building then falls off while business and public building continue to rise.

The lack of a lead on the part of the residential *number* data is difficult to explain. It is possible, however, to attribute it to a change toward smaller dwellings on the one hand and toward larger nonresidential buildings on the other. It is also possible that the rapid increase in the number of small contractors during the latter stages of a boom results in severe competition for a number of jobs which are increasing less rapidly, with a resulting decline in the average cost of dwellings of the same size and quality. Conversely, competition on the basis of price is less likely to take place in the construction of the larger business and public buildings. The number of contracting firms which possess the equipment and financial responsibility to construct large projects is probably so small that conditions bordering on oligopoly exist, in which each contractor is restrained from cutting prices severely by fear of retaliation or of spoiling his own market. The larger firms are also "on the spot" to a greater extent in the matter of maintaining union wages, hours, and working conditions. Thus, although in the case of residential, *number* may continue to increase while *value* declines; in the case of nonresidential, the opposite may occur. The lead which exists for the value of residential building may thus be wiped out for number.

### Synchrony in the Timing of Turning Points from City to City

In view of the immobility of the product of the building industry, it might be supposed that the industry in each locality would have great individuality and that if long cycles did occur in all cities the turning points of these cycles would vary greatly from city to city. Actually, although such individuality exists, long cycles do appear in all cities and the agreement of the turning points of these cycles is surprisingly high, especially with respect to the troughs. The synchrony is particularly high for the recent cycle: In both 1918 and 1933-1934, the average deviation of the individual city cycles was only a fraction of a year and even in the peak of the middle 1920's was not much more than a year. The violence of the movement seems to have much to do with this. The sharper the rise or the more severe the decline, the greater appears to be the tendency of building of all cities and indeed of all types to join in the movement. In this connection, it has been pointed out repeatedly that the least agreement between the peaks and troughs of different types of building and in different localities was manifested in the relatively mild trough around 1900 and in the subsequent plateau in the decade before the war.

TABLE 12

*Average Deviation of Turning Points in Building in the Various Cities*[11]

(Unit: one year)

| Building Type | | Last 19th-Century Cycle | | Pre-First-World-War Cycle | | Post-First-World-War Cycle | | |
|---|---|---|---|---|---|---|---|---|
| | | Trough | Peak | Trough | Peak | Trough | Peak | Trough |
| Detached Dwelling | Value Data | — | — | 2.6 | 2.2 | 0.1 | 0.8 | 0.3 |
| | Number Data | 1.7 | 3.5 | 2.2 | 2.4 | 0.1 | 1.1 | 1.4 |
| Multi-family | Value Data | — | — | 3.0 | 3.1 | 1.8 | 1.2 | 1.0 |
| | Number Data | 0.7 | 3.3 | 3.2 | 3.4 | 1.0 | 1.2 | 1.0 |
| Public Building | Value Data | — | — | 2.0 | 3.8 | 1.3 | 1.7 | 0.6 |
| | Number Data | 1.8 | 1.2 | 3.2 | 2.2 | 1.2 | 2.7 | 0.9 |
| Private Non-residential | Value Data | — | — | 3.3 | 2.0 | 1.1 | 1.4 | 0.4 |
| | Number Data | 2.6 | 1.5 | 4.0 | 4.5 | 1.6 | 1.8 | 0.2 |

Among the various classes of building, the largest degree of synchrony of cycles in different cities is found in residential building and is due to the high degree of syn-

[11] For names of cities from which these average deviations were taken, see Appendix B.

### TABLE 13

*Average Deviations of Turning Points in Building in the Various Cities*[12]

(Unit: one year)

| Building Type | | | Last 19th-Century Cycle | | | Pre-First-World-War Cycle | | Post-First-World-War Cycle | |
|---|---|---|---|---|---|---|---|---|---|
| | | Trough | Peak | Trough | Peak | Trough | Peak | Trough | |
| Residential | Value Data | — | 1.8 | 3.1 | 3.3 | 0.1 | 1.0 | 0.5 | |
| | Number Data | 1.4 | 2.7 | 2.8 | 3.0 | 0.2 | 1.2 | 0.3 | |
| Non-residential | Value Data | — | 1.8 | 3.3 | 2.4 | 1.4 | 2.1 | 0.7 | |
| | Number Data | 0.8 | 1.5 | 3.3 | 4.8 | 1.5 | 1.5 | 0.5 | |
| Alterations | Value Data | — | 5.4 | 4.6 | 3.1 | 1.7 | 2.5 | 0.7 | |
| | Number Data | 5.3 | 2.7 | 4.1 | 1.9 | 1.0 | 2.4 | 0.8 | |

chrony of detached dwelling construction, which in the value data varies only 60 per cent as much as apartment house building. Detached dwellings are of more uniform size than the other building types, and uniformity of size prevents disturbance in local timing arising out of the fortuitous occurrence of large projects at varying times. Apartment house building and factory, commercial, and public construction lack this uniformity and are exposed, therefore, to a greater element of random fluctuation.

In addition to possessing uniform size, dwellings supply a more homogeneous utility due to the fact already suggested that residential buildings are less specialized than nonresidential structures. Dwellings vacated by some may

[12] For names of cities from which these average deviations were taken, see Appendix B.

be used readily by others; probably all residences are ultimately substitutes for other residences. Construction of these dwellings will, therefore, fluctuate more as a unit. As contrasted with the relative fungibility of residential buildings, many nonresidential structures are highly specialized. The consequence of this specialization is that each local cycle of nonresidential building may be governed by the special factors entering into the industry for which the construction takes place. Cycles of nonresidential buildings are thus less apt to move as a unit, and cycles of residential will exhibit the greater degree of synchronization.

Although the synchrony of cycles in the various classes of new building is thus rather good, it is much less so for alterations. The inferiority of the synchrony seems to run through the peaks and troughs of all cycles from the earliest to latest. In the value of building for twenty-seven cities the average deviation of the individual city turning dates from the medians of alterations is 50 per cent greater than that of new nonresidential and nearly double that of new residential. The average deviation of alterations is substantially greater than that of even the least synchronous type of new building. This greater diversity is no doubt largely due to the inclusion of large additions sometimes involving hundreds of thousands of dollars. It has been pointed out that these large projects bear a great proportion to the total volume of alterations, because of the small volume of the latter. The proportion may often be greater than that borne by large *new* projects to the total of any class of new building, and thus may

have greater effect in shifting the timing of the cycle turning points.[13]

[13] Statistics gathered by the writer indicate that nonresidential alterations comprise 60 to 80 per cent of the value of all alterations, the
explanation being that most residential alterations are so small in value
as to be exempt from permit requirements or capable of being con-
cealed from inspectors. It has already been observed that new nonresidential buildings are miscellaneous in character and include many
enormous projects capable of distorting the total. These same characteristics must necessarily pertain to alterations.

# CHAPTER IX

## LONG BUILDING CYCLES AND GREAT
## DEPRESSIONS

FOUR great waves in the construction of new buildings have occurred since the Civil War and it is not too much to say that their turning points mark the most exciting and memorable episodes in the nation's history.[1] The earliest of the four began with a period of inactivity during the Civil War and rose rapidly thereafter to reach a high level during the last years of the 1860's and a peak in the early 1870's, the subsequent decline thus anticipating the panic of 1873 by one or two years. The cycle, as reflected by the value of building, was completed in 1877 or 1878, and, as reflected by the physical volume of

[1] The measures of fluctuations in general business are the *Business Annals* of the National Bureau of Economic Research, The Axe-Houghton-Annalist index of business, and the Carl Snyder-New York Federal Reserve Bank Clearings Index of business. As described by W. C. Mitchell, the compilation of the *Business Annals* by Dr. Willard Thorp involved "a digest of contemporary opinions concerning (1) industrial, commercial and labor conditions, (2) conditions in the markets for loans, securities, and foreign exchange, (3) agricultural production and prices, and (4) non-economic occurrences, such as political events, epidemics, floods or earthquakes, which seem to have influenced business appreciably. From such information as he could gather under these four heads, Dr. Thorp formed his own opinion concerning the phase of the business cycle through which the country in question was passing each year, and expressed his opinion in a brief caption." *Business Cycles: The Problem and Its Setting* (New York: National Bureau of Economic Research, 1927), pp. 361-2.

building, was completed in 1880 after a drastic and persistent decline that lasted throughout the greater part of the 1870's.[2]

The next cycle started with the revival in 1879 in the value data and in 1881 in the number data, and thereafter recovered slowly. A substantial volume of building was not attained until almost the middle of the 1880's, and the peaks in the various branches of the industry ranged from the late 1880's to the early 1890's, during and after the boom in railroad construction. The decline that followed took place for the most part in the face of the prosperity and expanding activity in manufacturing and trade of 1892 and, except in the medians of the number data and of the value of total new building, preceded the panic and depression beginning in 1893 by one to six years. The decline continued through the repeal of the Silver Purchase Act, gathered momentum with the deep depression and extensive unemployment of 1894;[3] persisted through the

[2] Inasmuch as data are available before 1873 for only New York and Philadelphia and before 1868 for only the number data of these two cities, a caution should be extended against placing too much faith in the findings concerning this early cycle. However, the close agreement in the timing dates of the data for total residential and total new building in these two cities—in each city the troughs were 1864 and the peaks were 1871—inspires confidence in the results. This confidence is shaken somewhat by the fact that the data of the two cities show less agreement in the timing of nonresidential building. In New York the Civil War trough and subsequent peak occurred in 1864 and 1869 respectively, whereas in Philadelphia, the two corresponding turns fell in 1861 and 1872. Of course, the nonresidential data, due to their miscellaneous character, do not deserve as much confidence as the residential data.

[3] For the winter of 1893-1894, estimates of unemployment in thirty-eight United States cities by C. C. Clossen, Jr., and Bradstreets were 491,000 and 582,000, respectively. C. C. Clossen, Jr., "The Unemployed in American Cities," *Quarterly Journal of Economics*, Vol. VIII (1893-1894), p. 260. Mr. Clossen's estimate was based mostly on cor-

revival of 1895-1896, the McKinley election, and the revival and prosperity of 1898, 1899; and reached troughs varying for different types of building from 1898 to 1902, although the typical terminal date seems to have been 1900. The variation from city to city was also considerable; in many cities building reached a trough in the middle 1890's, whereas in many others the trough was not reached until as late as 1905. The poor synchrony is probably largely due to the relative mildness of the depression, which for the value of nonresidential was hardly more than a decline in the rate of increase.[4]

The prewar cycle recovered gradually (in absolute volume for the number data, and in rate of increase for the value data) during the active prosperities of 1901 and 1902, gathered speed all through the recession of 1903-1904, and reached a high plateau that lasted from 1905 to 1916.[5] It seems certain that the declines in 1917 and the trough in all classes of new building in 1918 were a direct

respondents' replies that were prepared during the second or third week in November. He describes the Bradstreet estimate as being based on estimates telegraphed by correspondents in the same cities on Dec. 22.

[4] However, because of the excessive influence of the large eastern cities which suffered little from the building declines, the indexes underestimate the actual severity.

[5] This plateau is responsible for much confusion concerning the true date of the peak of this cycle. Slight changes in its tilt or contour were sufficient to change the date of the peak by five or six years. It is important to point out that the plateau was due to the dominance of residential building and did not occur in business building or in total nonresidential, which business building dominates. The value index of nonresidential moved up rapidly to a peak in 1912 and thereafter declined. The number index of nonresidential showed no cycle at all, seemed to have been obscured by the steep upward trend from 1900 to 1924.

and violent consequence of America's entry into the war.[6] Indeed, the high level to which building was sustained through 1916 and the precipitous fall thereafter suggests that, in the absence of war at this time, the second cycle might well have ended several years later.

The most recent cycle commenced, as did the cycle following the Civil War, with an exceedingly rapid revival. Although the revival was checked briefly by a recession in 1920 (in the annual data), between then and the middle of the 1920's, building rose to the well-known, most spectacular boom. Peaks for the various building types ranged from 1924 to 1929 and for the individual cities even more widely than that, but in spite of this variation the year 1925 may be designated as a highly typical turning point. The only real variations from this date were manifested by apartment house construction, especially in New York, public building, and alterations.[7] After 1925 the volume of building began to decline, first gradually and then following 1929 with great velocity, until the trough was reached—for nonresidential building, total new building, and alterations in 1933, and for residential building in 1934. In the seven years since those dates, in spite of occasional interruptions, the trend of building has been persistently upward; though its recovery has lagged heavily behind the improvement in general business.

[6] The discussion of the depressing effect and the causes for the depressing effect of war on building, particularly residential building, occurs below, pp. 209-12.

[7] The lag in public building was not at all unusual, but the lag in apartment building was, and the lag in alterations was distinctly contrary to the customary lead that is usually encountered in this type of building.

From the foregoing account of the fluctuation of building activity several observations may be made concerning the relative movements of building and business.

### The Agreement of Major Movements in Building and Business

One observation is that, in the absence of war, major movements in building and in general business appear to be associated.[8] On the one hand, when either building or business is depressed, the other does not seem to remain long at an active tempo; on the other hand, when either building or business is active, the other does not seem to remain long inactive. This agreement of the major movements is, of course, due to economic interdependence. Building activity is naturally a derivative of national income and depends upon the prosperity of business in general. If business is inactive and unemployment is rife, the real income which the nation can spare, or rather wishes to spare, for construction of buildings may sink rapidly to near zero, especially in view of the fact that, as shall be discussed later, volume of new buildings demanded in an expanding industrial system tends to depend in part upon additions to income rather than exclusively upon absolute flow. Inversely, through the process discussed in

[8] Opinion is not at one concerning this agreement. J. B. Hubbard observed in 1924 that the relationship between building and business seemed to be irregular. "An Analysis of Building Statistics for the United States," *op. cit.,* p. 32. J. R. Riggleman observed no close correlation between building and business, although he noted that the two tended to be above and below normal at the same time (*op. cit.,* p. 40). W. H. Newman expressed the opinion that major cycles in building were pretty much independent of the business cycle (*op. cit.,* pp. 11-16, 36).

Chapters II and III business prosperity is intimately dependent upon building activity.

## The Lead of Building in Depressions

Building tends to precede general business on major downturns. During the 1870's, the decline in number and value of every class except public preceded the business recession by at least one year. During the 1890's, the recession in value of all classes of building except public, preceded business by one to three years; but number manifested precedence only for residential, and for the total building classifications which were, of course, dominated by residential. During the 1920's, every class of building, except public again, started its downturn three to five years in advance of business. In the case of the number data, even public building led by a year.

Of course, part of this lead in building was undoubtedly attributable to the use of permit rather than actual building data. However, it was noted that the average time required from the date of commencement to complete a building has been approximately four months. In annual data, this precedence has manifested itself as an occasional lead, rarely more than one year. The lead of permit data could not, therefore, be sufficient to explain a *persistent* advance over business of *one to five years*. The evidence of lead of building over business on downturns of great depressions must be accepted as rather strong. For explanation of this lead, the reader is referred to discussion in Chapter III of the investment consumption interaction. The lead may be due to (a) the decline in the "relation" through full employment frictions, reversals of confidence and

expectations, rising wages and interest rates, exhaustion
of normal flow of innovations, and decline in marginal
efficiency of capital or to (b) the slowed expansion of
consumption from the diminishing marginal propensity
to consume, due to various psychological and institutional
factors. On the other hand, it is possible that investment,
because of contracts, physical production lags or high producer optimum, might occasionally hold up even while
consumption is falling.

### The Lag of Building Recovery

Except after great wars, building has been slower to
recover from great depressions than has business activity
in general, if not in the initial recovery, at least in the
subsequent revival. There are a number of explanations of
this tardiness. One of them is the excess of plant and
equipment that may hang over from the previous boom
and, until worn out, hinder the formation of new capital.[9]
Obviously, a great boom, followed by a rapid and deep
fall, would lay the basis for a slow recovery. A second
explanation is the resistance, on the one hand, of most
building cost elements to reductions and, on the other, the
distressing propensity of these elements to "jump the gun"
with increases before the rise in demand has a chance to
harden.[10] A third explanation is the technical lag in pro-

[9] Thus "excess" refers not to any necessary redundance under normal conditions of consumption demand, but to an excess relative to the
low depression consumption.

[10] See T. J. Kreps' interesting comparison of the prices of iron and
steel, brick and tile, and lumber with the wholesale price level. This
relationship, which he calls the "exchange value," showed a strong
upward movement during the early years of the 'thirties, especially dur-

duction of capital goods due to the length of the capital propagation period, accentuated by immobilization of millions of men after years of inactivity. Of course, this lag slows consumption also by reducing the practical multiplier. However, consumption can be expanded by using existing equipment at increasing cost—with consequent increasing prices. Thus ephemeral production can run ahead of capital goods production. A fourth explanation is the blow which a severe and prolonged depression deals to business morale. Years of falling prices and incomes, bankruptcies and liquidation, makes both borrowers and lenders skeptical about the future and this uncertainty is greatest for extremely durable investments such as business buildings and homes. Capitalized values of very durable goods will naturally be very low even after present rents and earnings have risen somewhat. One would expect that the greater the durability, the greater therefore the uncertainty, and the longer therefore the delay in reaching full recovery.[11]

ing 1932, and only an incomplete decline in the latter part of the decade. T.N.E.C., *op. cit.*, pp. 5447-51.

[11] Such a shattering of morale will occur only after exceptionally severe and prolonged depressions and this may explain the absence of any real lag in building recovery after ordinary recessions.

# CHAPTER X

## THE DURATION OF LONG CYCLES

ONE distinguishing feature of the major cycle in building is its length. William H. Newman has placed the duration between fifteen and twenty-one years.[1] C. F. Roos states that "typical major swings" in residential building occupy periods of ten to twenty years, with a mean of fifteen years.[2] Warren and Pearson estimate the long cycle in building to be about eighteen years.[3] And John R. Riggleman, who has made the most careful and comprehensive study of *total building* in this country, counted six long cycles in building in the one hundred and three years from 1830 to 1932. The cycles varied from thirteen to twenty-two years in duration, with an average of seventeen. According to Mr. Riggleman, the building fluctuation has on the average lasted three times as long as the "major business cycle."[4]

All of the foregoing estimates of duration were for the United States. For a brief survey of foreign building cycles, the recent work of Warren and Pearson, *World Prices and the Building Industry* provides a convenient source of reference.[5] The writers present charts of build-

[1] *op. cit.,* p. 10.                                    [2] *op. cit.,* p. 69.
[3] *op. cit.,* p. 109.
[4] *Variations in Building Activity in United States Cities,* pp. 38-9.
[5] *op. cit.,* pp. 119-31.

ing series in London, Glasgow, Hamburg, Stockholm, the Netherlands, and Montreal. In London, the cycles ranged from eighteen to thirty years; in Glasgow, from twenty to thirty-five years;[6] in Hamburg, from sixteen to twenty-one years; in the Netherlands, from twelve to eighteen years. In Stockholm, the cycle was twenty-seven years; in Montreal, the cycle was about nineteen years. Warren and Pearson feel that these data indicate the European building cycle to have been somewhat longer than the American fluctuation.[7]

On first consideration, it may seem that considerable variation exists even in the United States between the duration estimates of different writers. Actually, the cycles themselves vary over time, and the variations are due to differences in the period of time studied. The closest approximation is probably the one-hundred-year study of John Riggleman, which places the average duration for the entire six cycles at seventeen years and for the last three cycles at slightly more than eighteen years.

The results of the present study do not alter this estimate. Rather, the concern is with an aspect that has not yet been presented—a comparison of the durations of cycles in different types of building. In addition, the durations of long cycles are broken into their phases of rise and decline; and comparison is made between different types of building as to relative durations of those phases. All these measures are tabulated and from them the following conclusions may be derived:

[6] The Glasgow data offered by Warren and Pearson are supported by data secured directly from the Dean of Guild Court and loaned to the writer by the National Bureau of Economic Research.

[7] *ibid.*, p. 126.

(1) Since the Civil War, average length of fluctuations in all types of building has been eighteen or nineteen years, with close agreement between the various building types.

(2) Although from one type of building to another within the same period there has been little variation in length, from one cycle to the next there has been considerable. The shortest fluctuation, the one following the Civil War, lasted only fourteen to sixteen years. Only slightly longer than this was the cycle following the World War. At the other extreme was the movement ending about 1900, which lasted twenty-one to twenty-three years. Of the four cycles since the 1860's, the cycle before the World War was the only one to agree in length with the average.

(3) Except in the case of residential building, average period of rise exceeded that of fall.

## Why Cycles in Building are Long

A number of explanations for the fact that nearly twenty years instead of a shorter period, say three to five years, has been the average length of building fluctuations are inadequate because they fail to establish a one-way causal relationship. W. H. Newman has found a correlation in length and timing between long building cycles and long cycles in population increase,[8] but doubt may well arise as to whether population cycles induce building cycles or cycles in building and gross capital formation, by causing profound movements in income and employment, induce cycles in births and immigration. Equal doubt may exist as to the causal significance of the correlations found by

[8] *op. cit.,* pp. 36, 49.

Wenzlick and Roos in St. Louis between building cycles and long fluctuations in the mortgage foreclosure and marriage rates.[9, 10] Finally, with respect to income and employment, even if long-period, annual data were available and a good correlation could be found between fluctuations in these factors and building cycles, the same familiar problem of dissociating cause and effect would be encountered.[11]

As an independent determinant of the timing and duration of building cycles, serious consideration should certainly be given to war. A severe war stops nearly all residential building and a considerable volume of nonresidential building.[12] The effect of such stoppage is to create a shortage of shelter that may in turn cause an extreme postwar speculative boom, a boom that on the reaction principle may go far in the direction of overbuilding and thus result in further building depression. Eventually, of

[9] Roy Wenzlick, "The Problem of Analyzing Local Real Estate Cycles," *Proceedings of the American Statistical Association,* Vol. XXVIII (1933), pp. 201-6.

[10] C. F. Roos, *op. cit.,* p. 77. Chart XV. This doubt is not allayed by the fact that the foreclosure cycle precedes the building cycle or by the argument that foreclosures reflect the supply of credit. In the last years of a building boom foreclosures are bound to increase as the result of the mere increase in the number of mortgages accumulating from the boom itself and as the result of the accumulation of weak mortgages from years of increasing optimistic borrowing and lending. In the last years of the building depression foreclosures are bound to decrease as the result of the decrease in the number of mortgages from lack of building and as the result of the elimination by foreclosure of most of the weak mortgages susceptible to foreclosure.

[11] Even inventions and technological changes are robbed of much of their causal significance by the fact that their discovery and development usually wait upon booms in the industry itself.

[12] For explanation of the inhibiting effect of war on building, see pp. 209-12.

course, in the absence of further disturbance, such waves must be expected to subside, but several large fluctuations may ensue before this happens, and by that time another war may well whip up a new series of perturbations.[13]

In addition to the direct effect upon the building industry, it is reasonable to expect that wars will modify building cycles indirectly through repercussions on other economic and social phenomena. One of these repercussions, perhaps the chief, has been pointed out by August Lösch to be the creation of great waves in populations.[14] The deficit of births during the war and the excess that follows thereafter results in great population waves lasting about thirty-three years. These waves tend to flatten out and to disappear after a century, but not until about three cycles have been formed. Usually, before the force has exhausted itself, however, a new war appears to reinforce the previous waves or to create new ones. The waves, according to Lösch, have determined "the timing and form of most of . . . German business cycles."[15]

It can hardly be denied that wars have had far-reaching effects on cycles in the building industry. Wars certainly intensify the severity of building cycles and determine when at least some cycles occur. Still, it is difficult to fasten upon war the explanation of the historical length of the

---

[13] Homer Hoyt, although he does not seek to propound any "catastrophic theory of business fluctuations," points out: "It seems that the dislocations of the normal flow of economic activity caused by great wars produce a series of speculative tidal waves that do not subside until years after the echo of the last cannon shot has died away." *op. cit.*, pp. 422-3.

[14] "Population Cycles as a Cause of Business Cycles," *Quarterly Journal of Economics,* Vol. LI (1937), pp. 649-62.

[15] p. 662.

United States building fluctuations. The serious wars have not occurred often enough, even counting wars abroad, and the thirty-three year cycles in population, cited by Lösch as the product of war, are too long to furnish an explanation for the American cycles in population and building construction.

Some attention ought to be given to the connection between durability of a commodity and the length of the cycle in its production. However, why, if buildings are capable of lasting a hundred years or more,[16] does the length of the building cycle average less than a generation? Why has not the American building industry experienced a much longer cycle than the one recorded?

Since the potential physical life of buildings is much too long to furnish an explanation of the thirteen- to twenty-three-year length of long cycles, is it possible to fall back upon the "economic" life as reflected by depreciation rates? Unfortunately, economic life of goods as potentially durable as buildings is a result of inducement to invest new and can be taken to exercise only a psychological inducement to replace—though the conventions among business men as to what is "good business'" policy in regard to replacement may be more important than its intangible nature would suggest.

[16] The Real Property Inventory of Peoria reveals that 15 per cent of the dwelling structures in 1934 were over fifty years of age and that 1.3 per cent were over seventy-five years of age (Federal Housing Administration, *Analysis of Housing in Peoria* [Washington: G.P.O., 1935], p. 23) ; Frank J. Hallauer has analyzed the data of the Real Property Inventory "for some of the older cities, where age has had time to develop. . . ." According to Mr. Hallauer, the analysis indicates a "probable average age of 120 years, possibly even longer. Analysis of population and construction records for New England seems also to support such a figure." *op. cit.*, p. 17.

In one sense, however, the rate of depreciation could have a tangible influence on the length of the cycle. As explained in Chapter III, when a building matures on the books of a business concern, this releases current income to become available for consumer purchasing power. The rise in consumer expenditures may furnish a demand for new homes and business buildings. The higher the depreciation rate, the earlier the maturation and release of income for consumption and the sooner the upward acceleration. Unfortunately for this theory, the statistics reveal very little decline of business depreciation charges of industrial corporations during even severe depression. Fabricant's data show a decline for all industries from four billion, six hundred million dollars aggregate charge in 1930 to three billion, nine hundred million dollars aggregate charges in 1935, a fall of only 13 per cent. Of course, these figures are not to be taken too literally. There is strong incentive to maintain such nominal charges to keep down corporation income taxes; and if such charges are made for this purpose only, earned surplus is apt to be drawn on for dividend disbursals.

Moreover, there is a great area of capital goods which are not formally depreciated. For most residential buildings, for small, nonincorporated businesses, and for farms, all of which are not covered by Fabricant's business depreciation figures, depreciation charges are implicit in the amortization of mortgage debt. As the mortgages taken out in the previous boom mature, income is released for consumption expenditures with a potential multiplying and accelerating effect. Again, however, the statistics let us down for, according to reports of the *Financial Survey of Urban Housing,*[17] very little reduction in the burden of mortgages took place between 1930 and 1934. This is too short a period to expect great change, but even so it would, in the light of the data, be foolhardy to rely on maturation of mortgage debt payments as setting the duration of building cycles. There do not, therefore, seem to be any obvious tangible determinants of the length of long building cycles. We have seen that a number of the more obvious factors that might lend a clue to the length, e.g. population cycles, marriage rates, mortgage foreclosure cycles, are as likely to be determined instead by the length of building cycles. Wars have not occurred often enough to explain the period of population and building waves in this country. And explicit depreciation charges do not seem to decline sufficiently in depressions to offer an upward impetus to consumer purchasing power; the same is true of mortgage amortization payments on residential buildings.

We are left, therefore, with only the psychological feeling on the part of business men concerning the life of assets in a "progressive business." In a new country such as the United States, "psychological life" would be shorter and replacements would recover sooner, than would be true in old and mature countries. This may account for the shorter building cycles in this country than in Europe.[18]

In addition to the psychological life of buildings, we have the interesting suggestion of Norman J. Silberling that the practice of making ten-year mortgage loans may be partly responsible for the length of the cycle inasmuch

[17] Washington, D.C.: G.P.O., 1937, Table 31 (for each of the twenty-two cities).
[18] G. F. Warren and F. A. Pearson, *op. cit.,* p. 126.

as these loans tend to get into trouble about a decade after the boom has first begun to get under way.[19] Mr. Silberling would, no doubt, be the first to admit that this "trouble" into which mortgages get is partly due to the building cycles themselves and is not altogether adequate to explain them.

[19] "Some Aspects of Durable Consumer Goods Financing and Investment Fluctuations," *American Economic Review*, Vol. 28 (1938), pp. 443-5.

# CHAPTER XI

## SEVERITY OF LONG BUILDING CYCLES

THE extreme variations in building activity from boom to depression have not escaped unobserved. John Riggleman has pointed out that "while *general business cycles* usually fluctuate within a range of 20 per cent above or below normal, the major *building cycles* fluctuate from two to three times as far from normal."[1] The following is a summary of the various characteristics of fluctuations in the individual types of building.

Residential building fluctuations were much wider and more severe than the cycles experienced by any other type

---

[1] John R. Riggleman, "Building Cycles in the United States, 1875-1932," *op. cit.*, p. 182. It is hardly fair, however, to compare the fluctuation of a single industry such as building with an index of industrial activity (Index of the Cleveland Trust Co.) for the United States. The economic area covered by the latter is naturally so broad that one would expect the cycles to be less severe. A fairer comparison would be between building cycles and cycles in other industries taken individually. See A. F. Burns, *op. cit.* Even so, according to Burns' study, building manifested trend cycle amplitudes wider than all except beet sugar or raisins in the agricultural group; sulphur, asphalt, cement, natural gas, fluorspar or mercury in the mining group; vessels, aluminum, cigarettes or locomotives in the manufacturing group; or shares traded in the transportation and trade group. As compared with the great majority of production series, the amplitudes of building were very great. Of the ninety-nine industries studied by Burns, building permits manifested cycles at least twice as wide as those of seventy and at least three times as wide as those of forty (pp. 230-3).

of building here considered, though the greater variation does not hold in all cycles or in all phases of cycles.

Of the residential types, apartment house construction revealed more extreme variation than detached dwellings. Individually or together, both residential types varied more widely than did either nonresidential series (public or business building).

Public and business building manifested fluctuations of approximately the same degree.

Cycles in alterations were much less intense than those of new building.

With each cycle since the 1878-1900 fluctuation, severity of building cycles has increased. The same observation may be made in both number and value data, but the increase was greater in the latter than in the former. Residential building, both detached and multifamily, exhibited much greater increase than did the nonresidential classifications.

## The Greater Severity of Residential Cycles

In the index of twenty-seven cities, the value of residential building for the eleven years, 1920-1930, was $7,790,000,000; whereas in comparison the value of nonresidential was only $5,846,000,000, or about 75 per cent. From the operation of the principle of large numbers, therefore, one would expect the severity of residential, relative to that of nonresidential, cycles to be small. Actually, whether measured by number or by value data, residential cycles were on the whole wider than nonresidential cycles.

One explanation is based on the fact that a considerable proportion of residential building is done by speculative builders for anticipated sale. In this respect residential building bears an important difference to nonresidential building. Small stores, office buildings, hotels, and private garages are perhaps exceptions, but in general the nature of nonresidential construction is such that ready-made production is impossible. It is nearly inconceivable that public buildings such as churches, schools, public utility construction, municipal buildings; or private nonresidential buildings such as factories and workshops, banks, club houses, public garages and service stations, warehouses, theatres and moving picture houses, stadiums, and dance

TABLE 14

*Amplitudes of Long Cycles*[2]

(Peak Values as Percentages of Trough Averages)

(Average Annual Percentages)

| Building Type | Last 19th-Century Cycle | Pre-First-World-War Cycle | Post-First-World-War Cycle |
|---|---|---|---|
| Detached Dwelling | 14.4 | 18.8 | 151.4 |
| Multifamily Dwelling | 12.5 | 55.1 | 341.8 |
| Public Building | 18.0 | 12.1 | 86.7 |
| Private Nonresidential | 7.3 | 14.1 | 86.7 |

[2] Amplitudes were computed by subtracting the averages of the initial and terminal trough values of each cycle from the peak value, then dividing the trough averages into that excess. The result is further divided by the duration of the cycle and this result multiplied by 100. The formula may be expressed as:

$$\text{Average Annual Amplitude} = \frac{200\left[P - \frac{1}{2}(T_1 + T_2)\right]}{N(T_1 + T_2)}$$

[ 169 ]

## TABLE 15

*Amplitudes of Long Cycles*[3]

(Peak Values as Percentages of Trough Averages)

(Average Annual Percentages)

| Building Type | | Post-Civil-War Cycle | Last 19th-Century Cycle | Pre-First-World-War Cycle | Post-First-World-War Cycle |
|---|---|---|---|---|---|
| Total Residential | Value Data[4] | — | 6.9 | 22.0 | 165.3 |
| | Number Data[5] | 21.6 | 10.7 | 15.3 | 91.3 |
| Total Non-residential | Value Data | — | 10.5 | 10.2 | 63.1 |
| | Number Data | 27.2 | 4.4 | — | 22.2 |
| Alterations | Value Data | — | 2.7 | 3.8 | 17.3 |
| | Number Data | — | — | — | — |

[3] See footnote 2 to Table 14.
[4] Amplitudes of the value data are taken from the indexes of building in twenty-seven cities as measured by estimated cost of buildings for which permits were granted.
[5] Amplitudes of the number data are taken from the indexes of building in twenty-nine cities as measured by number of buildings for which permits were granted.

halls should be built in any other way except by order. Uses are so highly specialized that builders cannot anticipate requirements in advance. Specifications are rigid, markets are narrow, risks are great.

In contrast with this, the standardized utilities offered by residences serve so large a market that speculative or ready-made construction of homes has become an established phenomenon. Examination of the classified and display advertisements of real estate in the daily newspapers

TABLE 16

*Severity of Long Cycles*[6, 7]

(Rises and Falls as Percentages of Peak Values)

| Building Types | Post-Civil-War Cycle | | Last 19th-Century Cycle | | Pre-First-World-War Cycle | | Post-First-World-War Cycle | |
|---|---|---|---|---|---|---|---|---|
| | RISE | FALL | RISE | FALL | RISE | FALL | RISE | FALL |
| Detached Dwelling | — | 13.0 | 7.3 | 6.1 | 7.8 | 9.3 | 15.9 | 9.6 |
| Multifamily Dwelling | — | 9.5 | 9.5 | 4.2 | 28.3 | 7.2 | 9.2 | 24.4 |
| Public Building | — | 11.2 | 6.1 | 13.0 | 5.5 | 9.8 | 8.5 | 22.8 |
| Private Non-residential | — | 10.7 | 7.2 | 3.1 | 6.3 | 11.2 | 12.8 | 11.9 |

[6] The measurements of severity of falls are computed by dividing the difference between the previous peak value and the trough value by that same previous peak value; the result was converted into an annual percentage and multiplied by 100. The equation may be expressed: $\dfrac{100\,(P_p - T)}{N\,P_p}$. The severity of the rise is computed in the same way, but employing the subsequent peak value: $\dfrac{100\,(P_s - T)}{N\,P_s}$.

[7] The measures are computed from the same data as were those of Table 14.

## TABLE 17

*Severity of Long Cycles*[8],[9]

(Rises and Falls as Percentages of Peak Values)

| Building Type | | Post-Civil-War Cycle | | Last 19th-Century Cycle | | Pre-First-World-War Cycle | | Post-First-World-War Cycle | |
|---|---|---|---|---|---|---|---|---|---|
| | | RISE | FALL | RISE | FALL | RISE | FALL | RISE | FALL |
| Total Residential | Value Data | — | 11.1 | 8.5 | 3.1 | 23.2 | 6.6 | 13.7 | 10.7 |
| | Number Data | 11.3 | 8.4 | 8.2 | 5.6 | 7.1 | 9.1 | 13.1 | 10.6 |
| Total Non-residential | Value Data | — | 10.9 | 7.2 | 5.4 | 5.5 | 9.3 | 12.3 | 11.7 |
| | Number Data | 8.1 | 9.7 | 5.5 | 3.9 | — | — | 3.8 | 9.2 |
| Alterations | Value Data | — | 5.9 | 5.8 | 1.3 | 8.0 | 1.7 | 6.5 | 18.1 |
| | Number Data | — | — | — | — | — | — | — | — |

[8] See footnote 6 to Table 16.
[9] The measures are computed from the same data as were those of Table 15.

is a convenient index of the large amount of residential construction which is done by speculative builders for sale ready-made. Mr. Herbert U. Nelson, secretary of the National Association of Real Estate Boards, has made the statement: ". . . home building is normally done by great numbers of small operative or speculative builders who build only three or four houses a year."[10] And James Ford comments: "Most of the housing in the outlying boroughs (of New York City) has been of the speculative type"; and again: "Most of the dwellings in New York City in recent generations have been built by speculators with a view to sale."[11] Willard Thorp estimates that between a third and a half of all one-family, residential building is done for sale or rent.[12]

As a result of speculation in dwelling construction, room for miscalculation is much greater. During boom times builders, imbued with optimism, are apt to overestimate prospective demand for dwelling construction; and during periods of depression builders, rendered pessimistic by lean years, are apt to underestimate future requirements. This should help to intensify the cycle in residential construction.

A second explanation may be that during periods of prosperity buyers of residential buildings show less foresight than the nonresidential purchaser and are apt to undertake greater commitments than economic conditions warrant. It is hardly to be doubted that home buyers are

[10] *New York Times* (Nov. 7, 1937), 4 RE:1.
[11] *Slums and Housing* (Cambridge, Mass.: Harvard University Press, 1936), Vol. I, p. 477; Vol. II, p. 671.
[12] T.N.E.C. Hearings, Part 11, *The Construction Industry,* p. 5189.

less well equipped in knowledge and judgment to forecast trends in real estate and business than are the business man. They have less business acumen, suffer from inferior advice,[13] and are influenced by considerations of social prestige. Nonpecuniary motives naturally interfere with sound judgments. Here again, the business man in his office is better situated to make sensible decisions.

But home buyers, bold in prosperity, may be timid during depression. It has been pointed out earlier that the public is frightened after several years of severe depression. A large proportion of the public has been wholly or partly unemployed, and a still larger proportion has been in daily dread of becoming so. In such a frame of mind, few even of those financially able are willing to enter into twenty-year contracts to purchase dwellings or to move into more expensive apartments. A large price is put upon liquidity and few possess sufficient faith in the future to relinquish it. Such faith does not come until the wounds of the depression have healed and business has given rather convincing evidence of future stability. The timidity is intensified perhaps by the fact that the individual buying a home is risking his own money and his own security; whereas a business man faced with the decision of expanding his business quarters is emboldened by the reflection that the money he risks is at least partly that of others.

The timidity of the home dweller might have less significance if the standard of living of the family were not contractible. A wage earner, faced with an uncertain fu-

[13] *The President's Conference on Home Building and Home Ownership* (Washington: National Capitol Press, 1932), Vol. IV, p. 49.

ture, can retrench his standard of living, and one of the easiest ways to do this is to move into smaller quarters or take in paying guests. There is no compulsion except personal pride or family pressure to force him to expand his living standard again. So long as the fear of insecurity is great enough to counterbalance these forces he will engage no more commodious apartment or purchase no more expensive dwelling. On the other hand, the business firm may find it necessary to build because it is the most profitable or the least unprofitable course to take. Expanding business, pressure of more efficient competition, desire for better location, all these and more are the stimuli to business building. They are motives that are pecuniary in character, and as such are probably more immediately compelling in time of depression than the postponable and *nonpecuniary* motives of the home dweller to secure social approval, avoid social condemnation, or achieve a larger measure of physical comfort. If to these considerations is added the widespread development of consumer credit, the purchase and sale of buildings on installment or high ratio mortgage, there is little wonder the home dweller first overbuys and causes a higher peak and later underbuys and causes a lower trough in comparison with nonresidential building.[14]

## *The Severity of Cycles in Detached and Multifamily Residential*

The comparison of the severities of cycles in apartments and detached dwellings yields wide differences. Amplitudes

[14] For a discussion of purchase of homes on credit see pages 189-90, below. See also a recent article by N. J. Silberling, *op. cit.*, pp. 439-46.

of apartment cycles were double those of detached dwellings and intensities of rises and falls averaged 50 per cent greater.

The wider fluctuation of apartment construction may be due to a greater element of speculation in this than in detached dwelling construction. Not all detached dwellings are produced ready made. A substantial proportion is built by direct order of the owner dweller. For this portion of the detached dwelling industry there is much less uncertainty as to demand. The doors are shut upon at least one type of error, and the cycles are, therefore, less extreme than they otherwise might be.

Apartment house construction, however, is entirely ready made. Because the apartments are rented to the general public rather than occupied by the builder, the demand for living quarters must always be anticipated rather than "known in advance." For this type of residential construction, therefore, errors in estimation of future demand are liable to be made for all projects. It is not surprising if the cycles should be more extreme than those in the less speculative detached dwellings.

Another explanation for the greater severity of the cycle in multifamily construction is the much larger size of the average apartment house project.[15] In the last two cycles of building in fourteen cities, the average cost of multifamily dwellings was between eight and eleven times as great as that of detached dwellings. This being true, the severity of the apartment house declines may be due to the greater hesitancy of people during periods of low

[15] The average costs of apartment houses and detached dwellings for fourteen cities are compared in the table on the following page.

morale to make large investments than small ones. The greater size also opens the way for accentuation of the cycle by random influences.

## The Severity of Cycles in Business and Public Building

Business and public building agreed closely with respect to intensity of fluctuation. This agreement may come as a surprise. Other things being equal, the relatively small volume and large average size of public building ought to cause cycles in public building to be more extreme than those in business building.

| City | Post-First-World-War Cycle | | Pre-First-World-War Cycle | | Last 19th-Century Cycle | |
|---|---|---|---|---|---|---|
| | Multi-family (000) | De-tached (000) | Multi-family (000) | De-tached (000) | Multi-family (000) | De-tached (000) |
| Brooklyn ....... | $ 47 | $ 8 | $14 | $ 4 | | |
| Manhattan and Bronx ........ | 195 | 9 | 61 | 8 | $28 | $9 |
| Queens ......... | 49 | 6 | | | | |
| Richmond ....... | 123 | 4 | 16 | 2 | | |
| Atlanta ......... | 23 | 3 | | | | |
| Boston .......... | 52 | 8 | | | | |
| Cambridge ...... | 76 | 10 | | | | |
| New Haven ..... | 25 | 8 | | | | |
| Philadelphia ..... | 142 | 5 | 51 | 2 | | |
| Portland ........ | 47 | 4 | | | | |
| Richmond, Va. .. | 53 | 6 | | | | |
| St. Louis ....... | 11 | 4 | | | | |
| Springfield ...... | 37 | 5 | | | | |
| Washington ..... | 90 | 7 | 24 | 3 | | |
| | $69 | $6 | $33 | $4 | $28 | $9 |

However, there are several explanations. Failure of public building to fluctuate more than business building is explained perhaps by differences again in degree of speculation. For although some degree of speculation may exist in business building, for example, small stores, renting garages, hotels, office buildings, manufacturing lofts[16]—in public building ready-made construction is nearly impossible. Only with difficulty can one conceive of a speculative builder constructing a college dormitory, a church, or a public high school with the hope of selling the structure when completed in the open market. The needs of most public and quasi-public agencies are too specialized as to both form and place utilities to admit of such practices. As a consequence, less room will exist for error in estimating demand and, under equal circumstances, cycles in public building may be expected to be somewhat milder than they otherwise would be.

Another explanation for the unlooked-for mildness of public building cycles may lie in the fact that public and quasi-public agencies are protected somewhat from competitive vicissitudes. Possessing powers of taxation, government agencies, although they often suffer loss of revenue and impaired credit during depression, usually have more stable sources of income and credit than most businesses. Another factor is absence of fear of the future. Government will last as long as most institutions. And the politician fears little personal consequence from government default; his chief fear being that of losing political following through lack of patronage to dispense.

[16] This is particularly true in large cities. Considerable advertising of business space takes place in the New York newspapers.

Quasi-public agencies, such as hospitals, universities, churches and public utilities are sheltered from the most severe economic perturbations. Public utilities are commercial enterprises, it is true; but, protected from direct competition, they are in a position to enjoy inelastic income demands for their products. Universities, churches, and similar institutions enjoy much of their income from endowments invested usually in high-grade securities. And statistics as far as they go, indicate that no class of incomes held up better during the depression than income in the form of interest.[17]

Government also finds it less easy to dodge its responsibilities during depression than does private business. Social and economic obligations increase rather than decline. Unemployed young men and women decide to finish their educations. Demands upon relief facilities become greater. Need for parks and playgrounds does not fall off and crime and fire rates are likely to increase. All these factors form a comparatively large amount of government building even during severe depressions.

This discussion, therefore, indicates that if the volume of public building were larger and the size of the average project smaller, one would expect to find much less severe cycles in this type of building. As it is, the stable revenue of public agencies, the absence of personal liability of the policy-determining authorities and their freedom from pecuniary hopes, and the made-to-order nature of public construction—all compensate approximately for the greater

[17] See statistics of the Bureau of Foreign and Domestic Commerce in cooperation with the National Bureau of Economic Research, *Statistical Abstract* (1935), p. 270.

fluctuation which might be expected in an industry of small volume and large unit size. Both of the latter are factors that intensify cycles because they open the way for accidental variations not always compensated by similar variations in other directions. Thus, they doubtless rob public building of the stability that on other grounds would rightfully belong to it.

## The Mildness of Cycles in Alterations

All the indexes agree on much milder variations in alterations than in new building. Alterations cycles were only a third as severe as total new building cycles, and only a fifth as severe as residential cycles. The relative gentleness of the fluctuation in alterations is not astonishing, but perhaps a discussion will emphasize the contrast between this type of construction and new building, and strengthen the conclusions as to the causes of fluctuations in the former. The characteristics of alterations which distinguish them from new building are their relatively short life; their urgency; their small average size; and their substitutability for new buildings.

Perhaps the most plausible explanation for the severe cycles experienced in new building is the long life of all types of new structures.[18] Once erected, the building need not be replaced for one or even many generations. Both the time and the volume of replacements of new buildings are highly discretionary.

Alterations, however, have a shorter life than new buildings. All buildings even when new are in continual need of

[18] See the discussion of the durability of buildings in the chapter on Duration of Long Cycles.

repair. Plaster cracks; roofs need reshingling; the house must be repainted; show-cases must be remodeled or re-arranged; a new furnace must be installed. A succession of these operations occurs in the life of every building. No way of anticipating and performing them all at once exists. And so the milder cycles in alterations.

This is particularly true if the definition of alterations is restricted to repairs, and additions are thus excluded. Separate data for extensions and additions on the one hand, and for alterations and repairs on the other, are available only for Pittsburgh and Philadelphia, but the data for both of those cities indicate milder cycles in repairs than in additions and extensions which possess many of the characteristics of new buildings. The average annual amplitudes are as follows:

|  | First Cycle | | Second Cycle | | Third Cycle | |
|---|---|---|---|---|---|---|
|  | Rep'rs | Add'ns | Rep'rs | Add'ns | Rep'rs | Add'ns |
| Pittsburgh | 26 | 89 | 35 | 34 | 22 | 24 |
| Philadelphia | 23 | 34 | | | | |

Of course, the repairs data include some alterations which involve structural modifications and therefore bear resemblance to additions and extensions. If these could be excluded, and a great number of other repairs which now escape through legal exemption or defective administration could be included, one would expect to find the cyclical variation even milder.

The second reason for the relatively mild cycle in alterations is the urgency of this type of operation. The erection of a new building, especially a residential building, may be postponed until a rise in income or a return of confidence.

This is not always possible in the case of alterations, either physically or economically. If the heating and plumbing system breaks down, it may be physically impossible to put off the repair or replacement for even a short time. If the roof needs repairing, greater cost and damage may ensue if it is not fixed immediately.

The central reason for this relative urgency is the fact that the building upon which an alteration is made constitutes an overhead cost. So long as a building stands it is usually more profitable to utilize it than not. The building may be yielding an aggregate revenue much less than the aggregate costs of operation and carrying charges. To fail to use it, however, would not escape the taxes or recover the original investment. It is *less unprofitable* to use the building than not to use it so long as the revenue exceeds the special out-of-pocket expenses. One of these out-of-pocket expenses is alterations. If it is necessary to make the alteration in order to use the building or in order to adapt it to a purpose more productive by at least as much as the outlay, the alteration will be undertaken. This is one reason why the volume of alterations is comparatively well sustained at times when new building is unprofitable and declines heavily.

A third explanation for the less severe cycle in alterations is the smaller average size of the unit project. Building operations of small unit size are less likely to fall off during depression because of less hesitancy to make small commitments than large ones. The smaller hesitancy is probably due to the fact that there is less of a problem in financing. The building owner is more likely to be able to pay for the alteration out of his own savings, instead of being dependent upon the availability of mortgage loan funds.

A fourth explanation is that alterations are often substitutes for new building. As with nearly all durable goods, there comes a time in the life of every building when the decision must be made whether to alter or extend it on the one hand, or replace it with a new building on the other. During boom times, the amount to which a building can be altered in order to accommodate an increasing standard of living or an expanding business need is limited. If the prospect for future profits seems good, the business man is prone to build new rather than to alter or repair. Alterations and repairs will not tend to increase so greatly, therefore, because when business is best and incomes are highest, new building takes place instead. The reverse of this is apt to occur during depression. When incomes are low and the future uncertain, people are reluctant to build new and are much more likely to alter or repair existing structures. This prevents the trough in alterations from falling so low. Alterations are thus prevented from attaining so high a boom by substitution *of* new building, and from falling to so deep a trough by substitution *for* new building. The effect is to lend stability to alterations at the expense of instability in new building.

# CHAPTER XII

## SEVERITY OF LONG CYCLES EXPLAINED

In Chapters II and III we discussed the theory of investment fluctuations and noted some factors making for their severity. We have now to apply those principles and extend them in an effort to explain the extreme variations of long building cycles. The factors may be summarized as (a) those that enhance the size of the relation; (b) those that enhance the fluctuations in the size of the relation; (c) the postponability of replacements, together with the stability of depreciation reserves; and (d) great wars.

### *The Size of the Relation*

In Chapter III we pointed out that whatever makes for a large relation makes for extreme fluctuations in investment, for any variations in either the rate of increase or the absolute flow of consumption will induce a wider change in the stock of investment needed to produce for that consumption. Moreover, the wider variations in investment will, operating through the multiplier, naturally cause consumption to be all the less stable. The factors favorable to a large relation were pointed out to be (a) a high degree of capitalism in industry as a whole, and a long physical and economic life, which, of course, distinguishes building from all other industries of comparable size; (b) a high average level of expectations, which is apt to characterize a young and growing country like the United States; (c) a low investment rate of interest; and (d) a short capital production period.

Not much can be said about these factors. Buildings are the most capitalistic agents we have and almost any expenditure anywhere in the economy takes place in and involves the services of durable, expensive buildings. A high level of expectations is apt to characterize a young and growing country like the United States, although the more durable the investment the further such expectations are apt to remain on the average below the real marginal efficiency of capital, thus offsetting to some degree the effect of durability to induce a high relation. The rate of interest has not been traditionally low in this country especially in real estate mortgages but all evidence is that it has been steadily falling. Indeed, if the FHA mortgage insurance plan does permanently lower the mortgage rate of interest, and reduce the annual amortization payment by increasing the life of the mortgage, and increase the average level of confidence of loaning agencies, then, although it may improve the standard of housing, it may also increase the size of the relation and therefore the severity of cycles. On the other hand, operating to reduce the size of the relation, is the long capital production period that characterizes building. It is not possible to specify the length of this lag. Only a small part of it, probably, is the time required to erect a building.[1] The greater part arises

---

[1] Correspondence with a large number of building inspectors elicited the information that the time required to complete a building was four months or less for residential and small nonresidential and as much as

from the fact that after some years of depression in building, the supply of contractors and skilled workers is greatly
depleted, and a considerable period of time, as well as rather
certain prospects of high profits and sustained employment,
are required to attract a new supply. Time is also required
to build up the industries supplying materials and machinery. The resulting lag is likely to be lengthened still more
by the fact that building prosperity induces prosperity in
the consumption goods industries. As building expands, it
must bid against these industries for the (diminishing)
capital and labor available. The great size of the building
industry intensifies this difficulty. It can not tap the odds
and ends of unemployed resources. Thus many years are
required for the building industry to catch up with the demand. We saw that the delay has the effect of reducing the
relation of investment to consumption because consumption is naturally large for a longer period. On the other
hand, we noted the possibility for speculative excesses to
breed in the inflated prices and profits caused by the delay.

### The Fluctuations in Size of the Relation

Not only does a high relation make for wide investment
cycles, but a fluctuating relation may make them even
wider. The principal reason for this is the behavior, noted
in Chapter II, of expectations. The longer the life of an
asset, the greater the element of futurity and the less that
can be known about the wisdom of making the investment.
The investment decision is based purely on expectation

eighteen months for large nonresidential. In Richmond, Va., it was
found that most building is completed within the same calendar year
in which the permit is granted.

and expectation is based chiefly on psychology. Such psychology, though immeasurable and even unfathomable, does follow certain general empirical rules of behavior. It may interact with real factors to form cumulative movements upward and downward, reaching extreme positive confidence after long upward movements and extreme negative confidence after long downward movements, and tends to lean on the size of negative confidence in times of uncertainty; that is, it is likely to exercise a depressing effect more readily than an uplifting one.

A number of factors contribute to the fluctuation in expectations that forms the basis of a changing relation and intensifies the cycles of building. One of them is the large unit size that makes investment in buildings extremely risky, reduces the number of people who make decisions, increases the opportunity for operation of chance or special circumstance; and extends the dependence upon the capital market and general investment psychology.[2]

Another factor contributing to the fluctuations in expectations is the speculative organization of the industry, especially in the residential building industry where cycles have been most severe. The speculation is facilitated and enhanced by the widespread use of mortgage credit. Indeed, there has been a strong upward trend in both speculation and use of mortgage credit. Examination of the *New York Times* files since 1864 shows that before 1900 classified advertising was meager and display advertising was nearly completely lacking. Since 1900, however, and espe-

---

[2] Indeed, the increasing severity of cycles may be a natural outcome of increasing size of building units. For evidence of this increasing size of buildings there is the fact of increasing average cost. The average

cially since the First World War, the advertising of new, already-erected structures has been very extensive. The increase has extended not only to dwellings but also to stores and office and loft buildings. According to the criterion of advertising, speculation has increased substantially in re-

size of total new building for two or more cycles is given below individually for a number of cities:

| | Second Post-Civil-War Cycle $000's | Last 19th-Century Cycle $000's | Pre-First-World-War Cycle $000's | Post-First-World-War Cycle $000's |
|---|---|---|---|---|
| New York City | | | | |
| Brooklyn .................... | | 5 | 6 | 12 |
| Manhattan and the Bronx ........ | 18 | 28 | 47 | 77 |
| Queens ..................... | | | 4 | 6 |
| Richmond ................... | | | 3 | 4 |
| Atlanta ...................... | | | 3 | 6 |
| Boston ...................... | | 7 | 12 | 13 |
| Cambridge ................... | | | 12 | 13 |
| New Haven .................. | | | 5 | 10 |
| Philadelphia ................. | | | 3 | 8 |
| St. Louis .................... | | | 3 | 4 |
| Washington .................. | | 2 | 4 | 8 |

Haber suggests that the increase in size of building has been due partly to technology in building construction. The improvements he mentions include bessemer steel, portland cement, the pneumatic caisson process, and the steam and electric elevators. (William Haber, *op. cit.*, p. 264.) Also, of course, is the fact that the increase in size of buildings has been a concomitant of the rising price of land. But, as a measure of increasing size, average cost is not entirely satisfactory. It has in most cities increased only about 100 per cent, and such an increase may have been due to increases in the cost of construction itself. Of course, as a matter of observation it is well known that in both residential and nonresidential types, many buildings have increased greatly in size. The fact that these increases do not show up in the average value data may be due to the increase also of a large number of small buildings, particularly private garages, which have offset the large buildings in the statistics.

cent cycles. Moreover, as another index of speculation, data for Manhattan and the Bronx indicate that the ratio of the number of buildings per plan filed has increased steadily in those two boroughs: During 1878-1897, the ratio of buildings to plans filed was 1.2; during 1902-1918, the ratio was 1.4; and during 1919-1933, the ratio was 1.6.[3]

If speculation has increased during the last three or four decades in New York, an even greater increase has probably taken place in other areas. Speculative building relies for its existence upon a wide market. Since the development of automobile commutation the market of every suburban community has been extended to include the entire metropolitan area.

As for the use of mortgage credit, every decade since the 1880's has brought a decline in percentage of cash and

Proportion of Debt Involved in Transfers of Owner-Occupied, One-Family Dwellings, in Terms of Per Cent of Cost at Time of Acquisition: Twenty-two U.S. Cities[4]

| | Debt as Per Cent of Cost |
|---|---|
| Before 1889 .... | 12.8 |
| 1890-1899 ..... | 17.5 |
| 1900-1909 ..... | 25.4 |
| 1910-1919 ..... | 34.4 |
| 1920-1929 ..... | 46.1 |
| 1930-1934 ..... | 53.0 |
| Average ....... | 44.3 |

[3] If the buildings are projected by a speculative builder with the idea of selling them when completed in the open market, he will find it practicable and profitable to build a number of buildings according to the same identical specifications.

[4] *op. cit.* The survey includes only those houses still standing in 1934. It does not include all the houses that were transferred during all these decades.

an increase in percentage of debt that change hands when a building is sold. Computations from data published by the *Financial Survey of Urban Housing* show the proportion of debt involved in transfers of owner-occupied, one-family dwellings was nearly four times as great during the postwar decade as during the period before 1889. Purchase of houses still standing in 1934 but bought before 1890 was accomplished on the average by less than 13 per cent debt and more than 87 per cent cash.[5] In comparison with this, purchase of homes in the 1920's was accomplished on the average by 46 per cent debt and only 54 per cent cash. In some localities in the 1920's percentage of debt was even greater. A study of 619 Buffalo homes purchased in 1922 or later showed that on the average down payment constituted only 23 per cent of purchase price.[6] And further computations from data of the *Financial Survey of Urban Housing* indicate that in 1934 nearly a third of owner-occupied, residential properties were mortgaged for 70 per cent or more of their value; a sixth for 85 per cent or more; and a twelfth for 100 per cent or more.

The significance of this development is clear. Not only has the increase in the practice of "trading on the equity" encouraged, by broadening the market, ready-made or speculative construction;[7] it has from the individual, though not from the aggregate, view permitted purchase of buildings on future, anticipated, income, rather than on

[5] A very small per cent of the latter constituted trades.

[6] *The President's Conference on Home Building and Home Ownership,* Vol. IV, p. 103.

[7] It is well known that the existence of a mortgage on a property enhances both its value and its chances of selling.

already accumulated savings.[8] Inasmuch as from the view-point of either borrower or lender, anticipated income is a matter of confidence, building activity is placed further at mercy of the psychological.[9]

The importance of psychology to highly durable and large unit investments, accentuated by the speculative or-ganization of much of the industry, makes the relation of net building capital formation to increasing consumption highly fluctuating. On the upswing, under pressure of posi-tive confidence, enticed by competitive illusions, and de-luded by price rises during production lags, the relation becomes much greater than is justified by the underlying marginal efficiency of capital and underlying rate of inter-est. But, it may be asked, will not this swollen relation prevent a downturn?

Unfortunately not, unless the relation continues to in-crease. For the diminishing marginal propensity to con-sume would require an advancing relation, in order to keep absolute consumption expanding to sustain investment. But it is impossible for the relation to continue to enlarge indefinitely or to remain indefinitely at any given level above the marginal efficiency of capital. We saw that full employment frictions, diminishing productivity of capital,

---

[8] Although it can be shown that savings are a function of income, which is in turn a function of the volume of investment (see J. M. Keynes, *The General Theory of Employment, Interest and Money*, pp. 175-85), it is nevertheless true that a credit system which permits in-vestment to be based on future or hoped-for income will thereby cause the fluctuations in present income and investment to be greater than they otherwise would be. The effect of this will be to accentuate not only the cycles in building but also those in savings.

[9] The basing of the credit on the value of property does not alter this fact. The appraisals of real estate upon which loans are made are no more stable than the economic cycles that the loans facilitate.

restrictive prices and production policies (partly from operation of Harrod's diminishing elasticity of demand) would eventually cause the relation to fall in spite of innovation and increasing confidence. And the fall in investment flow would be all the greater because of the high relation that had been existing during the boom.

But we saw also that confidence is an uncertain base for continuous expansion and indeed is likely to become negative in time of doubt. Consequently, when the relation slows or stops its expansion, absolute consumption must slow or stop its rise. But the slowing up of consumption rise causes a fall in net investment flow whatever the level of the relation, and the subsiding flow of investment has a downward multiplier effect on consumption, not likely to be offset by rising replacements.[10] The stage is now one of uncertainty; and confidence, so potent in inducement to durable investment, is, therefore, likely to shift from positive to negative. And this shift causes a fall in investment related even to those consumption increases that have still persisted, adding to the fall in investment related to suspended consumption increases.

Widely fluctuating factors on the demand side, including not only current prices and rents, but also the expectations of future prices and rent would seem to make for a widely fluctuating relation and thereby accentuate the cycles in inducement to invest in buildings. But these fluctuations in demand factors would be powerless to disturb the inducement to invest were it not for the apparently unyielding nature of construction costs, operating costs, and interest rates.

[10] See *supra,* pp. 78-82.

The fact that building costs are slow to adjust to falling demand is as widely conceded as it is difficult to prove statistically. In 1922, the Joint Legislative Committee on Housing of the New York State Legislature said in its Intermediate Report:

"Your Committee found profiteering, restriction of competition, price-fixing, trade strangulation and similar abuses in almost every phase of the building and allied industries. The manufacturer, jobber, middleman, contractor, labor leader and the laborers themselves, were all found to be locked in combinations, having the cumulative effect of making the construction of a building well-nigh an economic impossibility."[11]

Among the causes of excessive costs of building which the report gave were the following: grafting, exclusiveness, and uneconomical regulations of labor unions; monopolistic combinations of the materials supply industries; monopoly in all types of insurance; exorbitant charges and discounts on loans by financial institutions.[12] Recently, T. W. Arnold, Assistant Attorney General of the United States, asserted before the T.N.E.C. that: "Throughout the history of the Antitrust Division about 25 per cent of the cases instituted have dealt with manufacturers and distributors of building materials or with building trades contractors or building trades labor."[13] "Building costs have moved flexible upward but not downward; and the aggregate effect of the restraints in the building industry appears to be a gigantic stairway of prices and costs in

[11] *Legislative Documents* (1922), No. 60 (Albany: J. B. Lyon Company, Printers, 1922), p. 9.
[12] *ibid.*, p. 18.
[13] T.N.E.C., *op. cit.*, Part 11, *The Construction Industry*, p. 5147.

which the level attained during the period of rising prices becomes the taking-off point for the next period."[14]

Some conception of the inflexibility of building costs may be had by examining Chart VI, which contains statistics of some of the principal cost factors in New York City building.

Only twice since 1874 have the hourly wage rates of building labor, skilled and unskilled, declined appreciably. From 1874 to 1879, the average wages of carpenters, bricklayers, masons' laborers and common laborers fell from 24½c to 18¾c an hour; and during the recent depression, wage rates fell from $1.51 in 1930 to $1.22 in 1932. The latter decline lagged behind the fall in building by several years. In neither case was the decline more than about 20 per cent. However, these rates apply only to a fraction of the laborers employed in building, so that for this and other reasons the actual decline was greater than the published rates would indicate; moreover, increase in the efficiency of labor during the slack periods has undoubtedly made the decrease in cost more significant than it seems.

The published wholesale building materials prices have been more flexible than the published wage rates, though the de facto prices have most certainly been much more stable than de facto wage rates. The index on Chart VI contains the average yearly wholesale prices at New York of brick, cement, pine, lime, and steel shapes. The index of building material prices fell during 1874-1878 from 53 to 33 and during 1926-1932 from 123 to 72; in both cases the declines were about 40 per cent. However, too much

[14] *op. cit.*, p. 5151.

1865 '70 '75 '80 '85 '90 '95 1900 '05 '10 '15 '20 '25 '30 1935

CHART VI:[1] Factors in the Cost of Building, New York City, 1868-1934[2]

Tax Rate

Tax Levy

Ratio of Assessed to Selling Value

New Mortgage Interest Rates

Wage Rates

Building Material Prices

[1] Semi-logarithmic scale.
[2] For explanation of these cost factors and sources of the basic statistics see Table 18.
-----Brooklyn, Queens, and Richmond were added to New York City in 1898.

1865 '70 '75 '80 '85 '90 '95 1900 '05 '10 '15 '20 '25 '30 1935

TABLE 18

*Factors in the Cost of Building, New York City, 1868-1934*

| Year | Tax Rate[15] (per $100) | Tax Levy[16] (Millions) | Tax Burden (Assessed ÷ Sale Value[17]) | New Mortgage Interest Rates[18] | Wage Rates[19] | Building Material Prices[20] |
|------|------|------|------|------|------|------|
| | | | | | (1926=100) | |
| 1868 | 2.66 | 24.1 | | | | |
| 69 | 2.27 | 21.9 | | | | |
| 1870 | 2.25 | 23.5 | | | | |
| 71 | 2.47 | 23.4 | | | | |
| 72 | 2.90 | 32.0 | | | | |
| 73 | 2.50 | 28.2 | | | | |
| 74 | 2.80 | 32.3 | | | 19 | 53 |
| 1875 | 2.94 | 32.4 | | | 17 | 47 |
| 76 | 2.80 | 31.1 | | | 16 | 41 |
| 77 | 2.65 | 29.2 | | | 15 | 36 |
| 78 | 2.55 | 28.0 | | | 14 | 33 |
| 79 | 2.58 | 28.2 | | | 14 | 51 |
| 1880 | 2.53 | 28.9 | | | 16 | 57 |
| 81 | 2.62 | 31.1 | | | 19 | 57 |
| 82 | 2.25 | 27.7 | | | 19 | 58 |
| 83 | 2.29 | 29.2 | | | 20 | 60 |
| 84 | 2.25 | 30.0 | | | 20 | 54 |
| 1885 | 2.40 | 32.9 | | | 20 | 51 |
| 86 | 2.29 | 32.4 | | | 20 | 53 |
| 87 | 2.16 | 32.4 | | | 20 | 49 |
| 88 | 2.22 | 34.3 | | | 19 | 48 |
| 89 | 1.95 | 31.1 | | | 20 | 52 |
| 1890 | 1.97 | 33.2 | | | 25 | 52 |
| 91 | 1.90 | 33.8 | | | 25 | 50 |
| 92 | 1.85 | 33.7 | | | 26 | 50 |
| 93 | 1.82 | 35.0 | | | 26 | 48 |
| 94 | 1.79 | 35.7 | | | 26 | 48 |
| 1895 | 1.91 | 38.4 | | | 26 | 49 |
| 96 | 2.14 | 44.9 | | | 26 | 50 |
| 97 | 2.10 | 45.3 | | | 26 | 46 |
| 98 | 2.01 | 77.5 | | | 26 | 48 |
| 99 | 2.45 | 72.8 | | | 27 | 51 |
| 1900 | 2.25 | 71.8 | | | 29 | 58 |
| 01 | 2.32 | 75.6 | | | 30 | 51 |
| 02 | 2.27 | 76.3 | | | 32 | 53 |
| 03 | 1.41 | 67.9 | | | 33 | 56 |
| 04 | 1.51 | 76.6 | | | 33 | 53 |
| 1905 | 1.49 | 78.6 | | 5.35 | 34 | 54 |
| 06 | 1.48 | 85.7 | | 5.32 | 35 | 57 |
| 07 | 1.48 | 93.6 | | 5.41 | 38 | 56 |
| 08 | 1.61 | 109.5 | | 5.00 | 38 | 55 |
| 09 | 1.68 | 115.2 | | 5.05 | 38 | 54 |
| 1910 | 1.76 | 124.9 | .86 | 5.03 | 39 | 49 |
| 11 | 1.72 | 136.1 | .91 | 5.31 | 39 | 47 |
| 12 | 1.83 | 144.7 | .93 | 5.29 | 39 | 49 |

TABLE 18—*Continued*

| Year | Tax Rate[15] (per $100) | Tax Levy[16] (Millions) | Tax Burden (Assessed ÷ Sale Value[17]) | New Mortgage Interest Rates[18] | Wage Rates[19] (1926=100) | Building Material Prices[20] |
|------|------|------|------|------|------|------|
| 13   | 1.81 | 145.9 | 1.08 | 5.75 | 39  | 50  |
| 14   | 1.78 | 144.4 | 1.07 | 5.44 | 40  | 46  |
| 1915 | 1.87 | 153.7 | 1.10 | 5.58 | 40  | 45  |
| 16   | 2.04 | 168.7 | 1.09 | 5.29 | 41  | 69  |
| 17   | 2.02 | 168.6 | 1.16 | 5.18 | 45  | 92  |
| 18   | 2.36 | 198.2 | 1.11 | 5.39 | 48  | 96  |
| 19   | 2.32 | 197.1 | .98  | 5.52 | 58  | 105 |
| 1920 | 2.48 | 215.9 | .85  | 5.76 | 74  | 123 |
| 21   | 2.77 | 278.2 | .77  | 5.99 | 76  | 110 |
| 22   | 2.75 | 282.5 | .96  | 5.74 | 76  | 97  |
| 23   | 2.74 | 290.4 | .85  | 5.85 | 80  | 114 |
| 24   | 2.74 | 306.0 | .85  | 5.88 | 88  | 109 |
| 1925 | 2.69 | 320.8 | .80  | 5.52 | 90  | 98  |
| 26   | 2.71 | 353.5 | .72  | 5.84 | 100 | 100 |
| 27   | 2.70 | 393.6 | .82  | 5.74 | 107 | 98  |
| 28   | 2.73 | 433.2 | .86  | 5.86 | 107 | 95  |
| 29   | 2.68 | 456.8 | .75  | 5.93 | 111 | 90  |
| 1930 | 2.70 | 487.4 | .73  | 5.85 | 114 | 86  |
| 31   | 2.72 | 504.2 | .76  | 5.86 | 102 | 80  |
| 32   | 2.68 | 526.2 | 1.19 | 5.51 | 92  | 72  |
| 33   | 2.43 | 449.4 | 1.29 | 4.92 | 95  | 85  |
| 34   | 2.72 | 472.5 | 1.07 | 5.20 | 94  | 88  |

[15] *Tax Rate* on real and personal property for 1868-1917; on real property only for 1918-1934. Area: 1868-1874, Manhattan; 1875-1895, Manhattan plus Wards 23 and 24 of the Bronx; 1895-1897, Manhattan plus entire Bronx; 1898-1935, entire Greater New York. Source: *Real Estate Record and Builders' Guide; Annual Reports of the Comptroller of the City of New York.*

[16] *Tax Levy*: Total tax levy on real and personal property and bank stock. Area: same; source: same. (1899-1934, real property only.)

[17] *Ratio of assessed to selling values of identical properties in Manhattan.* Source: *Real Estate Record and Builders' Guide.*

[18] *New Mortgage Interest Rates*: Weighted average of value of new mortgages in each of five interest categories: 4 per cent, 4.5 per cent, 5 per cent, 5.5 per cent, 6 per cent. Mortgages at nominal rates or rates not specified are ignored. The former category is 10 to 20 per cent of the total. Source of basic data the *Real Estate Record and Builders' Guide*. The datum for each year based on new mortgages loaned during four weeks of each year; usually the last week in March, June, September, and December.

[19] *Wage Rates*: Arithmetic mean of the yearly average of hourly union wage rates of carpenters, bricklayers, masons' laborers, common laborers, structural iron-workers (1908-34). Source: Engineering News-Record, *Construction Costs* (1935 edition), p. 13.

[20] *Building Material Prices*: Average yearly wholesale prices at New York of common brick, cement, lime, pine, steel shapes (1894-1935). *ibid.,* p. 10.

reliance should not be placed upon these data. As indicated, they represent wholesale prices which are much more flexible than retail; moreover, they represent prices only of a few of the staple materials. It is unfortunate that satisfactory indexes of prices of building equipment such as elevators, bathroom and other sanitary apparatus, furnaces, lighting fixtures, refrigerators, insulation, fire-escapes, do not seem to be available. But certainly, as they stand, the data are far from flexible. Throughout the period 1880-1915 prices were exceedingly stable, showing only slight and lagging response to fluctuations in building. Upward movements of prices have been much more rapid and extensive than the downward movements. Only five years (1916-1920) were required for building material prices to move from 45 to 123,[21] but twelve years (1921-1932) were required for prices to fall from 123 to 72. *In no important decline did the prices of building materials fall as far as the previous low level.*

*The Prices of Land*: One of the main factors in building cost is land. It is probable that land prices are highly

[21] See a statement by Corwin D. Edwards, assistant to the Attorney General: "Prices and costs in the construction field enhance the whole problem of maintaining prosperity because they remain too high during depression and rise too fast and too far during recovery. Although the prices of materials can be traced more definitely than other costs of construction, these other costs seem to move in the same way as the cost of materials.

"Though building costs readily go up with increased construction, even to the extent of choking off the revival, they do not readily go down when the demand for houses falls. . . .

"Within the last three months . . . prices of building materials throughout the nation appear to have increased between 3 and 4 per cent. Though some of these increases are natural consequences of the war, some of the most important ones cannot be readily explained by underlying costs and shortages." *New York Times,* Feb. 18, 1940, XI, 16:7.

inflexible, although it does not seem possible to secure any statistical corroboration for that belief. Homer Hoyt's study of the land value fluctuations of Chicago show movements about the same in timing and intensity as those in building construction, and he states that land values have been above normal only about 29 per cent of the time.[22] However, it is a mistake to impute the prices of urban land during a depression in real estate from the actual selling prices of the few properties that are conveyed voluntarily. The fact that actual sales at low prices do occur during depressions is not an index of the prices at which any specific sites could be secured by persons actually desiring to buy and build. It is true that any one wishing to sell land during a real estate depression must sell at low price; but it is also undoubtedly true that anybody wishing to buy at such times must pay prices higher than the value productivity of the land and therefore too high to permit building at a profit.[23] The actual situation with regard to the value of land is probably that each high level of value productivity of urban sites is rather promptly capitalized either implicitly or through sale or hypothecation; and that once capitalized upward, the new, high values become virtually conventional values and are readjusted downward only reluctantly and after great lag. The painfulness of the readjustment does not show in the statistics of land values because the latter include only those properties whose owners have made the readjustment; they do not show, they cannot show—except through the paucity of actual sales—the valuations of in-

[22] *op. cit.*, pp. 417-18.
[23] The same condition is undoubtedly true of most durable goods.

transigeant owners who refuse to lower their supply prices and who therefore make it expensive for building construction to occur.

Tied in closely with the problem of rigid cost is the fact that from the standpoint of a speculative builder or a contractor building costs are primarily direct costs that may be avoided by not building. The aggregate value of all equipment owned by reporting construction establishments at the end of 1929 was only 7 per cent of the total business done during that year. In fact, of the five and one-half billion dollars reported as having been received for construction work in 1929, the proportion paid out for expenses that might be listed as overhead was less than 14 per cent. The great bulk was for labor and building materials.[24] The building contractor then is under no particular compulsion to continue operations when rents and prices decline appreciably below average total unit cost. He simply drops out of business.[25]

However, although labor, materials, and land may represent direct costs, easily avoided by the builder, they are not so to the workers, the manufacturers, or the landowners. The fact that builders may exhibit elastic short-run supply curves on the downward side does not explain why the building material manufacturers, the laborers, and the landowners, all of whom have large overhead costs, possess

[24] Fifteenth Census of the United States, *Construction Industry,* 1930, pp. 96, 112. Many even of these so-called overhead expenses must necessarily be variable in any but the very short run.

[25] The assumption of relative elasticity of short-run supply for an industry of high out-of-pocket expenses is based on the relative constancy of marginal costs for the individual builder, and the greater uniformity of costs among builders than would probably exist if capital equipment played a bigger rôle.

short-run supply curves that are also elastic. The allegation of monopoly or oligolopy or impure competition is adequate to explain why these prices are at all times higher than their "proper" levels, but does not furnish adequate clue to why the prices are not continually adjusted to shifts in demand in order to attain the output that will maximize profits or minimize losses.[26] This failure of prices to adjust must be explained, for if it were not for the rigidity of all these prices the fact that they constitute direct cost to the builder would have much less significance in the study of disequilibrium in building.

Several factors may be cited as the probable reasons for rigidity in the face of large overhead costs. One is the familiar hesitancy of sellers to lower prices, even though it is of immediate advantage to do so, for fear that the prices, once lowered, cannot be raised again. Another is the fact that in many cases when it is believed that the future price and demand will be higher than the current price and demand, it pays sellers and leasers of land and lenders on long-term mortgages to allow their land and money to lie idle until the market situation becomes more favorable. Such belief in the future is apt to be particularly strong if there have been many generations of secular rise in land values or a long period of fairly high interest rates.[27] Still another, and perhaps the most important, explanation is the

[26] The monopolist does not differ from the competitor in the desire to maximize profits or the necessity he is under to adjust his price to shifts in demand in order to do so.

[27] Keynes feels that the farther the market rate of interest gets below the rate which banks consider the conventional long-run rate, the greater becomes the liquidity preference of the banks and the greater the resistance to further decline. *op. cit.*, pp. 202-4. However, see above, pp. 21-2.

knowledge of the workers, the materials manufacturers, and the landowners that buildings constitute joint demand for the various agents of production that provide the supply. The *Census of Construction* lists forty-five rather broad classes of building materials alone, not one of which in 1929 was as much as 5 per cent of the value of construction work done.[28] Each industry or each class of labor finds that its product is such a small part of the total cost of the end-product that for it to reduce its price by unilateral action would result in very little stimulus to building construction and therefore in very little increase in the demand for the product of that specific industry or class of labor. The same reasoning applies in the case of land, although to a much lesser extent inasmuch as land probably constitutes the largest single class of expense.

The effect of the jointness of demand coupled with the insignificance of the part played by any single industry or class of labor is that each such industry or class of labor is confronted with a very inelastic demand for its product or service, even though the joint demand curve might be very elastic. As an individual industry or class, it sees little additional business to be gained by price cutting and little to be lost by price maintenance. No one industry or class of labor then is willing to cut prices freely in time of falling demand unless it can be sure that the other industries or classes of labor will do likewise. Thus, paradoxically, in order to insure the free adjustment in building material prices, wage rates, and land prices, it is necessary to secure some kind of joint price convention between the different

[28] *op. cit.,* p. 120.

industries and classes of labor involved. Flexible prices apparently require cooperative (monopolistic!) action.

Every bit as important as original cost in the costs of ownership are the operating costs. And the importance of operating costs, including taxes, insurance, maintenance and repairs, and even heating since this expense is a fixed part of living on any given scale, is especially heavy for apartment projects. The following table presents the operating costs of eight Manhattan apartment projects. It will be noted that these operating expenses are even more unyielding than the wage rates and materials prices reviewed in the discussion of construction costs. Maintenance and repairs are important in these costs and would naturally be rigid to the same extent, and for the same reasons, as construction costs themselves.[29] Insurance seems to be comparatively unimportant but is no less stable for all that. Of course, many of the expenses, such as those under renting and administrative expense and those having to do with heating, elevator, garbage collection, and so on, merely reflect increased service rather than increased cost. Nevertheless, from the standpoint of inducement to invest, these operating costs represent a rigid deduction from a widely fluctuating actual gross income and from even more widely fluctuating expectations of real income.

For many building projects, one of the heaviest operating expenses is taxes. Three series are given in Chart VI to show the inflexibility of taxation: the tax rate; the tax

---

[29] Maintenance and repairs often include, beside the legitimate expenses of keeping the property in efficient running order, additions and betterments which should really be classed as capital investments.

TABLE 19

*Eight Manhattan Apartment Projects: Composite Operating Data, City and Suburban Homes Company*[30]

Per Room Per Annum

| Year | Gross Income Per Room* | Total Operating Cost Per Room | Income Available for Interest, Depreciation, Profit |
|------|------|------|------|
| 1909 | $ 63.35 | $ 31.41 | $ 31.94 |
| 1910 | 62.50 | 31.38 | 31.12 |
| 11 | 64.83 | 33.11 | 31.72 |
| 12 | 63.47 | 32.20 | 31.27 |
| 13 | 63.87 | 31.47 | 32.40 |
| 14 | 65.92 | 32.93 | 32.99 |
| 1915 | 69.18 | 34.32 | 34.86 |
| 16 | 67.32 | 34.03 | 33.29 |
| 17 | 70.41 | 33.91 | 36.50 |
| 18 | 72.97 | 37.08 | 35.89 |
| 19 | 76.98 | 40.74 | 36.24 |
| 1920 | 84.52 | 45.73 | 38.79 |
| 21 | 99.42 | 51.75 | 47.67 |
| 22 | 104.13 | 52.21 | 51.92 |
| 23 | 105.97 | 50.68 | 55.29 |
| 24 | 108.60 | 54.29 | 54.31 |
| 1925 | 113.44 | 56.09 | 57.35 |
| 26 | 118.39 | 59.66 | 58.73 |
| 27 | 118.75 | 54.75 | 64.00 |
| 28 | 119.99 | 56.51 | 63.48 |
| 29 | 121.21 | 55.86 | 65.35 |
| 1930 | 122.91 | 58.56 | 64.35 |
| 31 | 123.69 | 59.18 | 64.51 |
| 32 | 123.07 | 59.28 | 63.79 |
| 33 | 109.75 | 59.98 | 49.77 |
| 34 | 92.59 | 58.79 | 33.80 |
| 1935 | 95.31 | 65.19 | 30.12 |
| 36 | 96.02 | 72.54 | 23.48 |
| 37 | 101.11 | 72.42 | 28.69 |
| 38 | 109.16 | 71.01 | 38.15 |

*Actual Income from Rents.

[30] Federal Housing Administration, *Four Decades of Housing with a Limited Dividend Corporation*, Table 14, p. 106.

levy; and the ratio of assessed value to selling value of actual New York City conveyances.

Although the tax rate during the period, 1868-1934, showed some tendency to vary, the variation was small and anticyclical. As for the tax levy, it continued throughout the entire seventy-year period to increase almost without interruption, in spite of the fact that since 1898 no additions have been made to the land area of New York and in spite of the fact that during periods of building depression the wear and tear and depreciation of buildings has greatly exceeded the volume of new construction.

However, the real inflexibility of taxation as a cost factor may be seen in the variations in the ratio of assessed value to selling value. It was found possible to gather statistics of the aggregate assessed values of all Manhattan and Bronx real estate actually sold for which consideration was given in the conveyance. The annual ratio of the aggregate assessed value to the aggregate sale price of these identical properties gives, in the absence of appreciable changes in the tax rate, an accurate index of the variations in the burden of taxation on cost of owning and operating real estate. Examination of the index shows that, in general, the burden of taxation relative to value was quite low during the boom period of building and quite high during the depression years. In 1917 and 1918, years of depression in New York building, properties assessed in the aggregate at $49,063,000 and $39,566,000 sold for aggregate prices of $42,445,000 and $35,757,000, respectively; the ratios of assessed to selling values were thus 1.16 and 1.11. During all the boom years of building, the ratio of assessed to selling values of buildings varied from .96 to as low as .73, and during the depression of the early 'thirties the ratio rose to as high as 1.29. In 1933, 116 properties sold in Manhattan at an aggregate price of $7,790,000; while the assessed values of those same 116 properties aggregated $10,071,000.

Finally, interest, though less important in the cost of ownership than original cost and much less important in the inducement to invest than expectations,[31] is nevertheless usually more important than taxes, maintenance, land and insurance.[32] Consequently the stability of mortgage interest rates must be a strongly contributing factor in building cycle severity.

Data presented on Chart VI of interest rates of new mortgages on Manhattan real estate show little tendency to vary with the building cycle; in fact, the data show little variation of any kind. The greatest variation that occurred was the decline in the rate of interest from 5.93 in 1929 to 4.92 in 1933, but the decline took place only after long and painful lag.[33]

[31] See *supra,* Chap. II, pp. 18-30.

[32] See R. L. Davison testimony in T.N.E.C. Hearings, Part 11, *Construction Industry, op. cit.,* p. 4994; table and chart on pp. 5592-3.

[33] See Table 18 for description of the method of computation. The data are not altogether satisfactory: (1) They constitute a weighted average of value of new mortgages in each of five interest categories 4 per cent, 4.5 per cent, 5 per cent, 5.5 per cent, 6 per cent; thus mortgages at nominal rates or at rates not specified are ignored. The former category ranges from 10 to 20 per cent of the total. (2) The data include mortgages constituting both senior and junior liens and it is not possible to discover how these proportions vary, although such variations would have the effect of disturbing the homogeneity of the data. (3) The datum for each year is based on mortgages loaned during four weeks of each year: usually the last week in March, June, September, and December. They do not, therefore, cover all mortgages contracted during the year.

## *Depreciation and Replacement*

It may seem necessary to discuss replacements separately from net building investment because, whereas the latter is related to progress, the former seems to be related to events that have occurred in the past. Building that merely offsets current wastage is certainly a good part of gross building investment[34] and in the long run this aggregate is important to the question of welfare. As far as economic cycles are concerned, however, it may be questioned whether any distinction between net investment and replacements is significant to the problem of employment and purchasing power. For in spite of this apparent connection with the rather remote past, replacements of buildings are actually closely tied up with the volume of current net investment. Buildings are extremely durable and the more durable a commodity the greater is the difference between its minimum and maximum potential life. The time of replacement is not fixed by physical consideration of wear and tear, but primarily by economic considerations. Thus, it is idle to conceive of replacements running in cycles of the same pattern, but removed by a fixed number of years, from net investment cycles of the past. Indeed, even if replacements were governed by physical considerations the widely variable conditions of construction, care, and climatic conditions would gradually obliterate the cycles in their original construction and disperse the physical re-

---

[34] During the 1920's, it may have more than half of all nonfarm residential building. Compare Fabricant's estimate of twenty-two billion dollars depreciation charges for 1919-1935 (*op. cit.*, p. 143) with expenditures for residential nonfarm construction of forty-two billion dollars, the estimate of the Department of Commerce. (*Construction Activity in the United States, 1915-1937*, p. 43.)

placement need rather evenly over time.[35] As actually determined, replacements are entirely indistinguishable from net investment in purpose, method of financing, ap-

[35] See *supra*, p. 94, the allusion to P. de Wolff's study concerning the absence of the "echo" effect in replacement of automobiles.

The fact that buildings tend to be replaced long before their physical lives have been exhausted may be seen from the number and behavior of demolitions. Data quoted by the National Resources Committee indicate that, so far as residences are concerned, demolitions are negligible. During 1920-1930 demolition of nonfarm residences are said not to have exceeded thirty thousand a year (*Housing Monographs Series* No. 1, p. 14). Compare this with the half million or more family units started each year. As to the nature of demolitions, Homer Hoyt observes: "The continual growth of the central business district of Chicago for a century has required successive crops of buildings on the same site to meet the demands of different or more intensive uses. Since 1830 at least six different structures have occupied the southeast corner of Washington and LaSalle Streets, each of which in turn was expected to endure for many years. There are probably few spots in the downtown district which have not been occupied by at least three, if not four, sets of buildings. Along LaSalle Street, where the replacement has occurred more frequently than on any other street, thirteen-story skyscrapers with a structural life of a century or more have been torn down to give room for twenty-two- or forty-four-story tower buildings." *op. cit.,* p. 335.

Frank J. Hallauer in an article on "Population and Building Construction" presents the results of obsolescence studies in four cities, Philadelphia, Washington (D.C.), Portland (Ore.), and Oakland (Calif.), (*op. cit.,* pp. 17-18). In the case of Philadelphia, Mr. Hallauer quotes from a study of the Philadelphia Housing Association of demolitions on 936 residential sites: ". . . over 90 per cent of the loss in family accommodations was of buildings that still had a long period of usefulness before them." (Quoted from "Know Your City," March, 1935, by the Philadelphia Housing Association.) In Mr. Hallauer's study of demolitions of dwellings in the other three cities mentioned, he found a number of factors which made him feel that obsolescence rather than age was the controlling consideration: (1) The buildings succeeding the dwellings torn down were overwhelmingly commercial, industrial, or public in character. (2) Although buildings on adjoining lots might be much different in age, they would nevertheless frequently be torn down at the same time. (3) The age distribution of buildings demolished and buildings in use were practically the same.

pearance, and function. It would be impossible to identify any individual building as merely replacing others worn out. Consequently, the considerations governing replacement do not vary from those governing net investment. Indeed, only in one particular is the problem of replacements different at all in cycle analysis: in regard to depreciation charges. We saw in Chapter III that if a rise or fall in investment is accompanied by a rise or fall of the same amount in depreciation charges, the change in investment has no multiplier effect on consumption. If, then, depreciation charges fluctuated with the volume of investment a large part of the effect of building fluctuations on income and employment would be neutralized. But the extreme stability of depreciation charges, as reported by Fabricant, robs even this distinction of importance. We must conclude that replacements of buildings, extremely postponable and subject to all disequilibrations stemming from net investment, exercise little, if any, stabilizing or offsetting effect on gross building investment.

### The Depressing Effect on Building of Serious Wars

Finally, periods of severe war have been periods of severe building depression.[36] For one thing, construction is usually expressly prohibited in order to conserve the economic resources of the nation. During the First World

[36] Even a minor war, such as America's war with Spain, can be discouraging to building. In regard to the Spanish-American War, V. S. Clark writes: "But while Government orders piled in upon manufacturers, building operations were for a time checked or suspended, and some of the leading steel makers doubted whether the total effect of hostilities was beneficial to the trade." *History of Manufacturers in the United States, 1860-1914* (Washington, D.C.: Carnegie Institution of Washington, 1928), p. 632.

War, *Priorities Circular No. 21* (together with supplements) "decreed that except by special permit no new non-war building construction should be undertaken involving an expenditure of more than five hundred dollars and no extensions costing over twenty-five hundred dollars."[37]

But government prohibition is not the sole explanation for the wartime decline of building. All countries for which data are readily available showed the stagnating effect of the war upon building—whether those countries were belligerent or neutral. Warren and Pearson in *World Prices and the Building Industry* (pp. 119-31) present data graphically for building in a number of European cities. Not only did building decline to very low levels in belligerent countries such as England, Scotland, Canada and Germany (as indicated by experience in London, Glasgow, Berlin, and Hamburg, and about thirty-five cities of Canada) ; it fell off equally heavily in the neutral countries of Sweden (Stockholm) and the Netherlands.

There are consequently other and perhaps more important explanations for the wartime falling off in building. One is the fall in the flow of income or the failure of that income flow to increase at the same rate; this is naturally due to the diversion of a large amount of energy and resources to war purposes.[38] This diversion is reflected in disproportionate increases in costs of construction and operation. Costs increase both because of the increases in wage rates and prices of materials from the war demand,

[37] Grosvenor B. Clarkson, *Industrial America in the World War* (Boston and New York: Houghton Mifflin Co., 1923), p. 187. This circular seems to have been in effect for only a short time.

[38] Ian Bowen, "The Building Industry in War Time," *op. cit.*, pp. 663-9.

declines in the marginal efficiency of labor, delays in deliveries because of transportation difficulties, and increases in the rate of interest from the waste of wealth and decreases in savings.

In addition, the uncertainty as to the outcome of the war should not be underestimated—uncertainty felt not only by the participants, but also by the non-belligerents who are rarely free from anxiety. And, of course, both belligerents and neutrals realize that great and unpredictable adjustments will take place when the war is ended, regardless of outcome. The release from this uncertainty upon the termination of hostilities partly explains the rapid revival of building after both the World War and the Civil War. The cessation of building caused an accumulated shortage of shelter and pushed up rents and prices to the point that when technical, patriotic, and cost factors no longer interfered after the war, construction became excessively profitable.[39] In other words, the relation became abnormally large. As a result, then, of the war and its interference with the normal flow of capital formation, it is likely that building would have been pushed to high levels in the 1920's even without the enormous postwar growth in income, technology, population, and organizational efficiency. If the other factors creating and intensifying the building cycle are added, there emerges a rather complete explanation for the high amplitude of the recent long fluctuations. War is particularly discouraging to residential building,

[39] One may doubt whether the U.S. participation lasted long enough to accumulate a very great shortage, though throughout the years before our entry the expansion of war industries for export to Europe probably resulted in some replacement deficit of peace time construction.

[ 211 ]

because of the reduction in real income of the laboring and middle classes and the particularly heavy inflation of building costs. And this fact may help to explain the greater increase during the last two fluctuations in the intensity of residential as compared with nonresidential cycles.

Many businesses, on the other hand, secure an extra impulse from this same inflation. The temptation is strong to expand business quarters during such times, and this temptation partly overcomes the inhibiting effects of rising interest rate, increasing cost of construction, and uncertainty as to the future. Moreover, contrary to the situation with regard to residential building, much business building will be destined for the war industries and will not, therefore, come under the ban of the government at such times. For all these reasons business building does not fall so far as residential building during time of war. As an historical fact, this was not only true in the United States; it was also true of Glasgow, Scotland, the only European city for which detailed building data on that period seem to be available.[40] Although residential building fell off heavily during the First World War, the volume of warehouses, stores, and workshops constructed was as great as for many years both before and after the conflict.[41]

[40] *Memorandum of Linings Granted by the Dean of Guild Court,* City of Glasgow, 1872-1936.

[41] It should not be overlooked that a wealthy country such as the United States, with low marginal propensity to consume and high standard unemployment, may, if the war or armament program is not severe, experience a stimulation of building as a result of increased consumer spending by the government. But if the war is severe, government spending eventually competes with private building for transportation, labor, materials, and credit, and building costs become prohibitive.

# APPENDIX A

## THE MONTHLY INDEX OF BUILDING IN U.S. CITIES, 1868-1940

| | Index[a] | 43 Term[b] Gradua-tion 1868[1] | Index | 43 Term Gradua-tion 1869[1] | Index | 43 Term Gradua-tion 1870[1] | Index | 43 Term Gradua-tion 1871[1] |
|---|---|---|---|---|---|---|---|---|
| January | 4.7 | | 22.0 | | 8.1 | 15.7 | 8.3 | 22.4 |
| February | 12.4 | | 14.4 | | 13.9 | 15.4 | 18.0 | 22.9 |
| March | 14.9 | | 19.1 | | 12.6 | 15.3 | 34.7 | 23.2 |
| April | 28.5 | | 26.9 | | 32.4 | 15.4 | 40.5 | 23.2 |
| May | 21.6 | | 49.8 | | 20.8 | 15.7 | 25.3 | 23.0 |
| June | 20.8 | | 16.0 | | 21.5 | 16.2 | 31.0 | 22.7 |
| July | 12.6 | | 24.5 | | 14.1 | 16.9 | 24.3 | 22.1 |
| August | 9.0 | | 19.1 | | 23.4 | 17.8 | 14.4 | 21.4 |
| September | 21.1 | | 19.1 | | 20.7 | 18.8 | 21.4 | 20.6 |
| October | 17.3 | | 16.0 | 17.6 | 17.1 | 19.8 | 18.6 | 19.6 |
| November | 32.4 | | 11.4 | 16.8 | 14.2 | 20.8 | 12.3 | 18.5 |
| December | 13.5 | | 5.8 | 16.2 | 10.7 | 21.7 | 8.6 | 17.4 |

| | Index | 43 Term Gradua-tion 1872[1] | Index | 43 Term Gradua-tion 1873[1] | Index | 43 Term Gradua-tion 1874[1] | Index | 43 Term Gradua-tion 1875[2] |
|---|---|---|---|---|---|---|---|---|
| January | 6.6 | 16.3 | 8.1 | 14.3 | 4.8 | 8.0 | 6.5 | 8.5 |
| February | 10.8 | 15.3 | 8.7 | 14.4 | 10.5 | 7.5 | 5.9 | 8.2 |
| March | 17.2 | 14.4 | 15.4 | 14.5 | 8.7 | 7.3 | 10.6 | 8.1 |
| April | 32.2 | 13.8 | 32.7 | 14.4 | 12.4 | 7.3 | 10.6 | 7.9 |
| May | 22.9 | 13.4 | 21.5 | 14.3 | 12.1 | 7.5 | 14.1 | 7.7 |
| June | 19.9 | 13.2 | 18.2 | 13.9 | 12.3 | 7.7 | 10.7 | 7.5 |
| July | 8.5 | 13.2 | 9.6 | 13.4 | 5.7 | 8.0 | 4.4 | 7.3 |
| August | 7.8 | 13.3 | 15.8 | 12.6 | 5.6 | 8.3 | 7.4 | 7.1 |
| September | 12.3 | 13.5 | 6.0 | 11.7 | 7.4 | 8.5 | 4.9 | 7.0 |
| October | 12.3 | 13.7 | 8.7 | 10.7 | 11.6 | 8.6 | 7.2 | 6.9 |
| November | 7.3 | 13.9 | 2.5 | 9.7 | 4.9 | 8.6 | 4.4 | 6.8 |
| December | 10.9 | 14.1 | 3.7 | 8.8 | 4.7 | 8.6 | 3.6 | 6.8 |

| | 43 Term Gradua- | | 43 Term Gradua- | | 43 Term Gradua- | | 43 Term Gradua- | |
| | Index | tion 1876[2] | Index | tion 1877[2] | Index | tion 1878[2] | Index | tion 1879[2] |
| --- | --- | --- | --- | --- | --- | --- | --- | --- |
| January | 2.4 | 6.8 | 1.1 | 5.5 | 3.3 | 5.6 | 3.5 | 7.5 |
| February | 3.9 | 6.8 | 6.4 | 5.4 | 2.6 | 5.6 | 3.6 | 7.9 |
| March | 7.2 | 6.8 | 5.8 | 5.3 | 8.0 | 5.7 | 7.8 | 8.3 |
| April | 17.0 | 6.8 | 9.2 | 5.3 | 9.0 | 5.7 | 14.9 | 8.6 |
| May | 12.5 | 6.7 | 11.3 | 5.3 | 9.7 | 5.7 | 13.6 | 8.8 |
| June | 6.9 | 6.7 | 5.7 | 5.4 | 7.5 | 5.8 | 12.4 | 9.0 |
| July | 6.1 | 6.6 | 6.4 | 5.4 | 6.4 | 5.8 | 10.1 | 9.1 |
| August | 3.9 | 6.4 | 3.1 | 5.4 | 4.8 | 5.9 | 12.1 | 9.2 |
| September | 3.9 | 6.3 | 4.0 | 5.4 | 6.8 | 6.1 | 6.8 | 9.4 |
| October | 7.9 | 6.1 | 5.3 | 5.4 | 5.3 | 6.4 | 9.0 | 9.6 |
| November | 3.2 | 5.9 | 4.1 | 5.5 | 5.1 | 6.7 | 5.1 | 9.9 |
| December | 2.5 | 5.7 | 3.3 | 5.5 | 4.4 | 7.1 | 8.4 | 10.2 |

| | 43 Term Gradua- | | 43 Term Gradua- | | 43 Term Gradua- | | 43 Term Gradua- | |
| | Index | tion 1880[2c] | Index | tion 1881[3] | Index | tion 1882[5d] | Index | tion 1883[5d] |
| --- | --- | --- | --- | --- | --- | --- | --- | --- |
| January | 3.9 | 10.4 | 8.1 | 14.8 | 7.0 | 15.0 | 14.7 | 18.0 |
| February | 7.6 | 10.7 | 6.7 | 15.2 | 11.4 | 15.2 | 12.6 | 17.6 |
| March | 14.2 | 10.9 | 19.0 | 15.4 | 17.6 | 15.5 | 25.6 | 17.3 |
| April | 14.2 | 11.0 | 28.0 | 15.5 | 23.4 | 15.9 | 19.3 | 16.9 |
| May | 14.4 | 11.1 | 26.3 | 15.5 | 19.1 | 16.3 | 23.4 | 16.6 |
| June | 15.7 | 11.3 | 18.0 | 15.4 | 31.2 | 16.8 | 23.6 | 16.4 |
| July | 14.1 | 11.6 | 20.7 | 15.3 | 17.5 | 17.3 | 21.4 | 16.3 |
| August | 14.6 | 11.9 | 12.5 | 15.3 | 13.4 | 17.7 | 12.3 | 16.4 |
| September | 14.2 | 12.4 | 11.5 | 15.0 | 17.8 | 18.0 | 16.2 | 16.7 |
| October | 14.0 | 13.0 | 13.3 | 14.9 | 21.3 | 18.2 | 14.2 | 17.0 |
| November | 7.5 | 13.6 | 10.1 | 14.9 | 10.7 | 18.3 | 10.5 | 17.4 |
| December | 3.7 | 14.2 | 9.6 | 14.9 | 8.1 | 18.2 | 10.9 | 17.6 |

|  | 43 Term Gradua-tion 1884[5d] | | 43 Term Gradua-tion 1885[5d] | | 43 Term Gradua-tion 1886[5d] | | 43 Term Gradua-tion 1887[7d] | |
|  | Index | tion | Index | tion | Index | tion | Index | tion |
|---|---|---|---|---|---|---|---|---|
| January | 7.1 | 17.9 | 9.8 | 17.1 | 16.0 | 22.7 | 11.7 | 25.6 |
| February | 16.1 | 18.0 | 15.7 | 17.3 | 22.2 | 22.7 | 24.8 | 26.3 |
| March | 20.4 | 17.9 | 23.3 | 17.6 | 36.1 | 22.5 | 48.0 | 26.7 |
| April | 30.9 | 17.8 | 31.4 | 18.0 | 32.6 | 22.4 | 41.5 | 26.8 |
| May | 34.5 | 17.7 | 27.7 | 18.6 | 26.8 | 22.2 | 33.1 | 26.6 |
| June | 22.4 | 17.5 | 25.5 | 19.2 | 28.4 | 22.1 | 31.4 | 26.1 |
| July | 15.3 | 17.4 | 17.5 | 19.9 | 20.5 | 22.1 | 25.0 | 25.2 |
| August | 14.5 | 17.3 | 17.6 | 20.6 | 21.2 | 22.3 | 21.8 | 24.2 |
| September | 11.3 | 17.2 | 18.1 | 21.3 | 19.5 | 22.7 | 20.0 | 23.0 |
| October | 14.3 | 17.1 | 17.5 | 21.8 | 19.5 | 23.3 | 18.7 | 21.9 |
| November | 11.1 | 17.1 | 15.9 | 22.3 | 17.8 | 24.0 | 14.0 | 20.7 |
| December | 9.2 | 17.1 | 14.2 | 22.6 | 9.6 | 24.9 | 11.0 | 19.8 |

|  | 43 Term Gradua-tion 1888[9d] | | 43 Term Gradua-tion 1889[10d] | | 43 Term Gradua-tion 1890[11d] | | 43 Term Gradua-tion 1891[13d] | |
|  | Index | tion | Index | tion | Index | tion | Index | tion |
|---|---|---|---|---|---|---|---|---|
| January | 9.1 | 19.1 | 19.9 | 26.0 | 22.3 | 29.4 | 18.6 | 27.9 |
| February | 12.5 | 18.8 | 23.0 | 26.7 | 28.1 | 29.4 | 22.6 | 27.9 |
| March | 25.7 | 18.7 | 31.1 | 27.4 | 32.7 | 29.4 | 31.2 | 28.1 |
| April | 28.0 | 19.0 | 41.7 | 28.0 | 37.3 | 29.5 | 38.9 | 28.5 |
| May | 30.7 | 19.5 | 40.6 | 28.6 | 31.5 | 29.6 | 41.4 | 29.1 |
| June | 32.2 | 20.2 | 32.1 | 29.1 | 38.9 | 29.6 | 32.2 | 29.8 |
| July | 20.3 | 21.0 | 33.6 | 29.4 | 33.2 | 29.5 | 28.0 | 30.7 |
| August | 22.8 | 21.8 | 23.9 | 29.6 | 28.8 | 29.3 | 24.2 | 31.6 |
| September | 19.0 | 22.7 | 23.5 | 29.7 | 22.0 | 29.0 | 27.0 | 32.5 |
| October | 19.9 | 23.6 | 28.9 | 29.7 | 30.9 | 28.7 | 40.5 | 33.4 |
| November | 13.4 | 24.4 | 24.6 | 29.6 | 26.7 | 28.3 | 34.7 | 34.2 |
| December | 17.9 | 25.2 | 24.5 | 29.5 | 21.3 | 28.0 | 36.1 | 34.9 |

| | 43 Term Index | Gradua- tion 1892[15d] | 43 Term Index | Gradua- tion 1893[16e] | 43 Term Index | Gradua- tion 1894[25de] | 43 Term Index | Gradua- tion 1895[26d] |
|---|---|---|---|---|---|---|---|---|
| January | 21.6 | 35.4 | 21.6 | 32.0 | 16.0 | 18.0 | 25.6 | 28.0 |
| February | 30.1 | 35.7 | 24.7 | 30.7 | 15.6 | 17.9 | 22.8 | 28.7 |
| March | 39.8 | 35.9 | 40.7 | 29.2 | 22.7 | 18.0 | 38.1 | 29.1 |
| April | 46.5 | 35.9 | 39.1 | 27.7 | 25.4 | 18.5 | 40.5 | 29.3 |
| May | 37.1 | 35.8 | 42.6 | 26.1 | 29.2 | 19.1 | 44.3 | 29.1 |
| June | 44.4 | 35.7 | 27.5 | 24.6 | 24.1 | 20.0 | 27.4 | 28.8 |
| July | 33.6 | 35.5 | 18.9 | 23.2 | 19.5 | 21.0 | 29.7 | 28.2 |
| August | 35.5 | 35.3 | 14.7 | 21.9 | 18.4 | 22.2 | 23.7 | 27.6 |
| September | 32.9 | 35.0 | 11.9 | 20.7 | 17.2 | 23.4 | 17.8 | 26.9 |
| October | 31.8 | 34.6 | 13.4 | 19.7 | 23.0 | 24.7 | 22.2 | 26.1 |
| November | 31.2 | 33.9 | 21.9 | 18.9 | 23.0 | 25.9 | 19.4 | 25.4 |
| December | 25.8 | 33.1 | 14.7 | 18.3 | 18.2 | 27.0 | 24.4 | 24.8 |

| | 43 Term Index | Gradua- tion 1896[30d] | 43 Term Index | Gradua- tion 1897[30] | 43 Term Index | Gradua- tion 1898[33] | 43 Term Index | Gradua- tion 1899[33] |
|---|---|---|---|---|---|---|---|---|
| January | 17.6 | 24.3 | 24.3 | 24.0 | 16.4 | 23.0 | 19.2 | 27.0 |
| February | 22.1 | 23.9 | 19.9 | 24.2 | 16.1 | 22.7 | 19.2 | 28.0 |
| March | 32.0 | 23.7 | 30.6 | 24.5 | 29.1 | 22.5 | 39.3 | 28.9 |
| April | 27.3 | 23.5 | 40.0 | 24.7 | 35.5 | 22.3 | 38.6 | 29.7 |
| May | 32.4 | 23.5 | 27.2 | 24.9 | 20.4 | 22.3 | 40.0 | 30.4 |
| June | 29.8 | 23.6 | 28.4 | 25.0 | 25.8 | 22.3 | 32.2 | 30.7 |
| July | 29.7 | 23.6 | 22.3 | 25.0 | 21.2 | 22.6 | 32.7 | 30.8 |
| August | 19.5 | 23.7 | 19.0 | 24.9 | 24.5 | 22.9 | 26.3 | 30.5 |
| September | 16.5 | 23.8 | 21.9 | 24.6 | 21.5 | 23.5 | 22.5 | 29.9 |
| October | 16.3 | 23.8 | 21.8 | 24.2 | 24.2 | 24.2 | 26.4 | 28.9 |
| November | 18.7 | 23.8 | 26.2 | 23.8 | 20.9 | 25.0 | 15.8 | 27.7 |
| December | 19.4 | 23.9 | 21.8 | 23.4 | 20.8 | 26.0 | 47.8 | 26.3 |

| | 43 Term Index / Graduation 1900[33] | | 43 Term Index / Graduation 1901[33] | | 43 Term Index / Graduation 1902[33] | | 43 Term Index / Graduation 1903[33e] | |
|---|---|---|---|---|---|---|---|---|
| | Index | tion | Index | tion | Index | tion | Index | tion |
| January | 19.7 | 24.8 | 24.9 | 33.1 | 23.9 | 33.7 | 24.2 | 37.4 |
| February | 16.0 | 23.4 | 30.2 | 34.6 | 32.0 | 34.0 | 25.2 | 37.6 |
| March | 20.7 | 22.1 | 39.3 | 35.7 | 42.3 | 34.3 | 53.9 | 37.8 |
| April | 26.5 | 21.2 | 76.7 | 36.4 | 41.6 | 34.8 | 43.4 | 37.8 |
| May | 26.1 | 20.7 | 39.3 | 36.5 | 42.2 | 35.2 | 44.1 | 37.2 |
| June | 26.9 | 20.9 | 36.1 | 36.3 | 47.0 | 35.6 | 54.6 | 37.2 |
| July | 21.3 | 21.6 | 28.5 | 35.8 | 42.7 | 35.9 | 38.7 | 36.9 |
| August | 19.9 | 22.8 | 29.6 | 35.2 | 30.5 | 36.1 | 34.1 | 36.4 |
| September | 18.4 | 24.6 | 24.9 | 34.6 | 31.2 | 36.4 | 26.1 | 36.0 |
| October | 29.3 | 26.7 | 36.9 | 34.1 | 32.4 | 36.6 | 35.6 | 35.8 |
| November | 21.2 | 28.9 | 30.6 | 33.8 | 27.2 | 36.8 | 32.3 | 35.7 |
| December | 24.0 | 31.1 | 26.6 | 33.6 | 38.7 | 37.1 | 30.0 | 35.9 |

| | 43 Term Index / Graduation 1904[33] | | 43 Term Index / Graduation 1905[33] | | 43 Term Index / Graduation 1906[35e] | | 43 Term Index / Graduation 1907[35e] | |
|---|---|---|---|---|---|---|---|---|
| | Index | tion | Index | tion | Index | tion | Index | tion |
| January | 29.5 | 36.3 | 37.4 | 50.7 | 59.4 | 61.4 | 36.0 | 53.5 |
| February | 20.0 | 36.8 | 29.5 | 52.4 | 43.8 | 61.1 | 33.8 | 53.4 |
| March | 41.3 | 37.6 | 68.5 | 54.0 | 62.2 | 60.6 | 57.5 | 53.2 |
| April | 50.4 | 38.4 | 69.4 | 55.3 | 80.9 | 59.8 | 75.6 | 52.8 |
| May | 51.0 | 39.3 | 61.9 | 56.4 | 72.2 | 58.9 | 70.1 | 52.1 |
| June | 50.1 | 40.3 | 70.9 | 57.4 | 69.9 | 57.8 | 69.3 | 51.1 |
| July | 45.4 | 41.3 | 67.7 | 58.2 | 65.3 | 56.7 | 54.1 | 49.8 |
| August | 40.7 | 42.5 | 65.4 | 59.0 | 60.2 | 55.7 | 52.3 | 48.2 |
| September | 45.8 | 43.9 | 60.8 | 59.8 | 52.5 | 54.9 | 46.0 | 46.7 |
| October | 45.7 | 45.5 | 50.5 | 60.5 | 50.4 | 54.3 | 49.2 | 45.2 |
| November | 45.6 | 47.2 | 51.1 | 61.0 | 42.3 | 53.8 | 33.7 | 44.1 |
| December | 33.1 | 49.0 | 40.0 | 61.3 | 36.0 | 53.6 | 27.6 | 43.5 |

| | 43 Term Gradua-tion 1908[35e] | | 43 Term Gradua-tion 1909[35] | | 43 Term Gradua-tion 1910[35] | | 43 Term Gradua-tion 1911[34] | |
|---|---|---|---|---|---|---|---|---|
| | Index | tion | Index | tion | Index | tion | Index | tion |
| January | 27.4 | 43.6 | 47.7 | 71.4 | 41.7 | 63.5 | 47.1 | 64.4 |
| February | 22.1 | 44.4 | 53.7 | 71.1 | 43.9 | 63.8 | 36.5 | 64.8 |
| March | 38.8 | 46.1 | 76.8 | 70.2 | 81.9 | 64.2 | 73.9 | 65.2 |
| April | 69.2 | 48.6 | 78.4 | 69.0 | 87.7 | 64.4 | 75.2 | 65.5 |
| May | 57.8 | 51.6 | 89.0 | 67.7 | 75.6 | 64.6 | 71.8 | 65.7 |
| June | 81.7 | 55.1 | 72.1 | 66.5 | 74.2 | 64.6 | 81.3 | 65.8 |
| July | 74.2 | 58.7 | 75.3 | 65.3 | 57.8 | 64.4 | 74.9 | 65.8 |
| August | 51.9 | 62.4 | 63.5 | 64.5 | 74.5 | 64.1 | 88.2 | 65.9 |
| September | 54.6 | 65.4 | 62.4 | 63.8 | 54.8 | 63.9 | 68.1 | 66.2 |
| October | 80.1 | 68.1 | 56.5 | 63.4 | 62.0 | 63.8 | 61.7 | 66.5 |
| November | 72.8 | 69.9 | 58.3 | 63.2 | 74.4 | 63.8 | 57.4 | 67.0 |
| December | 60.2 | 71.0 | 53.7 | 63.3 | 50.8 | 64.0 | 49.4 | 67.4 |

| | 43 Term Gradua-tion 1912[33] | | 43 Term Gradua-tion 1913[34] | | 43 Term Gradua-tion 1914[34] | | 43 Term Gradua-tion 1915[34] | |
|---|---|---|---|---|---|---|---|---|
| | Index | tion | Index | tion | Index | tion | Index | tion |
| January | 40.9 | 67.9 | 46.1 | 66.7 | 44.2 | 62.4 | 37.2 | 52.6 |
| February | 41.0 | 68.3 | 48.1 | 65.2 | 43.9 | 62.2 | 44.1 | 53.5 |
| March | 75.6 | 68.6 | 71.0 | 63.8 | 71.3 | 61.7 | 65.7 | 54.9 |
| April | 91.8 | 69.0 | 82.4 | 62.6 | 70.0 | 60.7 | 68.7 | 56.5 |
| May | 91.1 | 69.4 | 72.1 | 61.8 | 77.4 | 59.5 | 85.8 | 58.2 |
| June | 89.1 | 69.8 | 77.2 | 61.2 | 78.6 | 58.1 | 62.2 | 58.8 |
| July | 79.0 | 70.2 | 64.3 | 61.0 | 70.0 | 56.5 | 63.9 | 61.5 |
| August | 73.8 | 70.4 | 60.2 | 61.1 | 55.6 | 55.0 | 66.3 | 63.0 |
| September | 57.9 | 70.4 | 59.7 | 61.4 | 47.2 | 53.7 | 68.8 | 64.4 |
| October | 61.9 | 70.0 | 54.6 | 61.7 | 46.9 | 52.7 | 64.0 | 65.7 |
| November | 62.4 | 69.2 | 45.6 | 62.1 | 34.0 | 52.2 | 63.3 | 67.1 |
| December | 66.0 | 68.0 | 66.3 | 62.4 | 33.9 | 52.1 | 63.5 | 68.5 |

| | 43 Term Index | Gradua-tion 1916[36] | 43 Term Index | Gradua-tion 1917[36] | 43 Term Index | Gradua-tion 1918[37] | 43 Term Index | Gradua-tion 1919[37] |
|---|---|---|---|---|---|---|---|---|
| January | 46.0 | 70.0 | 48.9 | 67.5 | 21.4 | 33.3 | 17.0 | 32.2 |
| February | 48.0 | 71.8 | 58.1 | 63.8 | 20.1 | 31.1 | 22.2 | 40.0 |
| March | 71.3 | 73.6 | 65.2 | 60.1 | 29.3 | 28.7 | 38.1 | 48.9 |
| April | 78.9 | 75.3 | 71.6 | 56.4 | 29.8 | 26.1 | 61.1 | 58.8 |
| May | 102.4 | 76.9 | 57.8 | 53.0 | 34.0 | 23.5 | 82.9 | 69.3 |
| June | 86.8 | 78.1 | 51.8 | 49.8 | 31.4 | 20.9 | 99.6 | 79.8 |
| July | 110.9 | 78.8 | 48.2 | 46.9 | 33.0 | 18.8 | 98.5 | 90.0 |
| August | 58.6 | 78.8 | 44.1 | 44.3 | 28.7 | 17.4 | 122.6 | 99.3 |
| September | 91.8 | 78.0 | 43.0 | 41.9 | 22.9 | 17.2 | 87.9 | 107.3 |
| October | 72.2 | 76.4 | 46.5 | 39.6 | 14.7 | 18.5 | 118.3 | 113.5 |
| November | 61.7 | 74.0 | 36.0 | 37.5 | 11.5 | 21.3 | 117.7 | 117.5 |
| December | 61.7 | 71.0 | 24.7 | 35.4 | 12.2 | 25.9 | 117.1 | 119.2 |

| | 43 Term Index | Gradua-tion 1920[37] | 43 Term Index | Gradua-tion 1921[37] | 43 Term Index | Gradua-tion 1922[37] | 43 Term Index | Gradua-tion 1923[37] |
|---|---|---|---|---|---|---|---|---|
| January | 95.8 | 118.4 | 44.7 | 73.9 | 111.5 | 146.1 | 173.0 | 204.0 |
| February | 85.5 | 115.4 | 74.7 | 77.8 | 119.7 | 149.1 | 198.2 | 205.8 |
| March | 112.6 | 110.4 | 93.0 | 82.7 | 220.3 | 152.1 | 340.2 | 207.1 |
| April | 147.0 | 104.1 | 109.3 | 88.7 | 160.3 | 155.4 | 255.9 | 208.3 |
| May | 88.7 | 96.9 | 112.5 | 95.3 | 186.9 | 159.7 | 205.0 | 209.6 |
| June | 104.2 | 89.7 | 113.9 | 102.5 | 198.6 | 165.1 | 185.8 | 211.3 |
| July | 96.6 | 83.0 | 132.3 | 110.2 | 161.8 | 171.4 | 182.0 | 213.4 |
| August | 84.8 | 77.4 | 122.2 | 117.9 | 169.1 | 178.4 | 212.9 | 215.6 |
| September | 69.6 | 73.3 | 114.9 | 125.3 | 161.1 | 185.5 | 165.5 | 217.8 |
| October | 65.6 | 70.9 | 140.1 | 132.0 | 159.3 | 191.9 | 214.9 | 219.9 |
| November | 51.4 | 70.3 | 116.6 | 137.8 | 169.5 | 197.2 | 208.1 | 221.6 |
| December | 48.8 | 71.3 | 117.2 | 142.4 | 193.6 | 201.3 | 210.6 | 222.7 |

| | 43 Term Gradua-tion Index 1924[36] | | 43 Term Gradua-tion Index 1925[36] | | 43 Term Gradua-tion Index 1926[36] | | 43 Term Gradua-tion Index 1927[36] | |
|---|---|---|---|---|---|---|---|---|
| January | 176.7 | 223.2 | 177.9 | 218.1 | 184.9 | 245.5 | 173.1 | 233.8 |
| February | 230.3 | 222.8 | 196.5 | 227.4 | 181.2 | 242.5 | 211.0 | 230.2 |
| March | 373.9 | 221.2 | 275.6 | 237.1 | 303.7 | 240.3 | 271.8 | 226.0 |
| April | 230.3 | 218.4 | 325.8 | 246.0 | 290.2 | 239.1 | 254.9 | 221.4 |
| May | 227.5 | 214.8 | 261.8 | 253.4 | 240.3 | 238.7 | 222.1 | 216.9 |
| June | 205.1 | 210.5 | 270.0 | 258.5 | 257.8 | 238.9 | 234.0 | 212.6 |
| July | 175.6 | 206.1 | 279.1 | 261.3 | 237.0 | 239.4 | 198.1 | 209.2 |
| August | 185.8 | 202.5 | 265.2 | 261.6 | 239.2 | 239.9 | 228.0 | 206.8 |
| September | 178.3 | 200.7 | 240.2 | 260.0 | 211.8 | 240.0 | 191.7 | 205.4 |
| October | 208.4 | 201.1 | 272.8 | 257.0 | 299.6 | 239.6 | 185.3 | 204.7 |
| November | 177.0 | 204.2 | 244.3 | 253.2 | 211.1 | 238.5 | 209.5 | 204.6 |
| December | 190.3 | 210.1 | 218.2 | 249.2 | 218.3 | 236.5 | 193.8 | 204.3 |

| | 43 Term Gradua-tion Index 1928[36] | | 43 Term Gradua-tion Index 1929[36] | | 43 Term Gradua-tion Index 1930[37] | | 43 Term Gradua-tion Index 1931[37] | |
|---|---|---|---|---|---|---|---|---|
| January | 166.8 | 203.6 | 174.6 | 220.8 | 84.7 | 107.2 | 74.7 | 97.1 |
| February | 114.5 | 202.7 | 193.0 | 219.6 | 76.0 | 100.6 | 73.9 | 95.3 |
| March | 271.7 | 201.5 | 308.8 | 216.8 | 114.0 | 96.7 | 122.4 | 93.2 |
| April | 224.6 | 200.5 | 418.4 | 212.0 | 122.5 | 95.3 | 125.4 | 90.5 |
| May | 252.3 | 200.4 | 185.7 | 205.0 | 120.1 | 95.6 | 91.9 | 87.2 |
| June | 249.6 | 201.4 | 143.5 | 196.0 | 104.7 | 96.9 | 68.6 | 83.4 |
| July | 218.1 | 203.6 | 176.9 | 184.8 | 119.0 | 98.3 | 66.9 | 79.0 |
| August | 210.7 | 206.9 | 141.8 | 171.8 | 93.9 | 99.5 | 102.0 | 73.9 |
| September | 172.2 | 210.9 | 131.9 | 157.4 | 100.2 | 100.1 | 60.6 | 71.4 |
| October | 182.2 | 214.7 | 155.9 | 142.9 | 89.7 | 100.0 | 60.9 | 62.5 |
| November | 165.0 | 217.9 | 131.2 | 129.0 | 87.6 | 99.5 | 54.0 | 56.0 |
| December | 161.1 | 220.1 | 85.9 | 116.8 | 87.7 | 98.5 | 44.7 | 50.0 |

| | Index | 43 Term Gradua-tion 1932[37] | Index | 43 Term Gradua-tion 1933[37] | Index | 43 Term Gradua-tion 1934[37] | Index | 43 Term Gradua-tion 1935[37] |
|---|---|---|---|---|---|---|---|---|
| January | 35.1 | 44.4 | 18.7 | 18.5 | 15.2 | 21.4 | 18.5 | 27.7 |
| February | 26.8 | 39.4 | 12.6 | 18.1 | 17.2 | 21.4 | 20.9 | 30.0 |
| March | 27.9 | 35.2 | 11.9 | 17.9 | 17.0 | 21.3 | 34.3 | 32.4 |
| April | 35.8 | 31.8 | 16.9 | 17.9 | 23.1 | 21.1 | 41.7 | 34.7 |
| May | 50.5 | 29.0 | 20.9 | 18.0 | 31.7 | 20.8 | 39.3 | 36.7 |
| June | 33.4 | 26.8 | 23.3 | 18.4 | 18.6 | 20.6 | 45.7 | 38.6 |
| July | 24.6 | 25.0 | 18.8 | 18.8 | 26.6 | 20.5 | 39.9 | 40.2 |
| August | 23.6 | 23.5 | 20.1 | 19.3 | 23.0 | 20.6 | 53.3 | 41.8 |
| September | 19.9 | 22.2 | 28.2 | 19.8 | 20.5 | 21.2 | 42.9 | 43.4 |
| October | 16.9 | 21.0 | 19.7 | 20.3 | 26.8 | 22.1 | 52.9 | 45.0 |
| November | 22.8 | 20.0 | 19.7 | 20.8 | 24.4 | 23.6 | 47.8 | 46.8 |
| December | 19.2 | 19.2 | 17.5 | 21.1 | 12.8 | 25.5 | 40.5 | 48.6 |

| | Index | 43 Term Gradua-tion 1936[37] | Index | 43 Term Gradua-tion 1937[37] | Index | 43 Term Gradua-tion 1938[37] | Index | 43 Term Gradua-tion 1939[37] |
|---|---|---|---|---|---|---|---|---|
| January | 44.5 | 50.4 | 45.2 | 66.4 | 142.7 | 68[t] | 71.4 | 70[t] |
| February | 30.4 | 52.3 | 76.7 | 65.5 | 41.0 | 66[t] | 84.2 | 72[t] |
| March | 45.5 | 54.2 | 87.7 | 64.8 | 47.0 | 64[t] | 70.6 | 74[t] |
| April | 51.3 | 56.4 | 78.5 | 64.6 | 50.6 | 62[t] | 66.1 | 75[t] |
| May | 54.5 | 58.6 | 58.3 | 64.9 | 47.0 | 62[t] | 85.5 | 77[t] |
| June | 93.5 | 61.0 | 66.6 | 65.7 | 61.4 | 62[t] | 93.4 | 78[t] |
| July | 85.8 | 63.4 | 55.8 | 66.5 | 122.7 | 62[t] | 84.5 | 80[t] |
| August | 69.9 | 65.5 | 56.3 | 67.5 | 73.5 | 63[t] | 94.6 | 82[t] |
| September | 64.5 | 67.0 | 56.9 | 68.4 | 74.3 | 64[t] | 80.6 | 84[t] |
| October | 57.9 | 67.8 | 63.4 | 69.0 | 59.8 | 66[t] | 77.4 | |
| November | 53.1 | 67.9 | 49.9 | 69.5 | 64.1 | 68[t] | 76.8 | |
| December | 61.9 | 67.3 | 108.3 | 70.1 | 62.7 | 69[t] | 60.0 | |

|  | 43 Term<br>Gradua-<br>Index tion<br>1940[37] |
|---|---|
| January | 64.3 |
| February | 70.5 |
| March | 73.4 |
| April | 87.5 |

Number of Cities

1. Manhattan.
2. Louisville added.
3. Detroit added.
5. Brooklyn and St. Louis added.
7. Cincinnati and Minneapolis added.
9. Cleveland and Nashville added.
10. Boston added.
11. New Haven added.
13. Chicago and St. Joseph added.
15. Indianapolis and Syracuse added.
16. Trenton added.
25. Omaha, Pittsburgh, Philadelphia, St. Paul, Denver, Kansas City (Mo.), Los Angeles, New Orleans and Washington (D.C.) all added.
26. Duluth added.
30. Cambridge, Fort Wayne, Atlanta and Milwaukee added.
31. Bronx added.
33. Alleghany and Buffalo added.
35. Newark and Everett added.
34. Cambridge subtracted.
33. Trenton subtracted.
34. Trenton added.
36. Richmond and Queens added.
37. Cambridge added.
36. Trenton subtracted.
37. Trenton added.

a. Monthly average in 1930 = 100. The number of cities in the index varies from one to thirty-seven. To adjust for this variation the base was also varied to include the 1930 average of building in the iden-

tical cities contained in the index at any one time (see above, p. 101).
Builders estimated costs of buildings for which permits were granted
or plans were filed.

b. Five-month moving total of a five-month moving total of an eight-month moving total of a twelve-month moving total; weights of $+7$, $-10,0,0,0,0,0,0, +10,0,0,0,0,0,0, -10, +7$, applied. Divided by 9600. See F. R. Macaulay, *The Smoothing of Time Series* (New York: National Bureau of Economic Research, 1931), pp. 24, 25, 73, 108.

c. Manhattan data estimated.

d. Alterations excluded in Brooklyn data.

e. Alterations estimated for Boston.

f. Estimated.

# APPENDIX B

| Year | Number of Cities | Detached Dwelling | Multi-family Dwelling[b] | Public Building[b] | Private Non-residential[b] | Altera-tions |
|---|---|---|---|---|---|---|
| 1868 | 1 | 76 | 5 | 9 | 5 | 6 |
| 69 | " | 79 | 6 | 9 | 7 | 12 |
| 1870 | " | 70 | 6 | 20 | 3 | 8 |
| 71 | " | 78 | 9 | 19 | 4 | 12 |
| 72 | " | 42 | 7 | 6 | 4 | 8 |
| 73 | " | 21 | 6 | 8 | 6 | 10 |
| 74 | " | 20 | 5 | 4 | 2 | 10 |
| 1875 | 2 | 21 | 5 | 4 | 2 | 13 |
| 76 | " | 25 | 3 | 5 | 2 | 10 |
| 77 | " | 17 | 4 | 2 | 1 | 9 |
| 78 | " | 21 | 3 | 2 | 2 | 7 |
| 79 | " | 34 | 5 | 4 | 2 | 9 |
| 1880 | " | 31 | 9 | 3 | 2 | 10 |
| 81 | " | 38 | 10 | 2 | 8 | 11 |
| 82 | " | 30 | 16 | 4 | 5 | 12 |
| 83 | " | 30 | 15 | 4 | 7 | 12 |
| 84 | " | 31 | 15 | 5 | 5 | 13 |
| 1885 | " | 46 | 15 | 2 | 5 | 20 |
| 86 | " | 60 | 18 | 9 | 5 | 16 |
| 87 | " | 65 | 22 | 13 | 6 | 19 |
| 88 | " | 35 | 16 | 8 | 7 | 20 |
| 89 | " | 49 | 22 | 8 | 12 | 18 |
| 1890 | 3 | 51 | 18 | 14 | 16 | 19 |
| 91 | " | 40 | 12 | 9 | 14 | 19 |
| 92 | " | 47 | 12 | 11 | 16 | 19 |
| 93 | " | 41 | 9 | 23 | 14 | 18 |
| 94 | " | 36 | 11 | 9 | 13 | 14 |
| 1895 | " | 45 | 23 | 10 | 20 | 18 |
| 96 | " | 38 | 15 | 9 | 22 | 18 |
| 97 | " | 38 | 21 | 24 | 18 | 20 |
| 98 | 6 | 15 | 20 | 8 | 10 | 15 |
| 99 | " | 17 | 33 | 12 | 19 | 19 |
| 1900 | " | 13 | 14 | 13 | 11 | 20 |
| 01 | " | 16 | 25 | 12 | 25 | 26 |
| 02 | " | 17 | 8 | 16 | 31 | 25 |
| 03 | " | 16 | 15 | 27 | 24 | 29 |
| 04 | " | 22 | 31 | 30 | 16 | 28 |
| 1905 | " | 31 | 54 | 24 | 25 | 35 |
| 06 | 8 | 34 | 43 | 22 | 28 | 44 |
| 07 | " | 33 | 26 | 25 | 27 | 43 |
| 08 | 9 | 30 | 19 | 22 | 27 | 31 |
| 09 | 10 | 44 | 45 | 16 | 33 | 35 |

| Year | Number of Cities | Detached Dwelling | Multi-family Dwelling[b] | Public Building[b] | Private Non-residential[b] | Alterations |
|---|---|---|---|---|---|---|
| 1910 | 12 | 33 | 34 | 23 | 32 | 38 |
| 11 | 14 | 34 | 25 | 29 | 41 | 42 |
| 12 | " | 30 | 32 | 28 | 46 | 40 |
| 13 | " | 23 | 25 | 27 | 33 | 39 |
| 14 | " | 23 | 24 | 22 | 23 | 34 |
| 1915 | " | 28 | 31 | 29 | 24 | 34 |
| 16 | " | 29 | 31 | 19 | 43 | 49 |
| 17 | " | 14 | 10 | 27 | 28 | 42 |
| 18 | " | 7 | 3 | 9 | 15 | 33 |
| 19 | " | 47 | 16 | 16 | 55 | 81 |
| 1920 | " | 33 | 12 | 28 | 66 | 110 |
| 21 | " | 81 | 42 | 39 | 56 | 77 |
| 22 | " | 131 | 83 | 86 | 73 | 88 |
| 23 | " | 150 | 104 | 95 | 90 | 100 |
| 24 | " | 164 | 96 | 92 | 109 | 102 |
| 1925 | " | 152 | 141 | 88 | 154 | 102 |
| 26 | " | 130 | 166 | 101 | 137 | 107 |
| 27 | " | 104 | 137 | 140 | 107 | 104 |
| 28 | " | 80 | 171 | 124 | 123 | 98 |
| 29 | " | 44 | 100 | 161 | 121 | 119 |
| 1930 | " | 31 | 48 | 140 | 64 | 91 |
| 31 | " | 33 | 40 | 100 | 49 | 68 |
| 32 | " | 10 | 4 | 88 | 11 | 35 |
| 33 | " | 7 | 9 | 14 | 7 | 37 |
| 34 | " | 6 | 6 | 26 | 10 | 47 |
| 1935 | " | 15 | 16 | 68 | 9 | 62 |

1. Manhattan.
2. Washington, D.C., added (Wards 23 and 24 annexed to Manhattan).
3. Philadelphia added.
6. Brooklyn, Queens, Richmond, N.Y., added. (Remainder of Bronx annexed in 1895.)
8. Atlanta and New Haven added.
9. Richmond, Va., added.
10. Cambridge added.
12. St. Louis and Boston added.
14. Portland, Oregon, and Springfield (Mass.) added.

a. 1920-1930 = 100. The number of cities in the indexes increases from year to year. In order to preserve uniformity, the aggregate of building volume in each year is divided by the average annual volume of building for the identical cities during the period, 1920-1930. The base is, therefore, a shifting one.
b. In the tables here presented the data have been rounded off to the nearest 1 per cent. In the charts, however, and in the computations of the amplitudes, the data were carried out to one decimal.

| Year | Number of Cities | Total Residential[b] | Total Non-residential[b] | Total New Building[b] | Alterations[b] | Total Building[b] |
|---|---|---|---|---|---|---|
| 1868 | 1 | 14 | 5 | 10 | 6 | 9 |
| 69 | " | 15 | 8 | 11 | 12 | 11 |
| 1870 | " | 14 | 5 | 10 | 8 | 10 |
| 71 | " | 18 | 6 | 12 | 12 | 12 |
| 72 | " | 12 | 4 | 8 | 8 | 8 |
| 73 | " | 8 | 6 | 7 | 10 | 7 |
| 74 | " | 7 | 2 | 5 | 10 | 5 |
| 1875 | 2 | 8 | 3 | 6 | 13 | 6 |
| 76 | " | 7 | 3 | 5 | 10 | 5 |
| 77 | " | 6 | 1 | 4 | 9 | 4 |
| 78 | " | 7 | 2 | 4 | 7 | 4 |
| 79 | " | 10 | 2 | 6 | 9 | 6 |
| 1880 | " | 13 | 2 | 8 | 10 | 8 |
| 81 | " | 16 | 7 | 11 | 11 | 11 |
| 82 | " | 19 | 5 | 12 | 12 | 12 |
| 83 | 3 | 17 | 6 | 12 | 11 | 12 |
| 84 | " | 17 | 5 | 11 | 12 | 11 |
| 1885 | " | 20 | 4 | 12 | 19 | 13 |
| 86 | " | 26 | 6 | 16 | 15 | 16 |
| 87 | 5 | 24 | 8 | 17 | 17 | 17 |
| 88 | " | 18 | 11 | 15 | 17 | 15 |
| 89 | " | 24 | 12 | 19 | 17 | 19 |
| 1890 | 6 | 24 | 16 | 21 | 17 | 20 |
| 91 | " | 18 | 14 | 16 | 17 | 16 |
| 92 | " | 21 | 15 | 18 | 17 | 18 |
| 93 | " | 16 | 16 | 16 | 16 | 16 |
| 94 | 7 | 16 | 12 | 14 | 13 | 14 |
| 1895 | " | 23 | 17 | 20 | 18 | 20 |
| 96 | 9 | 17 | 18 | 17 | 16 | 17 |
| 97 | " | 21 | 17 | 19 | 17 | 19 |
| 98 | 11 | 17 | 9 | 14 | 15 | 14 |
| 99 | 12 | 25 | 17 | 22 | 19 | 22 |
| 1900 | " | 13 | 12 | 13 | 20 | 14 |
| 01 | 13 | 20 | 22 | 21 | 25 | 21 |
| 02 | " | 13 | 27 | 19 | 25 | 19 |
| 03 | " | 16 | 24 | 19 | 28 | 20 |
| 04 | 14 | 26 | 22 | 24 | 28 | 25 |
| 1905 | " | 43 | 27 | 36 | 35 | 36 |
| 06 | 17 | 38 | 28 | 34 | 42 | 34 |
| 07 | 18 | 29 | 27 | 28 | 40 | 30 |
| 08 | 22 | 24 | 23 | 24 | 28 | 24 |
| 09 | 23 | 41 | 30 | 36 | 31 | 36 |

| Year | Number of Cities | Total Residential[b] | Total Non-residential[b] | Total New Building[b] | Altera-tions[b] | Total Building[b] |
|------|------|------|------|------|------|------|
| 1910 | 26 | 34 | 34 | 34 | 33 | 34 |
| 11 | 27 | 30 | 37 | 33 | 37 | 33 |
| 12 | " | 32 | 41 | 36 | 39 | 36 |
| 13 | " | 28 | 33 | 30 | 39 | 31 |
| 14 | " | 27 | 27 | 27 | 36 | 28 |
| 1915 | " | 32 | 28 | 30 | 36 | 31 |
| 16 | " | 36 | 40 | 38 | 49 | 39 |
| 17 | " | 16 | 32 | 23 | 41 | 25 |
| 18 | " | 6 | 18 | 11 | 33 | 13 |
| 19 | " | 38 | 56 | 46 | 78 | 49 |
| 1920 | " | 27 | 71 | 46 | 106 | 52 |
| 21 | " | 61 | 59 | 60 | 80 | 62 |
| 22 | " | 105 | 80 | 94 | 89 | 94 |
| 23 | " | 128 | 93 | 113 | 105 | 112 |
| 24 | " | 133 | 106 | 122 | 104 | 120 |
| 1925 | " | 151 | 136 | 144 | 103 | 140 |
| 26 | " | 147 | 127 | 138 | 106 | 135 |
| 27 | " | 117 | 116 | 117 | 105 | 115 |
| 28 | " | 120 | 118 | 119 | 100 | 117 |
| 29 | " | 72 | 118 | 92 | 117 | 94 |
| 1930 | " | 38 | 76 | 54 | 85 | 58 |
| 31 | " | 33 | 54 | 42 | 64 | 44 |
| 32 | " | 6 | 26 | 15 | 34 | 17 |
| 33 | " | 7 | 8 | 8 | 32 | 10 |
| 34 | " | 5 | 14 | 9 | 41 | 12 |
| 1935 | " | 15 | 21 | 18 | 54 | 21 |
| 36 | " | 30.9 | 23.8 | | | |

1. Manhattan.
2. Washington, D.C., added (Wards 23 and 24 of Bronx annexed).
3. Providence added.
5. Brooklyn and Minneapolis added.
6. Philadelphia added.
7. New Bedford added. (Remainder of Bronx annexed in 1895.)
9. Atlanta and Louisville added.
11. Queens and Richmond Boroughs added.
12. Watertown, Mass., added.
13. Baltimore added.
14. Indianapolis added.
17. New Haven, Rochester, Waltham, Mass., added.
18. Portland added.
22. Cleveland, Detroit, Newark, Richmond, Va., added.
23. Cambridge added.
26. Boston, Kansas City, St. Louis added.
27. Springfield added.

a. 1920-1930 = 100. See note (a) to Appendix B.
b. See note (b) to Appendix B.

| Year | Number of Cities | Total Residential | Total Non-residential[b] | Total New Building |
|---|---|---|---|---|
| 1856 | 1 | 23 | 16 | 21 |
| 57 | " | 19 | 16 | 18 |
| 58 | " | 19 | 12 | 18 |
| 59 | " | 25 | 16 | 22 |
| 1860 | " | 30 | 12 | 27 |
| 61 | " | 22 | 4 | 18 |
| 62 | " | 32 | 12 | 26 |
| 63 | 2 | 31 | 23 | 28 |
| 64 | " | 16 | 16 | 16 |
| 1865 | " | 22 | 23 | 22 |
| 66 | " | 31 | 28 | 29 |
| 67 | " | 44 | 26 | 38 |
| 68 | " | 56 | 26 | 47 |
| 69 | " | 66 | 26 | 54 |
| 1870 | " | 64 | 26 | 52 |
| 71 | " | 78 | 26 | 62 |
| 72 | " | 58 | 37 | 52 |
| 73 | 3 | 58 | 26 | 47 |
| 74 | 4 | 41 | 13 | 30 |
| 1875 | 5 | 41 | 12 | 29 |
| 76 | " | 34 | 12 | 25 |
| 77 | " | 37 | 9 | 26 |
| 78 | 6 | 26 | 10 | 19 |
| 79 | 7 | 23 | 12 | 19 |
| 1880 | 8 | 19 | 8 | 14 |
| 81 | 9 | 27 | 9 | 18 |
| 82 | " | 30 | 9 | 20 |
| 83 | 10 | 37 | 10 | 24 |
| 84 | " | 42 | 11 | 27 |
| 1885 | " | 53 | 12 | 33 |
| 86 | " | 60 | 12 | 37 |
| 87 | 12 | 64 | 15 | 34 |
| 88 | " | 61 | 14 | 30 |
| 89 | " | 74 | 16 | 36 |
| 1890 | " | 70 | 15 | 34 |
| 91 | 13 | 56 | 13 | 30 |
| 92 | " | 65 | 16 | 35 |
| 93 | " | 50 | 12 | 26 |
| 94 | " | 46 | 13 | 24 |
| 1895 | " | 56 | 13 | 27 |
| 96 | 17 | 49 | 13 | 25 |
| 97 | " | 55 | 11 | 26 |
| 98 | 20 | 36 | 10 | 20 |
| 99 | 21 | 38 | 11 | 24 |
| 1900 | " | 28 | 9 | 17 |
| 01 | 22 | 36 | 13 | 23 |
| 02 | 22 | 33 | 14 | 22 |
| 03 | " | 36 | 16 | 24 |
| 04 | " | 48 | 17 | 29 |
| 1905 | " | 66 | 20 | 39 |
| 06 | 23 | 72 | 21 | 42 |
| 07 | 24 | 65 | 21 | 39 |
| 08 | 26 | 60 | 19 | 37 |
| 09 | " | 79 | 20 | 46 |

| Year | Number of Cities | Total Residential | Total Non-residential[b] | Total New Building |
|---|---|---|---|---|
| 1910 | 27 | 72 | 28 | 46 |
| 11 | 28 | 71 | 29 | 46 |
| 12 | 29 | 66 | 29 | 46 |
| 13 | " | 60 | 28 | 43 |
| 14 | " | 61 | 29 | 42 |
| 1915 | " | 69 | 34 | 48 |
| 16 | " | 69 | 41 | 52 |
| 17 | " | 34 | 36 | 36 |
| 18 | " | 14 | 32 | 23 |
| 19 | " | 65 | 70 | 67 |
| 1920 | " | 37 | 75 | 58 |
| 21 | " | 75 | 83 | 81 |
| 22 | " | 123 | 103 | 112 |
| 23 | " | 143 | 121 | 133 |
| 24 | " | 149 | 129 | 139 |
| 1925 | " | 164 | 128 | 144 |
| 26 | " | 133 | 122 | 128 |
| 27 | " | 101 | 106 | 102 |
| 28 | " | 87 | 93 | 89 |
| 29 | " | 54 | 80 | 67 |
| 1930 | " | 32 | 60 | 48 |
| 31 | " | 31 | 52 | 43 |
| 32 | " | 10 | 29 | 20 |
| 33 | " | 7 | 22 | 15 |
| 34 | " | 7 | 23 | 15 |
| 1935 | " | 18 | 28 | 23 |
| 36 | " | 32 | 35 | |

1. Philadelphia.
2. Includes Philadelphia and Manhattan and Bronx.
3. Boston added.
4. Brooklyn added.
5. Washington added (Wards 23 and 24 of Bronx added).
6. Newark added.
7. Salem added.
8. Detroit added.
9. New Haven added.
10. Providence added.
12. Minneapolis and Cambridge added.
13. Indianapolis added.
17. Bridgeport, Atlanta, Louisville and Waltham added. (Remainder of Bronx annexed in 1895.)
20. Watertown, Queens and Richmond Boroughs added.
21. New Bedford added.
22. Baltimore added.
23. Rochester added.
24. Portland added.
26. Cleveland and Richmond, Va., added.
27. St. Louis added.
28. Springfield added.
29. Kansas City added.

a. 1920-1930 = 100. See note (a) to Appendix B.
b. 1887-1912, Philadelphia data excluded from *Total Nonresidential* and *Total New Building* because of excessive number of miscellaneous structures.

| Year | Number of Cities | Families | Year | Number of Cities | Families |
|---|---|---|---|---|---|
| 1871 | 1 | 167 | 1905 | 8 | 78 |
| 72 | " | 150 | 06 | " | 124 |
| 73 | " | 83 | 07 | " | 106 |
| 74 | " | 67 | 08 | 9 | 53 |
| 1875 | " | 67 | 09 | " | 61 |
| 76 | " | 33 | 1910 | 10 | 74 |
| 77 | " | 33 | 11 | 11 | 75 |
| 78 | " | 17 | 12 | " | 68 |
| 79 | " | 33 | 13 | " | 71 |
| 1880 | " | 33 | 14 | " | 59 |
| 81 | " | 33 | 1915 | 13 | 69 |
| 82 | " | 33 | 16 | 14 | 76 |
| 83 | " | 50 | 17 | " | 42 |
| 84 | 2 | 69 | 18 | " | 9 |
| 1885 | " | 75 | 19 | " | 32 |
| 86 | 3 | 44 | 1920 | 15 | 21 |
| 87 | " | 48 | 21 | " | 34 |
| 88 | " | 46 | 22 | " | 82 |
| 89 | " | 54 | 23 | " | 105 |
| 1890 | " | 63 | 24 | " | 139 |
| 91 | " | 73 | 1925 | " | 133 |
| 92 | " | 79 | 26 | " | 149 |
| 93 | 4 | 73 | 27 | " | 155 |
| 94 | " | 63 | 28 | " | 143 |
| 1895 | " | 73 | 29 | " | 96 |
| 96 | " | 69 | 1930 | " | 43 |
| 97 | " | 69 | 31 | 12 | 52 |
| 98 | " | 39 | 32 | " | 11 |
| 99 | " | 39 | 33 | " | 4 |
| 1900 | 5 | 32 | 34 | " | 7 |
| 01 | " | 47 | 1935 | 11 | 18 |
| 02 | 6 | 11 | | | |
| 03 | 7 | 21 | | | |
| 04 | 8 | 37 | | | |

1. New Haven.
2. Providence added.
3. St. Louis added.
4. New Bedford added. (Remainder of Bronx annexed in 1895.)
5. Evanston added.
6. New York City (includes all five boroughs) added.
7. All cities, New Jersey, added.
8. Salem added.
9. Cleveland and Detroit added. Providence subtracted.
10. Kansas City added.
11. Springfield added.
13. Cincinnati and Rochester added.
14. Boston added.
15. Providence added.
12. New Bedford, Evanston and Rochester subtracted.
11. Kansas City subtracted.

a. 1920-1930 = 100. See note (a) to Appendix B.

INDEX

# INDEX

Acceleration principle, conditions and limits of, 41-5, 57-60

Alleghany, Pa., 222

Alterations, 118; characteristics of, 180-3; cycles in construction of, 168-80; severity of cycles in construction of, 170, 172; substitutes for new building, 183; turning points in construction of, lead of, 140-1; synchrony of, 147

Amortization policies, 25-9

Amplitudes, building cycle, 106, 169, 170

Annalist index, 102, 104, 106, 107

Annual statistics of building, indexes of, 116-19, 130-3, 224-30; individual city, analysis of, 119-22; method of analysis of, 124-5; sources of (*see also* Monthly index of building), 116-17; uniformity of data of, 117-18

Anti-trust cases in building industry, 193

Apartment buildings, 118; large size of, 176-7; operating costs of, Table 19; severity of cycles in construction of, 168, Tables 14, 15; statistics of construction of, Chart II, App. B, Sect. 1

Arnold, 193

Assessed value v. sale value of buildings, Table 18

Atlanta, 134, 222, 225, 227, 229

Axe-Houghton index of business, 102, 104, 107, 150

Baltimore, 227

Berlin, 210

Bookholtz, 9

Boston, 132, 222, 225, 227, 229, 230

Bowen, 10, 210

Bowley, 9

Bradstreet's, 151-2

Bronx Borough, 134, 222, 225, 227, 229, 230

Brooklyn Borough, 97, 225, 227, 229

Buffalo, 222

Building, capitalistic nature of, 187; completion of, time required for, 185-6; cost of, 12-18; demand — elasticity of, 30-42; equipment, 198; industry, 13-14; life, 22-5, 93, 94, 165; permits data (*see* Building permits data); types of (*see* Detached dwellings, Apartment dwellings, Residential building, Business building, Public building, Nonresidential building, Alterations, Total building)

Building cycles, duration of (*see* Duration of building cycles); periodicity of, Table 8; phases of, 105-6; severity of (*see* Severities of building cycles); turning points (*see* Turning points)

Building permits data, boundary changes affecting, 97; building code changes affecting, 97; lags of building construction involved

INDEX

in, 98; lapses in, 98; shortcomings of, 96-8; underestimates of cost of building affecting, 97-8; uniformity of, lack of, 96
Bureau of Labor Statistics, 14, 96, 97, 98, 116, 126
Burns, A. F., 9, 128, 162, 167
Business activity, indexes of, 102
Business and building, 154-7, 173-5
Business Annals, 102, 150
Business building (private nonresidential), 118, Chart II, App. B., Sect. 1
Byer, Herman B., 7

Cairncross, 10, 128
Cambridge, 222, 225, 227
Canada, 210
Capital propagation period, 68, 90, 91, 185
Capital values, 11-12, 22
Capitalistic nature of building, 187
Capitalization and interest, 18-21
Chawner, 9, 14
Chicago, 208, 222
Cincinnati, 222
City and Suburban Homes Co., 17, Table 19
Civil War, 150, 153, 211
Clark, 62, 66, 78, 103
Clarkson, 210
Cleveland, 222, 225, 227, 229, 230
Cleveland Trust Co. index, 104, 167
Clossen, 157
Competition, 144-5
Competitive illusions, 191; restraints, 193
Confidence, shifts in, 192
Construction, census of, 202; gross value of, 5-6; nonbuilding, 6-8; residential (see Residential

building); total, 4; total private, 4
Consumers' outlay, 4
Consumption, 3-9; variation in, 53; interaction with investment, 70-92; investment and, Chap. III
Contracts awarded, 95
Costs of building, 12-18; capital requirements affecting, 13; competitive conditions affecting, 13; direct v. overhead, 13-15, 200, 201; downward inflexibility of, 193-8; factors in New York City, 194-8, Table 18; inadequacy of data on, 108-9; job differences in, 15; overhead v. direct, 13, 15, 200; slowness to adjust, 193; underestimates of builders in applying for permits, 97-8; upward flexibility of, 193-4; wage rates, 14
Costs of operation, importance of, 16; inflexibility of, 203-6
Costs of ownership, 16-18, Table I
Crum, 121
Curtis, 63

Davison, 206
Deflating, no —— of permit data, 120-1
Demand for buildings, elasticity of, 30-55; expenditure, 11-14; income (see also Acceleration), 38-45; price (Cost of ownership), 31-8; short-run (see also Acceleration), 42-55
Denver, 222
Depreciation, and replacements, 207-8; policies, 24-5; rates and length of cycle, 163-4; stability of, 83

# INDEX

Detached dwellings (*see also* Residential building), 133-4; dominance of, 134; freedom from random disturbances, 133-4; speculation in construction of (*see* Speculation); statistics of, Chart II, App. B, Sect. 1; uniform size of, 147
Detroit, 132, 222, 225, 227, 229, 230
Dewing, 25
De Wolff, 94
Diminishing elasticity of demand, 192
Dodge, F. W., 95
Duluth, 222
Durable goods industries, 3-5; growth of, 4
Duration of building cycles, 103-6, 127, Table 8, Chap. X
Dwellings (*see* Residential building); apartment (*see* Apartment buildings); detached (*see* Detached dwellings)

"Echo effect," 94
Economic life of buildings, 93-4, 163-4
Elasticity (*see also* Demand, Supply), 12, 14-16; investment demand, 12, 18; investment supply, 12, 92
Employment (*see also* Unemployment), 161; additional or off-site, 7-8; construction, 5-8; furniture manufacturing and dealing, 8; real estate, 8; upholsterers, 8
England, 210
European cycle, 159
Evanston, Ill., 230
Everett, Mass., 222
"Excess" plant capacity, 156

Expansion, continuous, 74-8, Table 5
Expectations, 11, 37-8, 44-55; and interest rates, 18-22; and size of building, 187-8; and the "relation," 89; characteristics of psychology affecting, 47-55; fluctuations in, 186-92; negative, 47; neutral, 47; positive, 47; probable behavior of, 53-4; real v. psychological factors affecting, 46; reversals of, 78; usefulness of concept of, 54-5

Fabricant, 25, 93, 94, 207
Federal Housing Administration, 14, 26, 28, 32, 33, 204
Financial Survey of Urban Housing, 24, 164, 190
Fisher, I., 21
Ford, 173
Foreclosures, 160-1, 165-6
Fort Wayne, Ind., 122
Foster, 10
Frisch, 78

Germany, 210
Ginzberg, 52
Glasgow, 159, 210, 212
Government wartime restriction of building, 209, 210
Great depressions, Chap. IX
Grebler, 10
Gross national product, 3

Haber, 188
Haberler, 41, 63
Hallauer, 10, 163, 208
Hamburg, 159, 210
Hansen, 57, 78
Harrod, 57, 62, 68, 69, 77, 78
Hayek, F. A., 20

Hicks, 29
Hotels (*see* Speculation)
Hoyt, 10, 162, 208
Hubbard, 154

Income, and consumption (*see also* Consumption), 3-6; elasticity (*see* Demand for building) ; expansion of, hypothetical cases illustrating possibility of, 43; acceleration of, hypothetical figures illustrating, 42-3; propagation periods (*see also* Capital propagation periods), 65, 66, 91; statistics of, 3, 5
Increasing number of cities, adjustment of indexes for, 125-6
Indianapolis, 222, 225, 229
Inducement to invest, Chap. II, VI
Insurance, 203
Interest rate, 18-30, 185; a minor factor in cycles, 27; and the "relation," 88-9; as barometers of financing conditions, 111; lack of good index for mortgage, 26-30; manipulation of long, 29-30; place of in capitalization, Table 2; short term, 19, 21; standard of housing and level of, 29-30
Inventions, 161
Investment, actual v. planned saving, 62-3; consumption downturn, inevitability of, 78; consumption interaction, 69-94; and marginal propensity to consume, 71-3; demand theory of, 30-55; goods industries (*see* Durable goods) ; market, an unorganized social group, 48

Joint Legislative Committee on Housing, New York Legislative, 193

Judkins, 9

Kalecki, 62
Kansas City, Mo., 222, 227, 229, 230
Keynes, J. M., 20, 21, 22, 46, 52, 53, 62, 191, 201
King, 37
Kreps, 30, 156
Kuznets, 3, 5, 8, 62, 93

Lag of building on upturn, 156-7; cost rigidities and, 156-7; depressed morale and, 156-7; technical delays as causes for, 156-7
Land, buying and selling prices of, 199
Lange, 63
Last 19th-Century cycle in building, 151-2, Tables 10-17
Lead of building, 103-4, 155-6
Length of building cycles, 103-5, 160-6
Lerner, 63
Life, of alterations, 180-1; of building, physical, 22-5; of building, economic, 93-4, 163
London, 159
Long cycles in building, characteristics of, 129-34; individual city analysis of, 118-24
Lösch, 162
Louisville, 134, 222, 227, 229
Lubin, 4
Lutz, 63

Macauley, 19, 109, 223
Machlup, 62, 65
Maintenance and repairs, 203
Manhattan Borough, 103, 134, 188, 197, 204, 205, 206, 222, 225, 227, 229, 230
Marginal efficiency of capital, 12,

# INDEX

Marginal propensity to consume, and investment-consumption deceleration, 68; and severity of cycles, 86-7

Marriage rate, 161, 165

Materials prices, 194-8, Table 18

Milwaukee, 222

Minneapolis, 120, 222, 227, 229

Mitchell, 102

Monopoly, 13-15, 193

Monthly index of building, 99-101, Chart I, App. A; analysis of, 102-6; cities included in, 100, App. A; coverage of, 100; explanation of, 100-1, App. A; smoothing of, 101, App. A; sources of, 100; statistical technique used in compiling and analyzing, 101

Montreal, 159

Morgenstern, 51-2

Mortgage credit, 189-90

Multiplier, and expectations, 67; and technical problems of production, 68, 90-2; and unemployment, 64-5; conditions and limits of, 62-8; practical v. theoretical, 66-8; statement of, 62-9

Nashville, 222

National Association of Real Estate Boards, 26, 172

National Bureau of Economic Research, 119, 150

National Income, 3, 5

National Resources Committee, 40, 208

Nelson, 172

Netherlands, 159, 210

New Bedford, 227, 229, 230

New Haven, 126, 134, 222, 225, 227, 229

New Jersey, 118, 127, 230

New mortgage interest rates, Table 18

New Orleans, 222

New York City, 125, 127, 132, 137, 151, 153

New York Federal Reserve Bank, 102

Newark, 96, 222, 227, 229

Newman, 9, 14, 102, 103, 110, 111, 128, 154, 158

Non-capital outlays (see also Operating costs) and the "relation," 89-90

Non-residential building, 118, 168, 169

Oakland, 208

Obsolescence, 207-8

Office building, 178

Omaha, 222

Operating costs (see also Non-capital outlays), apartment dwellings, 203, Table 19; mortgage interest rates affecting, 206; tax burden affecting, 205-6; tax levy affecting, 205; tax rate affecting, 205

Pearson, 10, 128, 158, 165

Period analysis (see also Income and Capital Propagation), 65-6

Periodicity of building cycles, Table 8

Phases of building cycles, 105-6

Philadelphia, 133, 151, 208, 222, 225, 227, 229

Pigou, 20, 21, 27-8, 50

Pittsburgh, 222

Population, 120, 165

Portland, 208, 222, 225, 227, 229

Post-Civil-War cycle in building, 150, Tables 10, 11, 15, 16, 17

# INDEX

Post-First-World War cycle in building, 153, Tables 10-17

"President's Conference on Home Building," 190

Pre-war cycle in building, 152, Tables 10-17

Price of land, 198-200

Providence, 134, 222, 227, 229, 230

Psychological factors (*see also* Expectations), 89, 91-2

Psychological life of buildings, 165

Public buildings, 118; and business building, 178; lag on downturn of, 139, 141-2; specialized nature of, 169

Queens Borough, 222, 225, 227, 229, 230

Rate of interest (*see* Interest rate)

Ready-made building (*see* Speculation)

Real Estate Analysts, 10

Recovery since 1933, 153

Reich, Emmy, 128

"Relation," 60-2; capital propagation periods and the (*see* Capital); elements in the, 62; expectations affecting the (*see* Expectations); income propagation periods and the (*see* Income); non-capital outlays affecting the, 89-90; precision of, 87-8; size of, 87-93; technical factors and the, 90-1

Renting and administrative expense, 203

Repairs and maintenance, 203

Replacements, and downturn of cycle, 78-82; behavior of, 78-82; depreciation charges and, 81-2; net investment and, 208-9

Residential building (*see also* Apartment buildings, Detached dwellings), in time of war, 161, 211-12; lead on downturn of, 140; magnitude of index of, 168; severity of cycles in, 168-9; speculation in, 169-73; synchrony of cycles in, 146-7

Residential buyers, lack of foresight, knowledge, judgment of, 173-4; timidity of, 174-5

Revival, factors inducing, 82-5; rôle of depreciation charges in, 83-4; rôle of marginal propensity to consume in, 83-4

Richmond Borough, 133, 222, 225, 227, 229, 230

Richmond, Va., 222, 225, 227, 229

Riggleman, 9, 116, 128, 154, 158

Robertson, 28

Robinson, 10, 14

Rochester, 227, 229, 230

Roos, 10, 158, 160

Rounds of income creation, 70-1

St. Joseph, 222

St. Louis, 222, 225, 227, 229, 230

St. Paul, 222

Salem, 230

Samuelson, 69

Saving (*see also* Investment, Income, Consumption), 62-4, 190-1

Schumpeter, 20, 27, 62

Scotland, 210

Severities of building cycles, 86-94; of long building cycles, 55, 105-7, 127, 167-83, Tables 14-17

Short term interest rates, 21

Silberling, 166

Size of buildings, 187-8

Smoothing, 119-20

Snyder, 104, 106, 121, 150

Spanish-American War, 209

Sparks, 17, 28

# INDEX

Speculation in building construction, 141-3, 169-73, 176, 178-80, 187-91

Springfield, Mass., 222, 225, 227, 229, 230

Statistical technique used in computing and analyzing, annual indexes, 116-27; monthly index, 100-1

Stewart, Ethelbert, 15

Stock prices, as index of expectations, 112; statistical association with building cycles, 113-14

Stockholm, 158

Stone, P. A., 17, 27

Store buildings, 212

Supply (*see also* Building, Costs of Building, Elasticity), 4, 5, 92

Sweden, 210

Syracuse, 222

Taxes, 203-5; burden (assessed v. sale value of buildings), Table 18; levy, Table 18; rate, Table 18

Technical factors and the "relation," 90-1

Technology, 211

Temporary National Economic Committee, Hearings, 4, 13-14

Thorp, Willard, 14, 104, 150, 173

Time and the multiplier, 65-8

Timing, 101-4, 127, Chap. VIII

Total building, Charts I, III, App. A, App. B, Sect. 2

Total new building, Chart III, App. B, Sect. 2, 3

Trenton, 222

Turning points, building and business cycle, Table 6; consensus of, 122; definition of, 121; investment- and consumption-, 74-8; lag of public building, 139,

141-2; lead of alterations, 140-1; leads and lags of, Table 7; long-cycle, 139-45, Tables 10-13; median dates of, 137-8; synchrony of (city-to-city), 145-9

Unemployment, 151

Unionization, 13, 15

Urgency of alterations, 181-2

Variation of long cycles, 159

Wage rates, building, 194, Table 18

Waltham, Mass., 227

War, and length of cycles, 162-3; and interest rates, 212; and population cycles, 162; and nonresidential building, 161, 211-12; and residential building, 161, 211-12; and speculative booms, 161; Civil (*see also* Post-Civil War), 211; cost inflation in time of, 210-11; depressing effect on building of, 211; rent inflation in time of, 211; Spanish-American, 209; uncertainty in time of, 211; World (First) (*see also* Pre- and Post-First-World War), 152, 209-12

Warehouses, 212

Warren, 10, 128, 158, 165

Washington, D.C., 126, 134, 208, 222, 225, 227, 229

Wastage of buildings, 207

Watertown, Mass., 227, 229

Wenzlich, 116, 128, 161

Wickens, 10

Wicksell, 20

Woodbury, 10

Workshop, 212

Yale University building program, 134